Fear Itself

Fear Itself

*Horror on Screen and in Reality
During the Depression
and World War II*

MELVIN E. MATTHEWS, JR.

McFarland & Company, Inc., Publishers
Jefferson, North Carolina, and London

LIBRARY OF CONGRESS CATALOGUING-IN-PUBLICATION DATA

Matthews, Melvin E.
  Fear itself : horror on screen and in reality during the Depression and World War II / Melvin E. Matthews, Jr.
      p.   cm.
  Includes bibliographical references and index.

  ISBN 978-0-7864-4313-0
  softcover : 50# alkaline paper ∞

  1. Horror films — United States — History and criticism. 2. Fear — United States — History — 20th century. 3. Motion pictures — Social aspects — United States — History — 20th century.   I. Title.
  PN1995.9.H6M3243   2009
  791.43'615 — dc22   2009014686

British Library cataloguing data are available

©2009 Melvin E. Matthews, Jr. All rights reserved

No part of this book may be reproduced or transmitted in any form or by any means, electronic or mechanical, including photocopying or recording, or by any information storage and retrieval system, without permission in writing from the publisher.

Cover images ©2009 Shutterstock

Manufactured in the United States of America

McFarland & Company, Inc., Publishers
  Box 611, Jefferson, North Carolina 28640
    www.mcfarlandpub.com

Table of Contents

Preface   1

1. The Horror Cycle Begins: *Dracula* and *Frankenstein* (1931)   5
2. Exploiting the Lower Classes (1932–1933)   37
3. The Banking Crisis (*King Kong*) and the Fascist Alternative (*The Invisible Man*)   75
4. Fade Out and Revival: From the Depression to the Eve of War (1935–1941)   95
5. The War Years, Part I: The Saga of the Wolf Man (1941–1945)   126
6. The War Years, Part II: Horror Goes to War   150
7. Beyond the Golden Age   178

Chapter Notes   185
Bibliography   197
Index   203

Preface

The inspiration for this book came during the 2005 Thanksgiving holiday season, shortly after I learned that my first book had been accepted for publication. That Friday after Thanksgiving found me at the Barnes & Noble bookstore in Roanoke, Virginia, where I purchased Ray Morton's new book *King Kong: The History of a Movie Icon: From Fay Wray to Peter Jackson*. It was published in connection with Jackson's forthcoming remake of the classic 1933 monster film. On this occasion I also purchased two DVDs: the original version of *Kong* and a box set of Val Lewton's horror classics of the 1940s. The combination of these purchases prompted me to want to do a book on the horror films of the 1930s and '40s and their relationship to the two great crises of those years: the Great Depression and World War II.

Until the 1970s I had not seen any of these films, save for *King Kong* in the 1960s. I had owned the Aurora movie monsters model kits and began learning about these films in high school. During my sophomore year a local television station aired them on weekends but I didn't watch them for a simple reason: They scared me! In the fall of 1974, shortly after the start of my second year at Virginia Western Community College, the films aired again and this time I began watching them. The coming of the home video and DVD revolutions afforded me the opportunity to buy these films for my personal enjoyment. Now what once frightened me provides relaxation, though I seldom watch these movies in their entirety any more as I've seen them before!

From the perspective of the early twenty-first century, when horror films are characterized by graphic special effects, the monsters of Hollywood's Golden Age seem antiquated as well as reassuring old acquaintances. Yet, in their prime, they were truly terrifying, largely because they were so new to movie audiences, who required time to assimilate and become familiar with them. In another sense, the classic monsters were perfectly suited to the escapist mood Hollywood conveyed in '30s America. Of all the mass entertainment media in America during the Depression years — music, radio, books, magazines, comics, sports — movies were the paramount diversion. In his history of Depression America, Robert S. McElvaine notes that nearly everyone who could afford to, as well as those who couldn't, frequently attended the movies during the 1930s. During the early part of the decade, when the Depression was at its worst, movie attendance was high: "Although part of this remarkable figure represented repeat customers, the number itself corresponds to more than 60 percent of the entire American population."[1] Arthur M. Schlesinger, Jr., was more direct in his assessment: In the '30s, "films mattered in American life...."[2]

Horror was nothing new to American cinema. What differentiated '30s horror films from their predecessors was their portrayal of the monster. The "monsters" of 1920s silent films were grossly disfigured social outcasts, yet still *human*, whose ostracism drove them to monstrous acts — the films of Lon Chaney come to mind here — or they were criminals masquerading as supernatural fiends, whose subterfuge was exposed in the last reel. Thirties horror films, beginning with *Dracula* (1931), presented genuine supernatural beings. The Depression no doubt contributed to this change.

American supernatural horror films debuted in the midst of the worst years of the Great Depression. During this interval they were especially immune to censorship. "Picture producers have discovered what is the first loophole in all forms of censorship as well as in their own Hays Production Code," declared *Variety* in 1931. "There is no provision, it is officially conceded, in any censor law which rules on the quality or extent of gruesomeness. Sex, crime, ridicule, politics, church and school — all are taken care of in the Code book. [Yet] the Hays Office admits that under the Code it is powerless to take a stand on the subject [of gruesomeness]."

State censor boards were another matter. There, the cutting of a film depended on the board members' personal views of what censorship required. *Frankenstein* was barred in Kansas as it displayed "cruelty and tended to debase morals." What displeased the state censor board were thirty-two scenes that, if deleted, would have cut the film's running time in half. "When it comes right down to cases," observed the *Kansas City Star*, "*Frankenstein*, the most popular picture of the year, is being kept from thousands of Kansans because it is not suitable for children and because three women do not like it."³ The intense editorial outcry compelled gubernatorial intervention, and the deleted scenes were restored.⁴ The likely explanation for the absence of strictures against horrific elements in the Hays Code was that its framers weren't acquainted with such. So long as they did nothing to incite social or political controversy, movie monsters were free to do virtually whatever they wished without fear of incurring the censors' displeasure.⁵

The Depression horror cycle introduced audiences to vampires, man-made monsters, mad scientists, zombies and the like. Initially horror films were high grossers, surpassing costly prestige films. After a flood of horror films in 1931 and 1932, the cycle stalled. Viewing one 1932 offering, *The Mask of Fu Manchu*, as "not as good as some that were released a few months ago," one exhibitor provided a view of film-going that became Hollywood's main rule during the Depression: "In these days of worry, people want light entertainment, comedy, drama; everyone has enough trouble. Why sit through a depressing picture? Let's have something that finishes up with adventure and optimism. People will leave our theater with their heads up, smiling, and we may expect them to return." Always counterintuitive, the horror boom greatly declined by the time the pre–Code period ended. When one film, *Black Moon* (1934), proved a dismal attraction, a small town exhibitor observed, "[T]he people out our way have had all the horror they can digest in their everyday life in the past few years and they just won't buy it."⁶

Added to this was an overseas development: the British horror ban of the mid–1930s, which curtailed Hollywood production of horror films for a brief time.

But just as supernatural beings aren't governed by the laws of nature, neither could the laws of censorship hold them down: The genre was revived in 1939, coinciding with the world war, and continued to thrive during the war, introducing moviegoers to the Wolf Man, the most successful screen monster of the war years, as well as the more sophisticated thrills of Val Lewton. At one point during the war, the *New York Herald Tribune* observed that "Hollywood is horror happy. Its monsters are making more money than ever before." Referring to the earlier British horror ban, the *Herald Tribune* noted that when "Hitler poured his pox over Europe ... film monsters crawled for cover. They knew they were licked — the public had enough horror without having to see more." In the wake of Pearl Harbor, "the public had different ideas. Mad ghouls, wolf men and Frankenstein monsters began to get more mail than contract cuties."[7]

Nevertheless, the wartime horror boom, like its Depression counterpart, proved short-lived. In the words of Curt Siodmak, who penned several of the '40s monster epics:

> When we made those pictures throughout the Second World War, we couldn't show an American with a machine gun mowing down five thousand Japanese. Nobody would believe it; it wouldn't work. So we had the Gothic stories....
> When the war ended, the bottom fell out of the horror film business. Then, when they began testing the atom bomb, it all started again.[8]

The postwar world was a different place indeed. The Cold War and the nuclear age made the classic Gothic monsters look antiquated. But they would once again prove resilient — revived for the television generation, marketed as plastic model kits, finally making their way into the home via videocassette and DVD editions. The story of their formative years is also the story of America during two critical eras in its modern history.

Several acknowledgments must be made. Gary Don Rhodes provided a copy, via email attachment, of his article on the 1938 horror revival. Once again Photofest provided the photographs that illustrate this book — except for one, which was found in an online search of the Library of Congress website. Kudos must also go to Rebecca Frazier-Smith, the manager of Journals Rights and Permissions for the University of Texas Press, who granted permission to use material from Rick Worland's article on the Office of War Information and wartime horror films that appeared in *Cinema Journal* in 1997. Finally, my computer repairman Chris Hartness once again came to my rescue, helping me prepare the manuscript and related material for transfer to CD before sending the entire package to the publisher. Thanks again.

1

The Horror Cycle Begins: *Dracula* and *Frankenstein* (1931)

For America, 1931 was a bleak year. The greatest economic crisis in the nation's history, the Great Depression, cast its shadow across the land. Visiting Lawrence, Massachusetts, formerly America's principle wool and worsted city, writer Louis Adamic chatted with an unemployed worker.

"I don't know nothing," Adamic's conversational companion declared emotionally. "Only that I have no job, no job — no job." In the Appalachian coal fields, journalist Morris Markey discovered a group of unemployed miners. "I don't say they can keep the hard times from coming," one of them said. "But they can make us understand the whys and wherefores, can't they? That's all I ask, and everybody in the mine is asking the same thing. You go back to New York and tell 'em the miners want to understand what's going on." Markey was slightly unnerved when one of the miners said, "You don't go singing no 'Star Spangled Banner' when you got hungry women and young 'uns in the cabin."

Breadlines were an inescapable sight in Chicago, St. Louis, and Detroit. There was hardly a single block of New York City that daily didn't have at least one evicted family sitting on a couch on the sidewalk. Passersby deposited nickels and dimes in a pot on the family's kitchen table.[1]

President Herbert Hoover, whom the Depression had transformed from a national hero into a scapegoat for the country's misfortunes, wasn't worried. He had told journalist Raymond Clapper, "What the country needs is a good big laugh. There seems to be a condition of hysteria. If someone could get off a good joke every ten days, I think our troubles would be over."[2] The evening of December 31, 1931, found men with inexpensive printed handouts prowling the streets of New York looking for people to occupy the two-thirds–empty cruise ships setting sail for the Caribbean at midnight. "There was a good deal of public drunkenness and numerous deaths attributed to alcoholic beverages made with antifreeze or chafing-dish fuel."[3]

Against this grim backdrop, two monsters, both European in origin, became superstars of the American cinema. Eventually becoming assimilated in their adopted land, they became as all–American as baseball and apple pie.[4] Moreover, as one film historian has noted, they became inseparable in the public mind, making their presence felt in every aspect of modern culture.[5]

Both released by the same studio, *Dracula* and *Frankenstein* not only inaugurated Hollywood's cycle of classic horror, but were perfect metaphors for the Great Depression. Count Dracula, the aristocratic, elegant Transylvanian vampire, seeking merely to satisfy his needs for survival at the expense of others, epitomized the well-to-do upper classes and businessmen who fell out of favor during the Depression. Frankenstein's Monster, by contrast a "proletarian clod,"[6] was ungainly and confused, wondering aimlessly about, seeking to comprehend, like the jobless miner Morris Markey met, what had happened to him and why. In a dark time, these two films would introduce "a new world of gods and monsters" to movie audiences,[7] completely revolutionizing the Hollywood horror film.

Origins: Mary Shelley and Bram Stoker

The ties between *Dracula* and *Frankenstein* extend beyond the fact that they were both movies released the same year by the same studio. Like so many of the classic horror films of Hollywood's Golden Age, both were based on literary works. But the monsters that emerged on screen were quite different from their literary interpretations. Again, in the case of *Dracula* and *Frankenstein*, both novels trace their creation to one event: a June 1816 house party at the Villa Diodati near Geneva.[8] Confined indoors by a downpour resulting from the previous year's eruption of Mt. Tambora and inspired by a group reading from the *Fantasmgoriana,* Lord Byron issued a challenge to his guests Mary and Percy Shelley and his physician John Polidori: each should write a ghost story.[9] "Byron eventually produced a fragment of a novel concerning a Romantic revenant that

Polidori elaborated as a popular novella, *The Vampyre* (1819), which was widely held to be Byron's work."[10] Mary Shelley required additional time to find her inspiration. It came to her one evening when a discussion about the principles of life and the possible construction and reanimation of human cadavers caused her to suffer a nightmare[11]: "I saw — with shut eyes, but acute mental vision — I saw the pale student of unhallowed arts kneeling beside the thing he had put together. I saw the hideous phantasm of a man stretched out, and then, on the working of some powerful engine, show signs of life and stir with an uneasy, half-vital motion." *Frankenstein; or the Modern Prometheus*, the literary work resulting from her nightmare, was initially published in three volumes in 1816.

Eighty-one years later, the ultimate vampire story appeared with the publication of Bram Stoker's *Dracula*. Stoker's tale centered on an undead Transylvanian nobleman who leaves his Carpathian abode to find fresh sources of blood in London.[12] Compared to earlier vampire stories, *Dracula* is significant for two reasons. First, Stoker placed Dracula in his ancestral home in Europe, then transported him to contemporary England. Second, Stoker's vampire is an aristocrat endowed with great physical and mental powers. Indeed, in the words of Bela Lugosi's biographer Arthur Lennig, Dracula is far more than just a vampire; "he is a kind of dark god, one who can command storms, transforms himself into bats, wolves, and mists, and one who has hypnotic powers."[13]

During the 1820s, Byron and Polidori's *The Vampyre* and Shelley's *Frankenstein* were translated to the stage in both England and on the Continent.[14] French audiences read political themes into Shelley's story, associating the monster with the threat of mob violence. In England, *Frankenstein* dramatizations annoyed conservatives who, as Steven Earl Forry observed, ever since the French Revolution "linked social reform with mob rule. The times themselves proved ripe for such a symbol.... Frankenstein immediately became associated with unbridled revolution, atheism, and blind progress in science and technology."[15]

Like *Frankenstein*, *Dracula* attracted social and cultural interpretations of its meaning. Professor Christopher Frayling has characterized Dracula's sea voyage to England as a journey from the East "to colonize the West." He continued that Stoker undoubtedly viewed his novel as "a simple adventure story about a gang of fine, upstanding chaps who defend their women-folk against the nasty Eastern Europeans who would make Britain part of their evil empire...."[16] In his 1999 DVD commentary for

Lugosi's *Dracula*, film historian David J. Skal elaborates further on this cultural theme:

> The novel *Dracula* was a departure from previous vampire stories, plays, and operas in that Stoker made no attempt to romanticize Dracula, and our twentieth century image of the count is a hybrid of Stoker's character and vampires from other literary sources. Stoker's Dracula engenders disgust rather than attraction. It is an amalgam of qualities that late Victorian England found repulsive and unsavory. There was a strong current of cultural xenophobia in the 1890s ... many Britons felt threatened by waves of immigration. Foreigners were frequently viewed as a threat to cultural and social purity and demonized as biologically degenerate — according to a very distorted understanding of the theories of Charles Darwin. Dracula himself is a perfectly Darwinian monster, changing shape up and down the evolutionary scale. He is an invading foreigner with a strong anti–Semitic coloration, much like Shylock, Fagan, or Svengali.[17]

On the morning of May 18, 1897, the Lyceum Theatre in London became the stage for the only dramatic production of *Dracula* Stoker witnessed during his lifetime. He arranged a lengthy staged reading of his novel, totaling five acts and forty-seven scenes. Whatever hopes Stoker may have had of impressing his employer Henry Irving with his work were dashed in a scene described by his biographer and great-nephew Daniel Farson:

> Legend has it that Sir Henry entered the theatre during the reading and listened for a few moments with a warming glint of amusement. "What do you think of it?" someone asked him unwisely, as he left for his dressing room. "*Dreadful!*" came the devastating reply, projected with such resonance that it filled the theatre.[18]

Having outlived his boss by several years, Stoker himself died in 1912. The official cause of his death was cited as "exhaustion."[19]

Two years before Stoker's death, American inventor extraordinaire Thomas Edison had been responsible for the initial film adaptation of *Frankenstein*, directed by J. Searle Dawley, and shot at the Edison Manufacturing Company at Bedford Park, the Bronx. Played by Charles Ogle, the cinema's initial Frankenstein Monster "was a Kabuki-like apparition in whiteface with a flyaway fright wig," attired in rags, ropes, and bandages, and with hands that resembled more vegetation than flesh. Instead of being fashioned from various body parts, this monster came to life by chemical means.[20]

The next American adaptation of *Frankenstein*, entitled *Life Without Soul* (1915), directed by Joseph W. Smiley, and released by Ocean Corporation, was a modernized and Americanized version of the story. This time Frankenstein's name was changed to Frawley — an alteration that perchance was occasioned by some anti–German feeling, though the United States was still neutral in World War I. William W. Cohill played the scientist Victor Frawley, while British actor Percy Darrell Standing played the monster.[21]

Dracula made his film debut nine years after Bram Stoker's death in a lost Hungarian movie, *Dracula's Death*, in which Dracula was portrayed as a deranged music teacher who pursues asylum patients. While the story, in one film historian's opinion, bears a greater resemblance to the Phantom of the Opera, it did feature the concept of a monster replete with fangs and a cape.[22] Shortly thereafter came the best pre–Lugosi *Dracula* film,[23] perhaps the best Dracula film of all time — the German silent classic *Nosferatu*.

Released in 1922, *Nosferatu— A Symphony of Horror* was created by Friedrich Wilhelm Murnau. A former disciple of German director Max Reinhardt, Murnau was no stranger to cinematic horror. A student of Eastern philosophy and the supernatural, he had done two horror films before turning his attention to Stoker's work. "In an act of flagrant copyright violation, he had scenarist Albin Grau change a few characters and locales while retaining a character that was unmistakably Dracula."[24] The film merely utilized the beginning portion of the novel depicting the solicitor's journey to Transylvania, the coach trip and stop at the inn, the vampire's welcome of his guest at the castle at midnight, followed by the vampire's sea voyage, the solicitor's escape, and, finally, the vampire's attraction to the solicitor's wife. The rest of the film was quite freely adapted. In essence, the film, set in 1838 — the theory being that a supernatural tale is better suited to an earlier time — recounts the solicitor's journey to meet Dracula and the former's return to his hometown of Bremen where his wife awaits him. Dracula has also moved to Bremen, taking up residence in an abandoned building across from the solicitor's wife's home. The vampire has moreover brought the plague with him; the pestilence now engulfs the town. Suspecting an evil presence is at hand, the solicitor's wife reads *The Book of the Vampires*, which confirms her suspicion. She then terminates Dracula's reign of terror by letting him drink her blood, keeping him up till sunrise, sacrificing her life for the sake of the others.

Unlike the cultured fiend so familiar to subsequent audiences, Murnau's Dracula is a repulsive being: "With his hairy, pointed ears, ... hideous fingernails, ... and lecherous ... lustful masklike face, he is an image of damned flesh and not of damned soul.... Although *Nosferatu* is frightening and draws upon the earlier and more ghoulish conception of the vampire, it also has a thematic richness and sense of poetry far beyond the Hollywood film."[25] Murnau's plagiarism didn't go unnoticed by Stoker's widow, Florence, who sought to suppress the film. Despite the fact that few American theaters could run *Nosferatu*, this failed to prevent every Hollywood studio from obtaining a copy of it. Murnau himself avoided any legal penalties and would go on to direct numerous other films.[26]

The year after *Nosferatu*'s release, Dracula's return to the stage was initiated when Hamilton Deane, an Irish actor-manager who had previously read Stoker's novel and had long since sought to get someone to write an adaptation of it, decided to do it himself.[27] Deane began the project at the time Florence Stoker was locked in legal combat over *Nosferatu*. Seeing Deane's proposal as an opportunity to regain control over a sanctioned adaptation of her husband's work, Florence accepted. Deane needed only four weeks to write the script, which featured major changes in the story. Deane's version was constructed as a conventional drawing-room melodrama, eliminating the novel's opening and closing chapters. The American character in the novel, Quincey Morris of Texas, one of Lucy's suitors, became a woman, supposedly to provide a third female character for a company member. Dracula himself was changed from the repulsive character of the novel to the well-bred aristocrat the world ultimately came to know — a makeup that allowed the count to interact with the other characters, instead of merely waiting outside their bedroom windows.

Deane's original intention was to play Dracula himself. When the vampire emerged as a relatively minor character in the finished script, Deane opted for the more substantial part of Dracula's nemesis, Abraham Van Helsing. The role of Dracula went to Edmund Blake. The play was an instant success. Despite offers to mount a London production, Deane opted to stay on the road, worried about the London critics' reaction, expecting that they would tear it to shreds.

The role of Dracula was ultimately taken over by Raymond Huntley. On February 14, 1927, Deane's *Dracula* began its London run at the Little Theatre. As Deane expected, the reviews were generally negative. The critics, however, couldn't keep the audiences away. The play presently began drawing capacity crowds in the 300-seat playhouse; before summer's end it would be necessary to relocate the production to a larger venue, the Duke of York's Theatre. It wouldn't be the last time *Dracula* had to change theatres. The following year it was revived under new management. Deane again took the play on the road, where it was such a hit that at one point there were three companies performing the play in separate engagements.[28]

One of those in attendance at the London production of Deane's play was the American publisher-producer Horace Liveright, who felt it would be a hit in America.[29] During the 1920s Liveright had enjoyed a meteoric rise, making his mark in both American publishing and the theatre. His 1927 adaptation of *Dracula* would be his greatest stage success. To obtain the American rights to it, Liveright engaged an American playwright and newspaperman living in London, John L. Balderston, to approach Stoker's widow. Liveright wanted Balderston to completely rewrite Deane's version, as the dialogue in it was terrible. Balderston's patience in dealing with Florence Stoker paid off. The major obstacle to be surmounted now was finding the right actor to play Dracula in the American version. No male paradigm for such a character existed, the closest being Theda Bara's "vamp." Their initial choice, Raymond Huntley, vetoed appearing in the American production over Liveright's proposed salary: a mere $150 a week. The dilemma was resolved when a producer who tried and failed to mount his own production of *Dracula* suggested the actor he had slated for the abortive project, supposedly saying, "I heard that he even came from Transylvania."

The actor, originally born in Hungary as Bela Ferenc Dezo Blasko, had come to the United States as a political refugee in 1921, performing as Bela Lugosi.[30] Lugosi's political problems stemmed from his backing, along with several fellow Hungarian artists, of the Communist regime of Bela Kun that seized control of Hungary after World War I. Kun's government was overthrown, and Lugosi's name wound up on a list of those to be arrested. Fleeing to Vienna in 1919, Lugosi subsequently went to Germany, where he found film work. Ultimately he came to the United States, working his way as third assistant engineer on a ship headed to New Orleans. Lugosi's prior political activities caused friction between him and the other crew members during the journey. When the ship reached New Orleans on December 4, 1920, Lugosi, aided by a sympathetic engineer, escaped with his life. Reaching New York City, he was assisted by Hungarian Americans there and avoided deportation. He was granted legal entry into the United States in March 1921, becoming an American citizen a decade later.

After achieving Hollywood stardom, Lugosi strongly supported California's Hungarian community. Moreover, he showed concern for little people, frequently citing the "working men" as friends, and befriending black actors such as Clarence Muse. He helped co-found the Screen Actors Guild in 1933. His prior, unpleasant memories of his political activities in Hungary may have prompted him to work behind-the-scenes in this new actors' union.[31]

During his Hungarian career, Lugosi had a reputation for versatility; his theatrical career in 1920s New York was largely restricted to such exotic characters as Arabs, bandits, fakirs, and apaches. His main problem was his English; "he learned American parts phonetically in a resonant, accented baritone that would become one of the most instantly recognizable, imitated, and parodied voices in theatrical history."[32]

After a five-performance engagement in New Haven, Connecticut, beginning September 25, 1927, *Dracula* moved to New York's Fulton Theater, where it set a record of 265 performances.[33] Critical reaction varied. Reviewers from *The New York Times* and *The New York Post* felt the play lacked passion and needed more fire. Other publications (*Variety* and *The New York Mirror*) enjoyed the production for the excellent, escapist fare it was. As was the case with Deane's British version, American audiences disregarded critical barbs and flocked to the performance. When the final curtain descended on the Broadway version on May 19, 1928, both the play and Lugosi headed West — to Los Angeles and the Biltmore Theater, where most likely, several movie studio bosses witnessed Lugosi's performance.[34]

Soon motion pictures would provide audiences nationwide the opportunity to witness Lugosi's Dracula in action.

Dracula *the Motion Picture (1931)*

Universal Pictures, the studio that would ultimately bring *Dracula* to the silver screen, had initially become interested shortly after the play's London run began. A studio reader was enthusiastic about the book's possibilities:

> For mystery and blood-curdling horror, I have never read its equal. For sets, impressionistic and weird, it cannot be surpassed. This story contains everything necessary for a weird, unnatural, mysterious picture.
>
> It is usually the case that if a story can be played upon the stage a screen version can be written from it as well. It will be a difficult task and one will run up against the censor continually, but I think it can be done. It is daring but if done there can be no doubt as to its making money.

This, however, was a minority opinion. The majority view was strongly negative, mostly regarding matters of censorship and good taste — the latter concerning the audience's ability to handle such a macabre tale. Rather than dismiss *Dracula* altogether, Universal decided to see how the play fared in New York and on tour. Other considerations came into play as well: the advent of sound movies resolved the problem of explaining vampire legends to filmgoers; finally, the censors, who occupied a position of great strength in 1927 when the Universal studio readers initially offered their views of *Dracula*'s suitability and the play opened in New York, "were again weakening against the onslaught of the producers. Such as unsavory topic became possible."[35]

Universal was the creation of a German immigrant, Carl Laemmle, who had come to America when he was seventeen. Before entering the movie business, he had worked a succession of odd jobs in different regions of the nation, finally winding up a clothing-store manager in Oshkosh, Wisconsin. His initial production studio had been situated in New York. Bucking the Motion Picture Patents Company (the "Trust"), which had been created to control every aspect of filmmaking, Laemmle relocated his company to Cuba. The island's susceptibility to tropical storms made it unsuitable for film production, so Laemmle moved again, this time making California his new base. He bought a 230-acre tract outside Los Angeles along the Camino Real highway. On this site arose an enormous motion picture production facility — "Universal City."[36] Laemmle was proud of what was dubbed "The Laemmle Foreign Legion," comprising roughly seventy relatives, friends, and hangers-on who were subsidized by the studio's payroll.[37]

Uncle Carl's crowning act of nepotism came on Sunday, April 28, 1929, when he named his son Carl Laemmle, Jr., general studio manager of Universal City. It was "Juniors'" 21st birthday gift. Seen in hindsight as a lesser figure among the Hollywood moguls, he was still responsible for such stellar movie fare of the '30s as *All Quiet on the Western Front, Counselor at Law, Imitation of Life,* and *Show Boat.* Added to the list were the landmark horror films *Dracula, Frankenstein, The Old Dark House, The Mummy, The Invisible Man, The Black Cat,* and *Bride of Frankenstein.*[38]

Many believed that even though Junior was the new studio chief, Uncle Carl would remain the true power. In reality Junior had big plans for Universal, and his father intended to support him in his ambitions. Junior's plans were much the same as those recommended by earlier

Universal executives Irving Thalberg and Al Lichtman, both of whom had desired to upgrade feature production and compete in the first-run market. Laemmle, Sr., had backed both of them only so far. By the beginning of Junior's tenure, Universal Theaters Inc. owned just over three hundred houses, the majority of them, however, were subsequent-run theaters in less desirable markets, more in sync with the studio's already established "program" strategy than to first-run releases. Feeling that the theaters didn't fit in with his upscale production ambitions and that converting them to sound films wasn't worth the expense, Junior sold them to subsidize his plans for prestige films. He trimmed shorts and programmers by some 40 percent, concentrating on A-level feature films. He sought presold properties and renowned actors, directors, and writers. He personally oversaw two of Universal's most grandiose films of the time, both adapted from prior successful properties: *Broadway*, an adaptation of a 1929 stage success, and *All Quiet on the Western Front*, adapted from Erich Maria Remarque's successful anti-war novel. Both were hits, with *All Quiet* copping the Oscars for Best Picture and Best Director of 1929–1930.[39]

These triumphs notwithstanding, Junior still experienced some costly fiascos; moreover, his successful films hadn't performed as well as they should, as Universal's sales and distribution system wasn't designed to exploit first-run releases. Because it had no real estate holdings that would be needed to obtain sufficiently large loans to replenish its cash reserves, Universal had no other recourse but to limit production and resume the method of operation that Uncle Carl had long utilized.

This crisis occurred as the Depression struck. Universal economized across the board. The emphasis now was on formula, or genre, films, including features. In this way Universal had no other option but to live within its means and utilize its own resources. In such a way did its house style and market strategy truly merge. And of all the genres Universal exploited during the early '30s, none came to be more associated with it than horror.

Long before the Depression descended on America, Universal had been developing the horror genre because it fitted in with the studio's strengths and assets. For a long time Uncle Carl had established a strong international distribution system, especially in Europe. He guaranteed the viability of Universal's films in Europe by hiring European moviemakers while he was abroad. Like Laemmle, numerous of these foreign talents were German. Additionally, they were well-acquainted with both the European tradition of gothic horror and German Expressionist films that flowered in the post–World War I era. These filmmakers were enthralled by cinema's extraordinary aspects, its ability to present a surreal panorama of eeriness. This style was successful in Europe and characterized Universal's American films. It was, moreover, comparatively cheap to translate on the screen. The atmosphere of Universal's horror films diminished the expense and intricacies of lighting and set design. It would become a routine film technique to build only that part of a set that would be seen through shadows or fog.

This sort of narrative frugality was essential to a studio like Universal with minimal financial assets and no big-name stars. The latter wasn't a drawback when it came to casting roles in horror films. The ideal horror star was an unconventional character actor. The sole major star in the Universal stable during the 1920s — Lon Chaney — fit that criterion. Chaney made his mark in horror roles playing disfigured characters in such films as *The Hunchback of Notre Dame* (1923) and *The Phantom of the Opera* (1925). Though Chaney had left for MGM, there were others in the Universal ranks (Conrad Veidt, Boris Karloff, and Claude Rains) whom the horror genre elevated to stardom.

In the late '20s, Universal's most talented artist in horror filmmaking was another Laemmle import from Germany, Paul Leni, whose specialty was converting Expressionism into a Hollywood form. A painter whose film career began in set design and art direction, he became a director at Ufa before moving on to Universal. His initial American film, *The Cat and the Canary* (1927), established Universal's "old dark house" film standard. This was followed by two other hits, *The Man Who Laughs* (1928) and *The Last Warning* (1929). The latter proved to be Leni's last film: he contracted a fatal case of blood poisoning. He was only 44.

Leni's premature death in no way affected Universal's interest in the horror film, which by 1930 was becoming a basic feature for the studio in both America and Europe. Despite his own apprehensions about *Dracula*, Junior Laemmle decided to go with it, motivated by the success of both the stage play and Universal's forays into "morbid" themes.[40]

As had been the case with the earlier hit *All Quiet on the Western Front*, Junior had to overcome his father's objections to filming *Dracula*. Laemmle, Sr., capitulated but with two stipulations: that Tod Browning direct the film and that its star be Lon Chaney.[41]

Thinking that Browning would be able to bring Chaney aboard, Universal signed the former to a three-picture deal. While he was at MGM, he had directed only one talking film, *The Thirteenth Chair*; despite that, he remained uncomfortable with sound. As Browning strove to comprehend the making of sound films, other events appeared to bode ill for the future of the proposed *Dracula* film. Owing to the Wall Street crash, Horace Liveright lost the screen rights. Acting on behalf of Balderston and Stoker, Harold Freeman in February 1930 approached MGM, Pathé, Columbia, and Universal about *Dracula*. Lon Chaney's dwindling health was known to all, and without Chaney, *Dracula* would be a no-go; it would be too hazardous from the censorship angle. Just the same, Junior Laemmle, owing to his experiences with *All Quiet on the Western Front*, knew there were ways around the Production Code.

Bela Lugosi was another interested party in *Dracula*. Seeking a studio to deal with the Stoker estate, Lugosi and his manager (and translator) Harry Weber succeeded in getting Universal's attention. What Lugosi failed to realize was that by assuming the role of self-appointed envoy between the studio and the author's estate, he was putting himself at a grave disadvantage as far as future negotiations with the studio. Thinking that if Lugosi wanted the role badly enough to be willing to act as an unsalaried representative, Universal believed that in all likelihood he could be signed to the role of Dracula far less expensively than a big-name star. By the time Freedman paid his respects to Universal in May 1930, the Depression was already exacting a toll on box-office profits. Despite his father's continuing resistance to *Dracula*, Junior directed writer Frederick "Fritz" Stephani to produce a treatment so that a budget could be prepared.[42]

All the while, various other machinations continued playing. As part of his ongoing quest for the role, Lugosi wrote Florence Stoker from a tour of *Dracula* in Oakland, California. Despite Uncle Carl's opposition to the film, Freedman continued his negotiations for the property's purchase. Steadfast in his support of the project, Junior turned it over to Tod Browning, complete with a budget of $355,000.

Junior's next move was to assign screenwriting chores to author Louis Bromfield. Then a pair of developments nearly sank it: *Nosferatu*, the bane of Florence Stoker's life, turned up for unlawful screenings in Greenwich Village; then the now insolvent Horace Liveright contended that a film version of *Dracula* constituted unfair competition to his future stage productions. The crisis was resolved when Universal finally obtained the rights to *Dracula* on August 22, 1930, only after paying Liveright a nuisance fee of $4000; suppressing Murnau's film by purchasing it (for Browning and his crew's perusal); and dividing $4000 between Florence Stoker (for screen rights to her husband's novel) and Hamilton Deane and John L. Balderston (for screen rights to their play). Four days after Universal obtained the rights to *Dracula*, Lon Chaney, one of the leading contenders for the role, died in Los Angeles of cancer.[43] Despite his passing, Browning wouldn't drop the picture, persuading Universal to screen test others for the role. Lugosi, who had played Dracula on the stage and collaborated with Browning on a prior film (*The Thirteenth Chair*), still wasn't the top contender. When he completed his screen test for the role, he remained uncertain of how it would all turn out, a feeling his protégé Carroll Borland observed:

> I remember that he wasn't sure at all that he would get the part. In fact, we both went up to Santa Barbara with the stage play *Dracula* to begin another Northern California road engagement. That's just how unsure he was. We were playing at Lobero Theater when he finally got the call from Universal to return for *Dracula*; he was really elated. I don't remember ever seeing him so pleased.[44]

Lugosi's jubilance quickly turned to rage when he learned that he would receive a flat $500-a-week salary for a seven-week shooting schedule, totaling $3,500 for the lead role in a major Hollywood motion picture. Lugosi was the paying the price for his imploration to Universal to secure the part. Universal was in a position of power, and Lugosi couldn't complain. He put a gloss upon the deal, consoling himself with the knowledge that he had the plum role in a big movie.[45] When Bromfield exited the production, final screenwriting chores fell to Browning and playwright Garrett Fort.[46]

Dracula's official screen debut before the public was scheduled for Friday, February 13, 1931, at New York's Roxy Theatre. Earlier stories of *Dracula*'s release have erroneously set its release date as Valentine's Day, 1931. In reality Universal had never considered issuing the film on that date, originally scheduling it for a Friday the 13th debut. *The New York Times'* February 11 edition featured a bogus telegram to S. L. "Roxy" Rothafel: DEAR ROXY DON'T BLAME ME BUT I WAS BORN SUPERSTITIOUS STOP JUST HEARD YOU ARE OPENING DRACULA FRIDAY STOP THAT'S BAD ENOUGH BUT FRIDAY THE THIRTEENTH IS TERRIBLE STOP I HAVE PUT EVERYTHING I HAVE INTO THIS PICTURE AND AS

A FAVOR TO ME CANT YOU OPEN YOUR PRESENTATION THURSDAY STOP BEST REGARDS TOD BROWNING. Thus *Dracula* debuted on February 12, 1931.[47]

As the film opens, a carriage makes its way to an inn in Transylvania. One of the passengers, Renfield, is making a business trip to see Count Dracula, who is relocating to England where he will reside in Carfax Abbey. When the coach reaches the inn and Renfield tells the innkeeper his ultimate destination, the horrified innkeeper warns him that Dracula is a vampire, an idea Renfield scoffs at as superstition. Viewing this scene in the context of the Great Depression, the villagers resemble working-class peons subservient to an all-powerful lord in the person of Dracula, a member of the upper class.

Renfield reboards the carriage, which transports him to his scheduled midnight appointment with Dracula's own carriage at Borgo Pass, then hurries off. Renfield boards Dracula's coach, which departs for the count's castle. As the carriage moves on its way, Renfield leans out the door to remonstrate the driver for going so fast — only to see in astonishment that the coachman has disappeared; in his place an enormous bat is seen flapping over the galloping horses. Audiences watching this scene in the Depression year 1931 might well have shared Renfield's unease, believing they themselves were "riding in a carriage without a driver"[48] (the driverless carriage signified a leaderless nation in a time of crisis).

The coach delivers Renfield to his host's abode. Once inside, Renfield meets Dracula, who greets him from atop a long staircase. This scene provides both Renfield and the audience their first good look at Dracula in his full attire, the latter clearly defining him as a member of the upper class: a black tuxedo with tail; a white vest adorned with mother-of-pearl buttons; and a white shirt. Topping off this finery is a black silk cape. (After he arrives in England, Dracula is shown walking the streets of London wearing a top hat and carrying a walking stick. His other accouterments include an enormous ring on his left hand; a pentagram pendant adorning his neck on the outside of his shirt; a white handkerchief; and a monocle.[49])

After leading Renfield upstairs, Dracula treats his guest to a late-night dinner and completes the final details of his departure to England, informing Renfield that they will be leaving via a ship the next evening. After Dracula bids Renfield good night, the latter falls unconscious from a drug in his wine. Dracula's undead wives approach him, only to be waved back by their master, who proceeds to drink Renfield's blood and enslave him. In becoming Dracula's servant, Renfield epitomizes a Depression victim, one who, like those real-life investors wiped out by the 1929 crash, fell from prosperity to despair, becoming, in one film historian's characterization, "a deranged shell of his former self. Locked up in asylum cell, he catches and eats flies, but only when he can't catch 'nice, fat spiders'"[50] — much like destitute people who scavenged for anything to eat. The desperation that hunger drove some people to was clearly illustrated by "food riots" that occurred that winter of 1931. On January 3, 1931, just weeks before *Dracula*'s New York debut, a group of farmers outside the village of England, Arkansas, unable to obtain sufficient relief food from the Red Cross, decided their sole recourse was to take matters into their own hands. "All you that hain't yaller," shouted one of them, "climb on my truck. We're a-goin' into England to get some grub." Once they arrived at their destination, this initial group was joined by others in a multitude that ultimately totaled from three hundred to five hundred. After receiving the Red Cross' pledge to compensate them, the town's merchants gave the disgruntled throng food to feed their families. Once the group had dispersed, city officials were cautioned, "The merchants of England either must move their goods or mount machine guns on their stores!" Other "food riots" followed in Oklahoma City, Minneapolis, and elsewhere at various times.[51]

Once the action shifts from Transylvania, with its nineteenth century look, to England, the film enters the contemporary world of the 1930s. Walking the streets of London, Dracula pauses to kill a flower girl. His ultimate destination is the operahouse, where he meets his new neighbor, Dr. Seward; the latter's daughter Mina; her fiancé John Harker; and Mina's friend Lucy. To gain admittance to the Seward party's box at the opera, the vampire hypnotizes an usherette to tell Dr. Seward a telephone call awaits him. Of this scene, David J. Skal has observed:

> Dracula movies tend to be very class conscious. The aristocratic vampire invariably dominates and controls an assortment of working-class characters — maids, nurses, and other economically subservient women. By 1931, the Depression had drawn very sharp lines between the world's haves and have-nots, and perhaps this accounts for some of the film's fascination for audiences of the period.[52]

After visiting the opera, Dracula attacks Lucy in her bedroom — an act that symbolizes the end of the Roaring '20s and the onset of the Depression. "When Bela Lugosi draws his black cape over sleeping jazz baby Frances Dade — the image of the Liberty dollar, according to her publicity — he is performing a rite of economic extreme unction." Subsequently Lugosi appeared as Dracula in a scene in a short film repeating the earlier sequence: Stalking "the quintessential flapper icon," Betty Boop (Mae Questal), he tells her "'You have booped your last boop' and summarily sinks in his fangs."[53]

After destroying Lucy, Dracula begins victimizing Mina, who complains of being weak, as if "all the life had been drained out of me." The sense of "wasting away" experienced by Dracula's victims found a real-life counterpart in the increase of malnutrition during the Depression. The year of *Dracula*'s release, 60 percent of all admissions to New York City hospitals resulted from malnutrition — an increase from 28 percent two years earlier. According to an Internet source, "the nation-wide food shortage would have affected some, if not most moviegoers, providing another link between the film and popular experience." The same source further notes: "The character of Renfield, the count's insane, bug-eating servant, as well as the setting of part of the story within the walls of a sanitarium also parallel the rise during the early Thirties of the numbers of the insane. Their official number rose from 439.2 per 100,000 in 1929 to 472.3 per 100,000 in 1933."[54] In another way Dracula was relevant to Depression-era America in that he represented a foreign invader. Just as Stoker's novel reflected the anxieties of late Victorian Britons over immigration to their shores, so, too, did the Lugosi film mirror America's unease over foreigners in its midst in the post–World War I era.

The war had witnessed an ebbing of the reforming spirit that animated the pre-war Progressive movement. In its place had arisen a spirit of patriotism and self-sacrifice that depleted the Progressive instincts of one of its champions, Woodrow Wilson. In the war's aftermath, Wilson devoted his energies, not to re-energizing the Progressive cause, but to an ultimately abortive campaign to win Senate approval of the Versailles Treaty and American entry into the League of Nations. By then, the majority of Wilson's fellow countrymen were eager to put the war and its attendant demands for selflessness behind them in favor of pursing their own private aspirations. The reforming impulse was over.

With its demise there arose an isolationist impulse, one that determined to shut Europe out of sight and out of mind and keep America safe from foreign contamination. This feeling grew out of Americans' conviction that the nation's investment in the war — both in the sacrifice of American lives and financial resources — had all been for naught. In the immediate postwar period, Americans had cast apprehensive eyes at the triumph of Communism in Russia, which contributed to Attorney General A. Mitchell Palmer's Red raids.

In the eyes of conservatives, immigration was the crux of the problem. Despite the fact that America had been created by a "melting pot" of various ethnic and national groups, despite Emma Lazarus' exhortation to the world to send their "huddled masses yearning to breathe free," America has seldom extended an emphatic welcome to foreign citizens, especially those who weren't completely the same as us. "In the twenties," noted historian T. H. Watkins, "the fear was much more intense, fired by a terror that American institutions would be subverted by uncontrollable foreign elements."

In the immediate post-war years, the United States received more than 600,000 southern European immigrants, mostly Italians, along with approximately 150,000 Poles, 50,000 Russians, and 150,000 people from other Central and Eastern European nations — not to mention almost 175,000 Mexicans; most of the latter would settle in rural areas of the Southwest. The lion's share of the others came to dwell in Northeastern and Midwestern cities. These newcomers greatly strained their new environs' political, economic, and social structures, which were already feeling the pressure occasioned by the arrival of southern blacks during the "Great Migration" before and during World War I. The presence of these myriad groups worsened the anti-urban sentiment of most rural Americans. An element of intolerance colored this attitude: Cities, in the eyes of numerous strict Protestants, were already controlled by two groups anathema to them — Jews with their supposed cunning monetary ways and rumored domination of America's financial institutions and Catholics who were completely in thrall to the Pope, a people of dubious ethics "and whose political corruption was legendary."

It was this sort of intolerance that played a major part in the enacting of legislation in 1924 imposing draconian limitations on future immigration to the United States, with special emphasis on limiting the number of Jews and Poles, Slavs, Russians, Italians, and other nationalities that weren't satisfactorily Anglo-Saxon or Nordic-Protestant. The reappearance

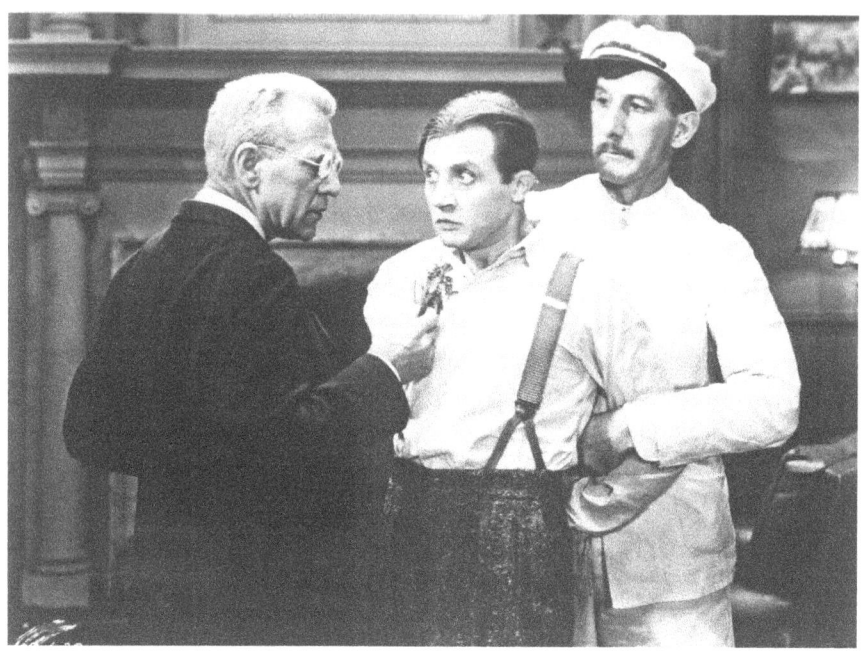

The agonies Dracula's on-screen victims suffered mirrored the real-life miseries Americans experienced during the Depression.

Above: Dracula's transformation of Renfield (Dwight Frye, center, between Edward Van Sloan, left, and Charles Gerrard) into a mentally unbalanced, insect-devouring patient in an asylum symbolized the rise of insanity during the early years of the Depression.

Left: Mina Seward's (Helen Chandler) sense of "wasting away" resulting from the vampire's feeding on her blood symbolized the rise in malnutrition (Universal Pictures/Photofest).

of the Ku Klux Klan during this time was another manifestation of the anti-immigrant sentiment of '20s America. Originally founded in the post–Civil War era as an anti-black organization, the revived Klan added Jews and Catholics to its list of unacceptables. The new Klan's greatest strength was found in the rural and small-town Midwest. Until its leader was tried and convicted of murder in 1925, an event that signaled the group's downfall to a handful of true believers, the Klan was a strong presence in the Midwest, completely ruling the political scene in Indiana and engendering anxiety among those peoples it despised.[55]

Given this climate of intolerance and anti-foreign attitudes, Count Dracula, an Eastern European, would have been most unwelcome in '20s America had he chosen to come here. Moreover, his attempts to recruit others, especially women, into his vampiric legions would have been viewed as cultural pollution of the nation's WASP majority, rendering him as an undesirable alien subject to deportation. Additionally, as the vampire malady was foreign-born, originating in Eastern Europe, it fit in perfectly with the thesis that the Depression was a foreign, not an American, problem. Immigration, in the view of one Congressman, was the source of the nation's unemployment problem during the Depression.[56] The economic crisis, explained the late Professor Robin W. Winks of Yale University,

> led many Americans to feel that they wanted even more isolation from European society because one view was that the Depression in America did not come because of deficiencies in the American economy but rather that it was the virus of Europe that had spread the Depression. After all, the first closure of banks took place in Austria, in Vienna, and there was a spread of those closures across Europe, which reached the United States a bit later. And this certainly gave many people, including Herbert Hoover, an opportunity to argue that the Depression had been brought to America because of European events. And if we could have only been more insulated from Europe, we might well not have fallen into the Depression ourselves.[57]

Another element of Depression imagery in *Dracula* involved the clash between Van Helsing and Harker over Mina's safety after she falls prey to the vampire, with an exasperated Harker at one point telling Van Helsing, "You're driving her crazy, professor," to which Van Helsing remonstrates that Harker's concern should be directed toward the setting sun heralding Dracula's imminent arrival after dark. Harker even tries to take Mina from Van Helsing's protective care to London, thinking she'll be safer there. Over a year after *Dracula*'s release, the on-screen Van Helsing-Harker dispute would be replayed in reality in the post-election clash between Herbert Hoover and President-elect Franklin D. Roosevelt during the interregnum between Roosevelt's election and inauguration. Believing that Roosevelt's proposed New Deal would be disastrous for the nation and unable to comprehend that his own policies were the source of the crisis, Hoover sought to obtain Roosevelt's promise that he would adhere to economic orthodoxy once FDR was president. Roosevelt declined the request. Nor would he accede to Hoover's wishes when the banking crisis began just before the inauguration in 1933, when Hoover requested that Roosevelt promise that there wouldn't be any toying with the economy, heavy borrowing, or unbalancing of the budget.[58] In the latter, Hoover fully understood what he sought: "I realize that if these declarations be made by the President-elect, he will have ratified the whole major program of the Republican Administration; that is, it means the abandonment of 90 percent of the so-called new deal."[59] Hoover's efforts to obtain Roosevelt's "cooperation" continued right up to inauguration eve, March 3, 1933, when the President-elect and his family paid a courtesy call on Hoover at the White House. The meeting ended abruptly and unpleasantly. When Roosevelt suggested that Hoover needn't return his call, Hoover replied, "Mr. Roosevelt, when you are in Washington as long as I have been, you will learn that the President of the United States calls on nobody." After the inaugural ceremony the next day, the two men never met again.[60]

Dracula concludes with Van Helsing and Harker, aided by an unwitting Renfield, tracking the count back to his Carfax Abbey hideaway, to which he has taken Mina. Thinking Renfield has led his pursuers to him, Dracula kills his servant, then carries Mina into his coffin lair just as dawn breaks. Finding the vampire in his coffin, Van Helsing pounds a stake into his heart, finally bringing Dracula's centuries-old reign of terror to an end, and releasing Mina from his grip. The action Dracula's pursuers take in the film's closing moments stand in sharp contrast to the general sense of helplessness then prevalent in America. Harker and Van Helsing's actions "may have provided hope for a demoralized society." In the words of one historian, it was "hope, after all, that drove people to acts of courage and determination.... When people rose ... they were acting not merely in desperation and fury, but in the hope that in doing so they were taking hold of their lives and changing them for the better."[61] Nevertheless, destroying a vampire on screen was a simple task; lifting America out of its economic morass in 1931 would be far more difficult.

In its first two days at the Roxy, *Dracula* sold 50,000 tickets, ultimately grossing $700,000, making it Universal's most successful film of 1931.[62] This success astonished film industry insiders, who strongly believed that audiences, who were confronting the grimness of life in the Great Depression, would never accept a supernatural horror thriller. The truth was that the Depression contributed to *Dracula*'s box office success. Such a film was perfect for the time. Hollywood quickly discovered that movies based on the Depression were box office poison. A story about a 500-year-old vampire was only slightly more incredible than other standard movie offerings of the time. The allegorical elements of a story where a malevolent alien menace jeopardizes average people who defeat the threat perhaps touched a nerve with audiences during the Depression. "The grimness of the theme was alleviated by its abnormality — viewers could [forget] the realities of the Depression and share vicariously in problems that they knew would never touch their own lives."[63]

In addition to surpassing nearly all expectations, *Dracula* vindicated Carl Laemmle, Jr. Whether one liked this type of film or not, it was clear that the horror genre was a new and lucrative one for Hollywood. By 1936, *Dracula* had grossed $1,012,189 worldwide. And though Universal would continually face financial problems all through the 1930s, *Dracula* had been the studio's financial savior in 1931, keeping the studio afloat.[64] Universal had found a winning formula in the midst of the Great Depression. As is the case with Hollywood, the success of *Dracula* prompted Universal's competitors to jump aboard the horror bandwagon with macabre projects of their own. This, combined with *Dracula*'s success, prompted Laemmle, Jr., to announce that Universal was going ahead with two other shockers, *Frankenstein* and *Murders in the Rue Morgue*. "The stories are well underway," he disclosed.[65]

Frankenstein *the Motion Picture (1931)*

Despite the box office punch *Dracula* packed, Universal's financial situation remained dire: In March 1931, just after *Dracula*'s release, the Laemmles laid-off 350 employees. This was followed by a brief closing of the studio. None of this dissuaded Carl Laemmle, Jr., from forging ahead with another horror production for Bela Lugosi, delegating it to 30-year-old French director-writer Robert Florey. Florey came to directing from a varied entertainment career — Hollywood correspondent for a French magazine and an assistant to several film stars and directors. In his directorial career, he had worked with the likes of Edward G. Robinson, Claudette Colbert, and the Marx Brothers, and knew everyone from D. W. Griffith to Fatty Arbuckle. After making his directorial debut at Paramount and directing in his native France, Florey had returned to Hollywood, where he met writer Richard Schayer, Universal scenario editor, to discuss the studio's follow-up production to *Dracula*. Florey's credentials, Schayer believed, made him the perfect choice for a horror film. Of all the ideas they considered, *Frankenstein* held the most interest for them.[66]

If he was to realize his dream of bringing a sound version of *Frankenstein* to the motion picture screen, Florey would have to convince Carl Laemmle, Jr. The first step in that process was Florey's five-page synopsis, which transformed the Monster from the calculating figure Mary Shelley originally presented into a marauding creature. Having secured Schayer's endorsement of the treatment, Florey than began toiling on the final script with Garrett Fort, who had worked on the *Dracula* screenplay.[67] The end result of their labor would virtually shape the final film.

During the preparation of his synopsis, Florey believed that Henry Frankenstein would be played by Bela Lugosi. Toward that end, the Fort-Florey script made Henry the principal character. Universal then unveiled a surprising casting decision: The role of the monster would be played by Lugosi.[68]

In wanting Lugosi to play the Monster, Universal had some logical motives. The studio wanted a "new Lon Chaney," and Chaney had made his mark playing grossly deformed characters. Moreover, Lugosi was nearly fifty years old and possessed a ponderous Hungarian accent that rendered him more a character actor than a leading man.[69] For his part, Lugosi regarded himself as a sexy, romantic man who had merely starred in a horror film, not Lon Chaney's successor.[70] Recalling her husband's attitude toward enacting the part of the Frankenstein Monster, Lugosi's fourth wife Lillian said:

> Bela wanted out! He said, "I'll get a doctor's excuse!" because it was a six hour makeup ordeal. Bela, you see, was the Actor and he couldn't see himself moaning and grunting — and that's all the Monster did in the original film. Bela thought, "You don't need an actor for that part! Anybody can moan and grunt! I need a challenging part — a part where I Can Act!"[71]

Different stories abound as to why Lugosi was dropped from the film.[72] What is definitely certain is that Carl Laemmle, Jr., seeing Lugosi as nothing more than a horror star, insisted that the Hungarian play the Monster,[73] and that Lugosi, in declining a part he viewed as unworthy of him, gave rise to a rival who would permanently outrank him as the King of Horror.

Lugosi wasn't the only one who would be off the project. Despite having been involved in filmmaking for a decade, Florey nevertheless had limited feature experience and only one talking film to his credit. Additionally, as he was a comparative newcomer to Universal, he had hardly established himself there. On the other hand, James Whale had perfect credentials. He was a veteran British stage director who was successfully moving on to film. He had helmed the movie version of the successful stage play *Journey's End*, which had been filmed in Hollywood because of the latter's better sound facilities. Whale's next project was another war film, Howard Hughes' *Hell's Angels*, on which Whale served as dialogue director. When Whale joined Universal, Laemmle wanted him to direct the film version of another play, *Waterloo Bridge*. Because Whale wasn't that greatly interested in the project and because Laemmle wanted Whale's services for a long time, Laemmle gave him the right to choose whatever project he wanted to do once *Waterloo Bridge* was completed. Whale selected *Frankenstein*.[74] Of his decision to undertake *Frankenstein*, Whale offered this explanation:

> I chose *Frankenstein* out of about 30 available stories because it was the strongest meat and gave me a chance to dabble in the macabre. I thought it would be an amusing thing to try and make what everybody knows to be a physical impossibility into the almost believable for 60 minutes. A director must be pretty bad if he can't get a thrill out of a war, murder, robbery. *Frankenstein* was a sensational story and had a chance to become a sensational picture. It offered fine pictorial possibilities, had two grand characterizations, and dealt with a subject which might go anywhere — and that is part of the fun of making pictures.[75]

Upon learning that he had been dropped from *Frankenstein*, the film he had scripted, Florey restudied his contract, only to discover that it stipulated he would direct a film — but not necessarily the one he wrote.[76]

When it came to casting the role of the Frankenstein Monster, no official record was kept of those who auditioned. Long after the fact, John Carradine would assert that he had tried for the role but, like Lugosi, declined it on the grounds that it wasn't sufficiently challenging. However, no evidence exists corroborating Carradine's story. David Lewis, Whale's companion, made a suggestion of his own: an actor who had appeared in Columbia's *The Criminal Code*.[77]

The actor whom Lewis had in mind originally entered the world in

Camberwell, south London, on November 23, 1887, as William Henry Pratt before ultimately changing his name, for stage reasons, to Boris Karloff.[78] Despite the hardships he encountered in the course of his acting career, Karloff persevered, barnstorming in stage productions before finally making his way to Hollywood, where he discovered his niche as a villain. Not until 1931, after roughly 80 film parts, stage appearances in California, and work as a truck driver, did he finally win a measure of recognition as an actor, playing a succession of villainous characters. By the time he appeared in Universal's *Graft*, Karloff was working so regularly, his school librarian wife had left her job, and they had left what she termed their "shack" atop Laurel Canyon, where they had treated guests to green beer they brewed in the bathtub.[79]

Following Lewis' suggestion, Whale sought out Karloff, eventually finding him in the Universal commissary. Of the occasion, Karloff recalled that he was having lunch, and Whale dispatched either his first assistant or secretary to request the pleasure of his company with Whale after lunch. Once the two were together, Whale began the conversation by mentioning the difficulties British actors faced in Hollywood, then got down to business: "Your face has startling possibilities." Karloff was surprised when Whale asked him to do a test.

"What for?"

"For a damned awful monster!" Despite Karloff's initial shock at the purpose of the test, he was thrilled, "because it meant another job, if I was able to land it. Actually that's all it meant to me. At the same time I felt rather hurt, because at the time I had on very good straight makeup and my best suit — and he wanted to test me for a monster!"[80]

Whale knew he had found his Monster, though Karloff's "physique was weaker than I could wish, but the queer, penetrating personality of his, I felt, was more important than his shape, which could easily be altered." Karloff, who suffered rickets during his childhood, needed padding; when playing classical stage roles he filled out his legs with "symmetricals," or padded undertights. Whale, who declared he was fascinated by Karloff's face, made his own sketches of it.[81]

Upon being contacted by Whale about the part, Karloff obtained a copy of Mary Shelley's novel. The key to being cast in the film would be the outcome of the test. As soon as possible, Karloff got together with Universal's maestro of makeup Jack Pierce to begin work on the Monster's appearance. At the time, Karloff was filming the motion picture *Graft*.

"Who am I and what am I?" the Frankenstein Monster (Boris Karloff) seems to be asking in this photograph—much as the American people sought an explanation for their plight in the Depression (Universal Pictures/Photofest).

When the day's work on the latter wrapped, Karloff would remain at the studio with Pierce and together the two would experiment on the makeup. Meeting three hours a night, they spent three weeks on the task. Pierce utilized layers of cheesecloth and collodion to enlarge Karloff's forehead. To enhance the Monster's sunken, emaciated appearance, Pierce had Karloff remove his partial bridge. Karloff himself made a contribution to the Monster's creation when he examined his makeup in a mirror: "We had the problem that if your eyes were alive and normal — and, I hope, intelligent — it would simply destroy the makeup and it would destroy the illusion. And that's why we used putty over the eyes — to distort them and to veil them a little bit, so they wouldn't be too clear and too sharp."[82]

When finally made up, Karloff stood seven feet tall, with an additional 48 pounds, including a hidden five-pound spine (the latter described by Pierce as "the rod which conveys the current up to the Monster's brain") and the enormous asphalt-spreaders boots — each weighing 13 pounds. Pierce had also made it possible for Karloff's made-up face to show emotion. It was this latter element, more than anything else, that resulted in Karloff winning the role.[83]

Budgeted at $262,000 and with a 30-day shooting schedule, *Frankenstein* began filming on Monday, August 24, 1931, with the cemetery scene the first to be shot. Principal photography had run five days over schedule when filming finally wrapped on October 3.[84]

Accompanied by *The New Adventures of Get-Rich-Quick Wallingford* with William Haines, *Frankenstein* had its initial public preview at Santa Barbara's Granada Theater on October 29.[85] The film opens at a funeral, where, unknown to the mourners, Henry Frankenstein and Fritz, his hunchbacked assistant, are watching, waiting for the proceedings to end. Once the mourners have departed and the corpse finally buried, the duo hurriedly disinter the body, then depart. After leaving the cemetery, Frankenstein and Fritz discover a dead body hanging from a roadside pole. Reluctantly obeying his master's order, Fritz scrambles up the pole and cuts the body down. It proves useless: the deceased's neck is broken, rendering its brain useless for Frankenstein's experiments. The only other source for a suitable brain is the local medical college. There, following a lecture, Fritz breaks in, finding a pair of human brains — one normal, the other belonging to a criminal. Fritz initially takes the former but an accident causes him to drop it to the floor, smashing its container and destroying the brain. Fritz now has no choice but to take the remaining, criminal brain.

Concerned over Henry's experiments, his fiancée Elizabeth reveals her unease to their mutual friend, Victor Moritz. Together, they see Henry's old medical school instructor, Dr. Waldman, who tells them that Frankenstein was obsessed with creating human life. The bodies that the university used for dissecting weren't good enough for Henry, who told the university to find other cadavers — no matter where they came from. Elizabeth persuades Waldman to take her and Victor to Henry's laboratory. The three of them arrive there on a stormy night, just as Frankenstein and Fritz are making final preparations to bring Frankenstein's creation to life. Frankenstein reluctantly grants them admittance, allowing them to view his experiment. Waldman asks his former student, "And you really believe that you can bring life to the dead?" That body, Henry retorts, has never lived, for he had created it from parts obtained from other bodies. He intends to bring it to life.

When the storm is at its greatest, Frankenstein and Fritz raise the body to an opening in the laboratory ceiling so that the body can attract lightning. After being lowered back inside the lab, the body's hand moves. "It's alive. It's alive. It's alive...!" Frankenstein deliriously exclaims. "...In the name of God, now I know what it feels like to be God!"

The laboratory special effects were handled by Hollywood technician Kenneth Strickfaden, who made money leasing his props for use in Universal's subsequent *Frankenstein* projects. By the time of Universal's 1931 adaptation, cosmic rays were a topical subject, hence in the film, Henry Frankenstein informs Waldman that, in his experiments, he has discovered the ray responsible for bringing life into the world. After *Frankenstein*'s release, fraudulent cosmic ray commercial products, such as the Bioray, were promoted; the Bioray, touted as something of a radioactive air freshener, promised "to bathe the user in a constant stream of benevolent, health-restorative gamma radiation."[86]

Waldman believes Frankenstein's creation should be kept under guard ("He will prove dangerous"). Frankenstein scoffs at the idea, asking, "Have you never wanted to do anything that was dangerous? Where should we be if nobody tried to find out what lies beyond? ...If you talk like that, people call you crazy...." Informed by Waldman that the Monster's brain belonged to the criminal, Henry, though momentarily shocked, again assumes a dismissive attitude: "It's only a piece of dead tissue." "Only evil can come of it," Waldman insists, adding, "You have created a monster, and it will destroy you." "I believe in this monster, as you call it," says

Henry. "And if you don't, well you must leave me alone.... I've got to experiment further."

The above exchange again personifies the Hoover-Roosevelt clash: Waldman personifies Hoover who clings to the old ways in dealing with the Depression, while Henry Frankenstein embodies Roosevelt, who believes his New Deal experiments will succeed. Waldman (Hoover) wants Henry (Roosevelt) to discontinue his experiments, believing they're dangerous.

When Frankenstein's Monster finally comes into full view on the screen, Whale treats the viewer to quick close-ups of his face, no doubt shocking 1931 audiences with them. Then the Monster reacts in wonderment to the sunlight flooding in when Henry opens a skylight. When the latter is closed, eliminating the light, the Monster shakes his hands disappointedly, yearning for the light's return. The Monster's joy at his discovery is shortlived: When Fritz enters, carrying a torch, the Monster, fearing the fire, goes berserk, requiring his confinement, in chains, in the cellar. Ultimately Fritz, who revels in torturing the Monster with the torch, is hung by the creature. Waldman overcomes the Monster with an injection in his back. Henry agrees to return home with his father and Elizabeth, while Waldman preserves the records of his experiments and destroys the Monster. However, just as Waldman is about to dissect the Monster, the latter regains consciousness, strangles Waldman, then escapes into the countryside.

Once free, the Monster ultimately encounters Maria, a small girl at her father's home by the lake. Befriending him, she shows the Monster how to make flowers float on the lake. The Monster imitates her but, when he runs out of flowers, he tosses her in, drowning her. Confused by what he's done, the Monster flees. After accidentally drowning Maria, the Monster intrudes upon Elizabeth's and Henry's wedding, terrorizing the bride-to-be in her bedroom. Just as Henry Frankenstein was powerless to protect Elizabeth from the Monster's ravages, so, too, were numerous real-life husbands unable to shield their wives from the ravages of the Depression.[87]

The wedding festivities are further disrupted when Maria's father, carrying her dead body in his arms, walks almost trance-like into town. Leaving Elizabeth in Victor's care, Henry joins the search party in pursuit of the Monster. Becoming separated from his group, Frankenstein encounters his creation, who overpowers him and carries him to a windmill. Once there, both Frankenstein and the Monster are cornered by the villagers. When Frankenstein tries to escape, the Monster hurls him from atop the windmill but his fall is broken when he lands on one of the windmill blades. The villagers then torch the windmill. As the fire consumes the structure, the Monster is pinned under a falling bean and seemingly destroyed.

Frankenstein's climactic moments clearly resonate with the economic hard times the film was released in. The mob pursuing the Monster resembles an enraged populace lashing out in frustration against the Depression — and the man they perceived as indifferent to their plight, Herbert Hoover. In chasing the Monster to the windmill, the mob signifies the angry voters who turned Hoover out of office in 1932. Just as the Monster himself strove to find his place in the world, so, too, did the common man seek to understand the Depression and what had happened to him. A contemporary view, offered by British critic G. A. Atkinson, saw racial

Uniting for a common cause. People of all social classes must band together to overcome a mutual danger — be it the destruction of the Monster, shown here at the conclusion of Frankenstein, or the Great Depression (Universal Pictures/Photofest).

connotations in the Monster's destruction, equating his demise with "a Georgia lynching.... The parallel may be unkind, but it is irresistible."[88] Another assessment holds that the mob, comprising people from every level of society — upper- to lower-class — signified the notion that, if the Great Depression was to be vanquished, then everyone — upper, middle, and lower class — must join together to achieve this goal. This plea for united cooperation found its greatest expression in the birth of the New Deal. Henry Frankenstein's realization that his wedding to Elizabeth must be delayed until his "horrible creation" is reined in intimates that the fulfillment of personal endeavors also depends on the elimination of the monster — and, by extension, the Depression.[89]

David Lewis, who joined Whale for the Santa Barbara preview, recalled the audience reaction to *Frankenstein*: "As it progressed, people got up, walked out, come back in, walked out again." Terrified at the preview reaction, Junior Laemmle termed it "a disaster."[90] Based on *Dracula*'s success, *Frankenstein* had been scheduled for viewing in all of RKO's theaters, beginning with Seattle, Detroit, and Milwaukee on November 21, then Kansas City, Minneapolis, and New York in early December.

"I didn't know enough at the time to say anything," recalled Lewis, "but I was Eddie Montagne's assistant at Paramount, and he used to be at Universal. I talked to him the next day. He said, 'My God, they've got the hit of all time. When you can stir an audience like that, you've really got them.' I told Jimmy, and Jimmy got Junior to call me — they were taking things out — and he said, 'Have Eddie Montagne call me.'"

"I didn't see it," Montagne told Junior, "but from what David tells me, you've got the hit of the year."

Junior disagreed: "They were walking out!"

"You're insane," Montagne retorted. "If we had a picture like that, we'd clean up."[91]

In the wake of the Santa Barbara preview, Universal excised a number of offending scenes: the drowning of Maria, Fritz tormenting the Monster in the dungeon, and a closeup of Waldman's hypodermic needle being injected into the Monster's back. Also eliminated was Frankenstein's triumphal cry, "In the name of God, now I know what it feels like to be God!" In its place would be heard a peal of thunder.[92]

There were also some additions. When *Frankenstein* was considered for viewing in Canada, the film drew protests from Quebec censors — Catholics who were offended on religious grounds by its concept of divine presumption. To mollify Catholic demurrals, Universal's T. B. Fithian arranged a screening for two Catholic priests in Los Angeles. Their verdict after seeing the film: It in no way affronted Catholic tenets. Still, they concurred with Fithian that the best way to appease the Canadian censors might be "through the agency of a suitable foreword or some preface that would indicate the picture was a dream. Perhaps we could open it on the book with the off-scene voices of Shelley and Byron and Mrs. Shelley discussing a fantastic tale and dissolve into the picture. We would be willing to do anything like this." Ultimately, *Frankenstein* received Canadian endorsement for viewing in basically its initial form. Still this didn't prevent the addition to every print of an opening prologue featuring Edward Van Sloan:

> Mr. Carl Laemmle feels it would be a little unkind to present this picture without just a word of friendly warning. We are about to unfold the story of Frankenstein, a man of science, who sought to create a man after his own image, without reckoning upon God. It is one of the strangest tales ever told. It deals with the two great mysteries of creation — Life and Death. I think it will thrill you. It may shock you. It might even horrify you. So if any of you feel that you do not care to subject your nerves to such a strain, now is your chance to.... Well, we've warned you!

Another edition was the closing scene in which Frankenstein didn't die, followed by Baron Frankenstein toasting his son's recovery and marriage while Elizabeth ministers to Henry in the background.[93]

Frankenstein, shorn of its "offending" scenes, debuted Friday, December 4, 1931, at the Mayfair Theatre in New York's Times Square, and was an immediate hit, earning an unprecedented $53,000, selling out the Mayfair's 1,734 seats several times and prompting further screenings of the film. By contrast, *Suicide Fleet*, the film that had played the Mayfair immediately before *Frankenstein*, earned a mere $19,000.[94] Presently, *Frankenstein* proved as much a sensation internationally as it had been in America: When it debuted in London later that month, *To-day's Cinema* proclaimed:

Pulpit Protests Against
Frankenstein
A Week of Packed Houses the Result"[95]

Why had *Frankenstein* been such a huge success? A contemporary explanation was provided by *Motion Picture Herald*: "Morbidity is not without its claim to a high place among humanity's respectable emotional interests," it noted in analyzing the film. The latter had appeared, "if the psychologists can be believed, at the familiar psychological moment. Say the savants, people like the tragic best at those time[s] when their own spirits are depressed, and the economists tell us that even more than their spirits are at a low ebb."[96] The *Herald*'s judgment, tying *Frankenstein*'s appeal to the Depression, has stood the test of time. In the 1970s, film historian Paul M. Jensen felt: "Large sections of the public, having difficulty dealing with the Depression, were glad to spend some time in the company of a monster that could more easily be defeated."[97] Going a step further, David J. Skal linked *Frankenstein* with *Dracula* as metaphors for the Depression: "A general anxiety about the prospects of resurrecting a dead economy was curiously refracted in the back-from-the-grave themes of both films."[98]

More immediately, in 1931 *Frankenstein* elevated Boris Karloff to the summit of stardom in the horror field, forever displacing Bela Lugosi who had scoffed at playing the Monster, beginning a rivalry that would end only with Lugosi's death. Lugosi, the embodiment of the aristocratic Carpathian vampire, would ultimately descend into virtual obscurity and drug addiction, while Karloff, the proletarian monster, soared to stardom. There were other immediate consequences of the 1931 horror revolution initiated by *Dracula* and *Frankenstein*: First, the supernatural became an established element of the American horror film; second, in the midst of the Great Depression, moviegoers were now anxious for more horrors, and Hollywood was now eager to satisfy their desire.

2

Exploiting the Lower Classes (1932–1933)

The end of 1931 found Universal number one in the horror field. Other studios had forayed into the genre: Paramount with *Murder by the Clock*; Warner Bros. with *Svengali*. While the latter productions weren't supernatural in nature, like Universal's offerings, they did enhance the horror cycle. However, voices inside and outside the film industry were raising concerns as to the suitability of horror. Within the industry Colonel Jason Joy of the Studio Relations Committee (SRC) worried over the censorship issues that horror films raised; such films, in his view, prompted local censor boards to grievously rend them — something Joy's department was supposed to prevent from happening. Writing to Motion Picture Producers and Distributors Association chairman Will Hays, Joy inquired: "Is this the beginning of a cycle that ought to be retarded or killed?"[1]

When it came to presentations of sex on the screen, the Production Code had succeeded in some measure in reining them in. "If something equally as effective could be done about the so-called horror pictures we'd be very much happier than we are," Joy informed Hays just as 1932 was beginning. "The fact that the supply of such stories is necessarily limited will lead eventually to straining for more and more horrors until the wave topples over and breaks," Joy asserted in reference to the burgeoning number of horror films Universal was turning out. The other studios "are much intrigued by the fact that *Frankenstein* is staying for four weeks and taking in big money at theatres which were about on the rocks." The latter point was significant. The income generated by horror films had been a financial blessing to the studios, making them resistant to the objections that such films raised. The MPPDA couldn't prevent a film from either being produced or distributed, as its rulings were reviewed by a panel of none other than the film producers themselves, who were certain to render final judgments on the basis of the profit motive. While conceding that "[t]alking out here won't have much effect," Joy hoped that a popular backlash on the public's part was fermenting. "How could it be otherwise if children go to these pictures and have the jitters, followed by nightmares?" Joy stated that he wouldn't want his children viewing such films.[2]

Joy's concerns were followed shortly thereafter by those of film critic Nelson B. Bell, expressed in the pages of *The Washington Post*'s February 21, 1932, issue:

> Those neurotic individuals who find agreeable occupation in following ambulances and pursuing fire engines, find themselves, at the moment, the unexpected beneficiaries of an era in the motion picture theaters dedicated largely to them and their quaint amusement tastes....
> It is not impossible that this disquieting and startling manifestation of public preference may be traced directly to the trying period of economic stress through which we, in company with the rest of the world, are passing. Many are without employment, many are employed only by virtue of having accepted drastic curtailment of income, many live their daily lives in a state of constant dread of the disaster that may overtake them at any minute. This is a state of mind that creates a vast receptivity for misfortunes more poignant than our own. There is, paradoxically enough, a distinctly heartening effect in the sorry spectacle of someone worse off than ourselves. But however that may be, the end of the "horror" pictures is not yet.[3]

Bell's forecast was accurate: The horror cycle had only just begun. The coming months witnessed a succession of horror films. In them would be themes of class struggle in which the strong would exploit the weak, a feeling those Americans struggling with the Depression daily felt.

The Distrust of Experts: Dr. Jekyll and Mr. Hyde *and* Murders in the Rue Morgue *(1932)*

An early casualty of the Depression was the people's trust in all manner of experts — scientists, bankers, and politicians. Emblematic of this sentiment was an article, "Scientists as Citizen," appearing in the March 1933 issue of the journal *Social Forces*. Its author, Read Bain of Miami University, was scathing in his denunciation of scientists: "Scientists, with a few notable exceptions, are the worst citizens of the Republic; they, more than any other single factor, threaten the persistence of Western culture. They are wholesale, though unconscious traitors to the civilization they have created." Bain continued:

> Racketeers are running sores on the social body, but unsocialized scientists are a foul corruption in the very heart's blood of society. They are not prophets of light and leading but workers of Black Magic, workers of weird spells, progenitors of destruction. Their calling has become a cult, a dark mystery cult. They have opened Pandora's box. They have released mighty forces that are pulverizing ancient social structures, producing personal and social disorganization; but they refused to accept any responsibility in the creation of new modes of social control to counteract the devastation produced by machine technique.

Bain further disputed scientific pretense of detached impartiality: "They sell their services to the exploiters of human life. They make a fetish of 'research' and 'scientific method.' They produce powerful mechanisms and proudly proclaim that they do not care how they are used — leave that to the moralists.' They are blatantly a-moral, un-moral or non-moral.... They are parasites upon the body politic but they refuse to accept any political responsibility." Mocking artists and the civic-minded, they are satisfied to "let things in general run merrily to the devil. Practical things do not concern the 'pure' scientists." The latter "has to be a moral eunuch or a civil hermit."[4]

Those subscribing to Bain's thesis, particularly his argument that scientists were "workers of Black Magic," could well point to *Frankenstein* as proof of this argument: By creating life, Frankenstein had recklessly and foolishly ventured beyond boundaries that man was not intended to go, consequently bringing calamity upon himself and others. *Frankenstein* was only the beginning; audiences would witness further tales of science run amuck.

The first of them had begun with a nightmare in the mind of its initial author.

"In the small hours of one morning," remembered his wife Fanny, "I was awakened by cries of horror from Louis. Thinking he had a nightmare, I awakened him. He said angrily, 'Why did you wake me? I was dreaming a fine bogey tale.'"

When Robert Louis Stevenson experienced his "fine bogey tale," he was beset with financial worries and was under pressure from his publishers to turn out what one author described as "a popular adventure book."

Now, the morning after his dream, Stevenson's mood was more upbeat. "I've got my shilling shocker," he declared. Such was the genesis of what became known as *The Strange Case of Dr. Jekyll and Mr. Hyde*.[5]

Thomas Russell Sullivan was the first to adapt Stevenson's tale as a dramatic presentation, in this case performed by Richard Mansfield, who first played the dual part in Boston in May 1887. It would remain part of his repertory until he died in 1907.[6] When Mansfield performed the part in London during Jack the Ripper's murderous spree in 1888, his performance convinced someone that he was the Ripper, and the police were informed of this hypothesis. "Mansfield gallantly closed the play, giving a benefit performance and a final curtain speech, saying, 'There are horrors enough outside.'"[7]

The early years of silent films witnessed eleven versions of the story.[8] Of these, the best (the "Rolls-Royce of the silents," Denis Gifford called it) was Paramount's 1920 version, starring John Barrymore — a film memorable, not only for Barrymore's performance, but for the fact that it was the first horror film to feature the element of frank sexuality — in this instance Hyde's sexual exploits in the seedier part of town with Nita Naldi.[9] Barrymore's film formed the template that characterized subsequent *Jekyll and Hyde* productions — with many aspects originating from another tale of split personality, Oscar Wilde's *The Picture of Dorian Gray*.[10] The success of Barrymore's *Jekyll and Hyde* prompted a quickie feature, set in 1920, the protagonist of which was dubbed "An Apostle of Hell!"[11]

A decade after Barrymore's take on the story, Paramount returned to it as its answer to Universal's *Frankenstein*, then in production.[12] The need to be competitive with a rival studio wasn't the sole reason for Paramount's interest in the tale. Owing to the Depression, Paramount hoped that its remake of *Jekyll and Hyde* would be a hit.[13]

To direct the film, Paramount assigned Russian-born Rouben Mamoulian. Paramount initially wanted John Barrymore to reprise the role but he wanted more than the $25,000 he was offered. The studio's second choice, Irving Pichel, failed to pass muster with Mamoulian, who felt that, while Pichel would be perfect for Hyde, he definitely couldn't play Jekyll. Mamoulian intended to remake Jekyll from Stevenson's original interpretation — that of a middle-aged man — to a young leading man.[14] "I insisted that he be somebody young, [because] rebellion and transformation is more interesting when it is the result of the ferment of youthful aspirations," Mamoulian would recall forty years later.[15] Mamoulian believed that the man he had in mind, Fredric March, brought two essential qualities to the title role: the ability to become another character and, more significantly, the sexual charisma needed to present the new interpretation of the story Mamoulian sought. That vision, achieved with the assistance of scenarists Samuel Hoffenstein and Percy Heath, was to transform Stevenson's original premise as a struggle between good and evil into a struggle between Victorian repression and sexual expression. March's off-camera behavior made him well-qualified to achieve Mamoulian's conception for, as film historian Mark A. Vieira explained: "It was widely known that March, after playing a sensitive scene on a Paramount soundstage, would become a singleminded seducer, luring a starlet into his dressing room." Mamoulian transferred March's sexual prowess to the screen "but put it into a pressure cooker." "I wanted a replica of our ancestor," Mamoulian said, "the Neanderthal man that we once were, to show the struggle of modern man with his primitive instincts."[16]

Another component in the film's sexual element was the prostitute Ivy, whose roots were in the dance-hall girl appearing in Barrymore's film. Mamoulian's production made Ivy a significant character.

Dr. Jekyll, a London physician of high social standing, is regarded by his peers, Dr. Lanyon and General Carew, as unconventional — in Lanyon's case, because of Jekyll's scientific theories; in Carew's, what he regards as Jekyll's unseemly haste to marry his daughter. Speaking before the University, Jekyll declares, "As men of science, we should be curious and bold enough to peer beyond [the fog that] has clouded our vision." His analysis of the soul of man, "the human psyche," has led him to the conclusion "that man is not truly one, but truly two. One of him strives for the nobilities of life ... his good self. The other seeks an expression of impulses that bind him to some dim animal relation with the earth ... the bad. These two carry out an eternal struggle in the nature of man, yet they are chained together. And that chain spells repression to the evil. Remorse to the good. Now, if these two selves could be separated from each other, how much freer the good in us would be.... And the so-called evil, once liberated, would fulfill itself and trouble us no more. I believe the day is not far off when this separation will be possible. In my experiments, I have found that certain chemicals have the power" to achieve this result.

His social position notwithstanding, Jekyll spends time helping patients in a charity ward — another illustration of his unconventionality.

One such patient, a young girl on crutches, is encouraged by Jekyll to discard them and walk unaided. Jekyll's willingness to devote time to help his lower-class patients, even when he's late for dinner with his fiancée, further annoy the more traditional Lanyon and Carew, with the latter grousing, "Jekyll gives entirely too much time to his charity patients.... He ought to come down to earth." Such an attitude can be read as emblematic of the anti–New Deal sentiments of those who opposed Franklin D. Roosevelt's reforms and of those wealthy Americans who considered FDR "a traitor to his class." The scenes of Jekyll in the charity ward, especially those of him helping the crippled girl walk without crutches, also bring FDR to mind: Here Jekyll becomes FDR helping, not only the handicapped girl, but, by extension, all of America during the Great Depression. Like Jekyll, Roosevelt spent time helping fellow polio patients, establishing the Warm Springs Foundation to that end. That experience not only enabled Roosevelt to lift the patients' morale, even if their paralyzed condition didn't improve, but to prepare himself for the greater task of lifting America's morale when it was stricken by economic paralysis — even when, like polio, the victory was more spirit than reality.[17]

After leaving the dinner with his fiancé, Jekyll comes to the aid of Ivy Pearson, who has been assaulted by one of her "callers." Following Jekyll's advice to get some bed rest, Ivy, who is quite taken by him, teasingly disrobes in his presence. As Jekyll departs, Ivy, covering herself with her bed cover and provocatively swinging her leg back and forth, pleads, "Come back soon, won't you...? Come back."

In his laboratory, Jekyll puts his thesis of the duality of man to the test, mixing up the potion he spoke of earlier, and drinks it, liberating the evil side of himself in the form of Mr. Hyde, who resembles a cross between a Neanderthal man and an ape. Feeling tempted by Ivy, Jekyll tries to get Muriel his fiancée to marry him immediately, rather than wait for the date set by her father. Muriel instead tells him she's going away with her father for a time, and that Jekyll must wait. Alone, urged by his man servant Poole to amuse himself, Jekyll downs his potion again, becoming Hyde, and steps out into the rainy night, reveling in the rain falling on his face. Searching for Ivy, he eventually finds her performing at a music hall. Becoming violently possessive of her, Hyde tells her he wants her — "and what I want, I get." He ultimately turns sadistic toward her. In a scene undoubtedly quite shocking for the time, he passionately kisses her breast.

Reunited with Muriel after she and her father return from their holiday, Jekyll is desperate to marry her: "I've played with dangerous knowledge.... Help me to find my way back.... Let us be married at once." Muriel finally overcomes her father's objections to an early marriage. Ecstatic, Jekyll returns home to find Ivy waiting for him. She pleads with him to save her from Hyde. This Jekyll agrees to, promising her that Hyde will never trouble her again. The following evening, however, while walking through the park to a formal dinner where his wedding will be announced, Jekyll pauses to admire a bird in a tree, only to see a cat kill it. Upset, Jekyll transforms into Hyde without benefit of his potion. Going immediately to Ivy, he divulges his secret to her, then murders her. Fleeing back to his residence as Hyde, Jekyll is refused entry by Poole. Hyde then sends word to Lanyon to secure a package for him. When Hyde appears at Lanyon's to claim the package, Lanyon refuses to let him take it unless he knows Jekyll is safe. Lanyon then watches, stunned, as Hyde prepares his potion from the package, and reverts to Jekyll after drinking it.

Still believing in Jekyll, Muriel refuses to part from him when he tells her they can never marry. Watching her cry from outside her drawing room doors, Jekyll once again becomes Hyde without taking his potion, enters the room and attacks Muriel, then tangles with her father and their butler, killing her father, before running back to his lab, the police in hot pursuit. Once in the lab, Hyde reverts to Jekyll just as the police and Poole enter, looking for Hyde. Unfortunately for Jekyll, Lanyon, who identified Jekyll's cane to the police as the weapon used to kill Muriel's father, arrives to identify him as the man they seek. Right before their eyes, Jekyll becomes Hyde. After a mad chase through the lab, Hyde is shot dead as he is about to hurl a knife at his pursuers. In death, he reverts to Jekyll for the last time.

In a 1995 analysis of Mamoulian's film, Annalee Newitz placed it within the context of the concerns that somewhat characterized the 1932 presidential election, especially the threat confronting liberalism arising from the Depression and FDR's emerging New Deal. She quoted Michael Rogin, who maintained that liberalism insisted upon man's independence from his fellow man and other forms of attachments; "work, instinctual repression, and acquistive behavior"; the importance of private property; and the foundation of liberal relations upon the fulfillment of promises and personal responsibility.[18] Roosevelt's proposed New Deal signaled a sharp break with such a philosophy. Newitz refers to a speech Roosevelt made and the response it elicited from Al Smith, Roosevelt's one-time friend turned rival. In a nationwide radio address on April 7, 1932, Roosevelt criticized the incumbent Republican administration for helping big banks and corporations and "shallow thinkers" who had no solution to the plight of farmers. "These unhappy times," Roosevelt declared, "call for the building of plans that put their faith once more in the forgotten man at the bottom of the economic pyramid." An enraged Smith replied at a political dinner: "This country is sick and tired of listening to political campaign orators who tell us what is the matter with us," and that "this is no time for demagogues. I will take off my coat and vest and fight to the end any man who persists in any demagogic appeal to the masses of the working people of this country to destroy themselves by setting class against class and rich against poor!"[19]

While noting that FDR had employed the singular term "man" in his address, "or in other words had remained rhetorically within the boundaries of the liberal imagination," Newitz observes that this still didn't deter Smith "from seizing upon the perhaps socialistic (and certainly populist) edge to Roosevelt's statement in order to discredit it."[20] Seen in this context, Jekyll's lecture concerning the duality of man at the film's beginning suggests that "radical theoretical positions, unchecked (be they Jekyll's separation of the good and bad elements of man, or Roosevelt's proposal to aid the 'forgotten man,' are always dangerously close to becoming radical practice."[21] Where Jekyll's conservative peers viewed his theories and assistance to the poor untraditional, Smith viewed Roosevelt's ideas as incitement to class warfare.

The boundary between the tradition-bound, upper-class world of Jekyll's peers and the working-class milieu of Ivy is quite pronounced, with Newitz characterizing the latter as "both sexually uninhibited and emotionally volatile."[22] Unable to satisfy himself sexually because Muriel's father insists on honoring tradition by observing a protracted engagement between them, Jekyll as Hyde finds sexual satisfaction through Ivy. Moreover, Hyde is Jekyll's means of functioning in the working-class world, becoming acquainted with it. However, Newitz continues, the film must present class consciousness in a negative light to make valid the argument that any pragmatic and theoretical divergence from liberalism is hazardous. When he becomes aware of Hyde's monstrous conduct, Jekyll feels remorse. Hyde, by contrast, is enraged that Jekyll can step out of his own proletarian world. The film makes Hyde's violent behavior — whether it is abusing a waiter at the dance hall or Ivy — a normal element of his world. Only in this manner can Jekyll experience a world outside his own upper-class

2. Exploiting the Lower Classes (1932–1933)   45

Ivy the street lady (Miriam Hopkins) met her doom at the hands of Mr. Hyde (Fredric March) in Paramount's *Dr. Jekyll and Mr. Hyde* (1932). One analysis argues the film mirrored the anxieties Roosevelt's New Deal generated concerning deviations from traditional liberalism in favor of a new sense of class consciousness (Paramount Pictures/Photofest).

realm. "Hyde arouses the liberal audience's worst fears about class consciousness. Rather than allowing Jekyll to experience a new sense of community and social awareness, Hyde forces Jekyll to perform criminal, and even primitive acts already associated with proletarian culture."[23]

In addition to providing Jekyll, as Hyde, with sexual release, Ivy is significant in that she is a member of the working class who is exploited by one of the upper class.[24]

Dr. Jekyll and Mr. Hyde enjoyed critical and popular success, going on to become one of the most financially successful films of 1932.[25] The film earned greater stature when Fredric March won the Academy Award for Best Actor, sharing the honor with Wallace Beery for *The Champ*; in reality, March beat Beery by one vote. The next time an actor received the Oscar for a horror performance would be 1991, when Anthony Hopkins was honored for *The Silence of the Lambs*.

Released just after *Dr. Jekyll and Mr. Hyde*, Universal's *Murders in the Rue Morgue*, though credited to Edgar Allan Poe, would more accurately be rooted in the timely and controversial subject of Darwinian evolution — specifically eugenics. The latter, which sought to enhance humanity through manipulation of the gene pool, enjoyed support both in America and Britain.[26] In a message to the third annual Congress of Eugenics in New York City in 1932, Charles Darwin's son, Major Leonard Darwin, proclaimed his "firm conviction" that "if widespread eugenic reforms are not adopted during the next hundred years or so, our Western civilization is inevitably destined to such a slow and gradual decay as that which has been experienced in the past by every great ancient civilization. The size and importance of the United States throws [sic] on you a special responsibility in your endeavors to safeguard the future of our race." Added to this alarming, though racist, warning was that of a doctor advocating "biological investigation," internationally, of all immigrants for "recessive characteristics."[27] "In Germany, the Nazis embraced an extremist version of eugenics in their diatribes on Aryan purity."[28]

Despite the success of *Dracula* and the anticipated success of the forthcoming *Frankenstein*, Universal's financial situation in the early months of 1931 was precarious, owing to the Depression, hence the studio's reluctance to pursue additional horror properties. Rather, the studio sought inspiration in works in the public domain, finally settling on Edgar Allan Poe's *Murders in the Rue Morgue*. A treatment was prepared and after some vacillation on the studio's part, the project commenced, with Bela Lugosi as the film's star and George Melford director. Still the effort to turn Poe's story into a workable screenplay was a difficult challenge. Poe's tale was not so much a horror but a detective yarn. All during the summer of 1931, Universal's writers struggled to come up with a script. Concurrently, Lugosi and Robert Florey were released from *Frankenstein* and assigned to the *Rue Morgue* project. As Universal's financial woes worsened, the studio's executives began doubting the advisability of yet another horror film after *Frankenstein*. As he was reluctant to invest in costumes and period sets, E.M. Asher, supervisor at Universal, decided to move *Murders in the Rue Morgue* from its initial setting, 1845, to the present— a decision that was dropped when it was pointed out that a story about an attempt to validate evolution would be more plausible in an earlier age. The ultimate solution was to slash *Rue Morgue*'s budget from $130,000 to $90,000— a move that prompted Florey to walk off the project. Florey was eventually persuaded to return.[29] Francis Edwards Faragoh's script for *Rue Morgue*, submitted on September 17, 1931, went far beyond Poe's initial story of a Paris murder committed by an ape. Poe made no mention of either a mad scientist or evolution; both were Faragoh's invention.[30]

Murders in the Rue Morgue began filming on October 19, 1931, and "wrapped" the following month five days over schedule yet within its budget.[31] Once filming was completed, Universal shelved the film while *Frankenstein* ran its course before unleashing its latest horror offering upon audiences. Universal executives used this interlude to review Florey's finished product. Based on their examination, they decided to rearrange the sequence of events in the film. That done, *Murders in the Rue Morgue* debuted at New York's Mayfair Theatre on February 10, 1932.[32] Originally *Murders in the Rue Morgue* was to begin with a scene, set on a Paris night in 1845, featuring a fight between two men at the edge of the River Seine over a screaming woman watching the battle. The combatants kill each other. The woman is then accosted by a mysterious figure who has arrived in a carriage: Dr. Mirakle (Lugosi), who asks, "A lady in distress?"

"Who are you?" she asks.

"Come with me."

"Where?"

"My carriage," Mirakle answers.

"No ... no.... Your hand is cold. It chills me."

"Come, I will help you."

Mirakle then takes the woman to his laboratory, where he binds her and draws a sample of her blood — the latter now commingled with that of an ape. When Mirakle's experiment fails and his unwilling "bride of science," as he calls her, dies, he disposes of her body. The woman's death is one of three "suicides" that have occurred recently. After the latest body is found in the Seine, Pierre Dupin (Leon Ames) studies the corpse, observing "the same marks" and "the same foreign substance in the blood of each victim," and nothing that "all three died of the same cause."

Universal's re-editing of *Rue Morgue* shuffled this original opening sequence to later in the film. The film, still set in 1845 Paris, now begins with Pierre Dupin and Camille (Sidney Fox), his fiancée, taking in the exhibits at a carnival. The barker at one exhibit declares:

> Behind this curtain is the strangest creature your eyes will ever behold: Erik, the ape man, the monster who walks upright and speaks a language — even as you and I. The ruler of the jungle whose giant hands can tear a man in half.

Erik, the ape man, the beast with a human soul. More cunning than a man and stronger than a lion.

Entering the tent, Pierre and Camille are greeted by Mirakle: "Take a seat in front, where you can see everything." Mirakle then takes the stage and addresses the assembled audience:

> I'm Dr. Mirakle, messieurs and mesdames, and I'm not a sideshow charlatan, so if you expect to witness the usual carnival hocus-pocus, just go to the box-office and get your money back. I'm not exhibiting a freak, a monstrosity of nature, but a milestone in the development of life! The shadow of Erik the ape hangs over us all. The darkness before the dawn of man.

Mirakle now displays the caged Erik to the spectators before resuming his discourse.

> Listen to him, brothers and sisters, he's speaking to you. Can you understand what he says, or have you forgotten? I have learned his language. Listen. I will translate what he says. "My home is in the African jungle where I lived with my father and my mother. And brothers and sisters. But I was captured by a band of hairless white apes and carried away to a strange land. I'm in the prime of my strength! And I am lonely."

When Mirakle then delivers a discourse on evolution, his words provoke a cry of "Heresy" from the audience.

> Heresy? Do they still burn men for heresy? Then burn me, monsieur. Light the fire. Do you think your little candle will outshine the flame of *truth*? Do you think these walls and curtains are my whole life? They are only a trap to catch the pennies of fools. My life is consecrated to a great experiment. I tell you I will *prove* your kinship with the ape. Erik's blood shall be mixed with the blood of man!

At this point the majority of Mirakle's listeners leave the tent. Camille and Pierre remain. Mirakle convinces Camille to meet Erik, who seizes Camille's bonnet, then Pierre. Mirakle commands Erik to get back. Erik damages Camille's bonnet, prompting Mirakle to offer a replacement. When Pierre declines to provide Camille's home address, Mirakle tells his servant Janos to follow them. In the version of the film released to the theaters, this sequence is followed by the one of the street fight over the woman and her death in Mirakle's lab.

Honoring his promise to Camille, Mirakle sends her a replacement bonnet and, with it, a handwritten note: "You are lovely. Who knows what the future holds for you? Great things are written on the stars. Erik and I will read them for you. Tonight — the carnival — come." Disturbed that Mirakle sent the bonnet, Pierre calls on him at his carnival tent, telling

Another street lady (Arlene Francis, tied to crossbeams) fell prey to unscrupulous science in *Murders in the Rue Morgue* (1932). In this instance, Dr. Mirakle (Bela Lugosi, kneeling left) tried to use her to prove the kinship between man and ape by mixing Francis' blood with that of an ape. The popularity of mad science films such as *Rue Morgue* and *Dr. Jekyll and Mr. Hyde* reflected a distrust of experts arising from the Depression (Universal Pictures/Photofest).

him that Camille won't be coming. Further saying he's a medical student, Pierre then inquires of Mirakle if he's authored any papers. "None — to be shown," Mirakle says. He goes on to say that he is leaving Paris that evening. When Pierre learns that Mirakle is in fact remaining, he follows Mirakle's carriage, finding his residence.

When Mirakle fails to persuade Camille to come with him, he dispatches Erik for her. The ape murders Camille's mother, then absconds with Camille herself. Learning that the foreign substance found in the screaming woman's blood is simian in origin, Pierre rushes to Camille's residence to check on her safety. But by then Camille's abduction has already occurred. While Pierre argues with the police, Mirakle begins experimenting with Camille's blood, discovering that it is perfect for his experiment. Finally convinced that Pierre has told them the truth, the police arrive at Mirakle's residence, shooting Janos when he attempts to block their entry. Attracted by Camille, Erik kills Mirakle, then carries her off over the rooftops, a sequence presaging *King Kong* by more than a year. After Erik is shot, Pierre and Camille are reunited in a scene that, *Variety* noted, engendered much derision from the audience during the film's New York debut.[33]

The unflattering images of the scientist presented by *Dr. Jekyll and Mr. Hyde* and *Murders in the Rue Morgue* aside, scientists were as much victims of the Depression as other Americans were. As a group, they suffered greatly as the Depression cut off academic and corporate research funds. With their own self-interest at sake, numerous scientists championed the cause of reform. Especially in Great Britain, notes David J. Skal, "the scientific mainstream moved politically to the left, espousing a mistrust of capitalism and denouncing the exploitation of scientists by industry and the military." Moreover, the scientific community became antifascist in international endeavors to aid German scientists who had fled Nazi Germany.

Despite this outpouring of beneficence on scientists' part, public suspicion of them remained.[34] And if any American in 1932 had justifiable cause to distrust experts, it was Franklin D. Roosevelt, whose skepticism stemmed from the misdiagnosis of his polio when he was initially stricken in 1921. "[It] cured him permanently of any belief in the conventional wisdom of experts," wrote columnist Max Lerner, "whether in medicine, politics, economics, warfare or diplomacy." From then on, experimentation, a willingness to try new ideas, became Roosevelt's motto. Delivering a commencement address at Oglethorpe University in Atlanta in 1932, he declared, "This country needs and, unless I mistake its temper, the country demands bolds, persistent experimentation." To this he added, "It is common sense to take a method and try it. If it fails, admit it frankly and try another. But above all, try something."³⁵ The key to Roosevelt's success as president was rooted in his convalescence at Warm Springs, where, as "Doctor Roosevelt," he listened to expert opinion, tried out the available polio treatments, learning which were beneficial and which weren't, perfecting the technique he would employ as president, first as "Doctor New Deal," then as "Doctor Win the War." To him, the struggles he faced during the Depression and the war were no greater than those he had previously surmounted in his fight against polio.³⁶

Like the public, Franklin D. Roosevelt (seen here in a 1933 photograph) cast a skeptical eye toward expert opinions. FDR's wariness, born of his polio experience, led him to abandon conventional wisdom in favor of experimentation with new ideas to solve national problems (Library of Congress).

The "Little People" vs. the "Big People": Freaks (1932)

Of all the films made during the Golden Age of Hollywood Horror, it was the most controversial — *The Exorcist* of its day. During its preview in San Diego, a woman ran screaming up the aisle. That incident may well have been a publicity stunt, as perchance was another: a woman watching the film suffered a miscarriage and sued.³⁷ Such were the reactions generated by MGM's 1932 release *Freaks*, a film using real-life human oddities to tell a grisly story of greed and revenge against the backdrop of a traveling circus.

Like Paramount's *Dr. Jekyll and Mr. Hyde*, *Freaks* was an effort to cash in on the horror boom Universal had initiated. "I want you to give me something even more horrible than *Frankenstein*," was how MGM executive Irving Thalberg phrased it to screenwriter Willis Goldbeck.

Obviously Goldbeck more than met Thalberg's expectations for, when Thalberg finished reading Goldbeck's completed work, he could only say, "I asked for something horrifying, and I got it."[38]

To direct MGM's foray into horror, Thalberg turned to the director of Lugosi's *Dracula*, Tod Browning, a man who previously explored the dark side of the circus milieu in two Lon Chaney vehicles of the silent era, the original version of *The Unholy Three* (1925) and *The Unknown* (1927). Browning's latest film excursion into the circus realm would trod over territory previously unexplored in his prior journeys: This time he would show filmgoers "a *real* world of freaks," one "where normal people were in the barely tolerated minority."[39]

The basis of the film was a 1923 magazine short story, "Spurs," written by Tod Robbins. MGM bought the rights to the tale in 1929 for $8,000. When the horror boom took off, the studio finally decided to transform it into a movie.[40]

Thalberg's original choices for the roles of the malevolent female circus performer Cleopatra and the heroine Venus had been, respectively, Myrna Loy and Jean Harlow. Possibly because he perceived both the inherent problems of the script and the ultimate storm the film stirred up, Thalberg decided instead to go with less stellar names: for Cleopatra, Olga Baclanova, the erstwhile star of the Moscow Art Theater, now in the twilight of her Hollywood career and, for Venus, contract player Leila Hyams. Wallace Ford was cast as Phroso, and British actor Henry Victor Hercules Roscoe Ates provided comic relief. Two other actors — Michael Visaroff and Rose Dione, both of whom had appeared in earlier Browning films — now appeared in his latest: Visaroff, the innkeeper who warned Dwight Frye not to go to Dracula's castle in the opening scenes of *Dracula*, played a groundskeeper distressed by the Freaks' appearance on his property; Dione, who played the barkeeper in *West of Zanzibar*, played the Freaks' guardian, Madame Tetrallini.

Leading the company of real-life "freaks" in the film was Harry Earles, who had starred in *The Unholy Three* as a tiny criminal posing as a baby. Joining him in *Freaks* was his real-life sister Daisy, playing his betrothed Frieda. They, in turn, were joined by an array of other real-life Freaks: Johnny Eck, "the Half Boy," so named because his body ended at the waist; Francis O'Conner, "the Living Venus de Milo," who lacked arms; Schlitze, rumored to be a transvestite, supposedly a "he" passing as a "she," and who acquired a fortune in jewelry and real estate from admirers; Prince Randian, the armless, legless "Human Torso," who wore earrings and rolled his own cigarettes; Siamese twins Violet and Daisy Hilton; beared lady Olga Roderick (whose real name was Jane Burnell); Koo Koo ("the bird girl from Mars") who apparently suffered from a rare malady, progeria, which causes swift and premature aging; Betty Green, the "Stork Woman," physically normal but quite ugly, who exploited her condition; Josephine/Joseph the Austrian hermaphrodite; a pair of dwarves (one of whom, Angelo Rossitto, would be the only Freak to continue in Hollywood); a fat lady, a "turtle girl," a sword swallower, fire eater, and others.[41]

Freaks began filming on November 9, 1931. The shoot, art director Merrill Pye remembered, went quite well; moreover, its sensational nature notwithstanding, it didn't attract spectators. Most likely, the latter resulted because many at the studio had no desire to behold the Freaks, particularly when it came to the studio commissary. When producer Harry Rapf spearheaded a formal protest about the nauseating effect the Freaks' presence in the commissary had on other diners there, a separate outdoor dining facility for the majority of the oddities was set up "so people could get to eat in the commissary without throwing up."[42] Despite such complaints. Thalberg remained committed to the project. "If it's a mistake, I'll take the blame," he said.[43]

Freaks wrapped production on December 16, 1931, followed by retakes beginning seven days later.[44] Of the film's preview, Merrill Pye recalled: "Halfway through the preview, a lot of people got up and ran out. They didn't walk out. They *ran* out."[45] While not questioning the fact that "the production is bold and novel in conception and execution," *Motion Picture Herald* in its January 23, 1932, review nevertheless had serious misgivings concerning "the taste that prompted it." Of greater concern to the paper was "the moral effect it will have upon the industry ... [*Freaks*] is evidently aimed at the great god Box Office and may very well reach its target." The *Herald* hoped that the film would offend enough people to force Hollywood to "stem this rising tide of goose-flesh melodrama."[46]

In the wake of the disastrous preview, the film was trimmed from almost 90 minutes to slightly over an hour. As part of the revisions was a more upbeat postscript, showing the reconciliation of Hans and Frieda, observed by Phroso and Venus.[47] Another revision, a "Special Message" at the start of the film, explained that "history and religion, folklore and legend abound in tales of misshapen misfits who have altered the world's course. Goliath, Caliban, Frankenstein, Gloucester, Tom Thumb, and

Kaiser Wilhelm, are just a few...." After explaining how freaks were ostracized in the past, the message explains that "the majority of freaks are endowed with normal thoughts and emotions." Fortunately, "never again will such a story be filmed, as modern science and teratology is rapidly eliminating such blunders of nature from the world."

Another passage of the "Special Message" detailed "the Code of the Freaks":

> ...They are forced into the most unnatural of lives. Therefore, they have built up among themselves a code of ethics to protect them from the barbs of normal people. Their rules are rigidly adhered to and the hurt of one is the hurt of all; the joy of one is the joy of all. The story about to be revealed is a story based on the effect of this Code upon their lives....

The newly revamped *Freaks* debuted at the Fox Criterion in Los Angeles on February 10, 1932.[48] As the film opens, a barker tells his audience the story of a freak on display and the Code of the Freaks: "Offend one and you offend them all." The barker then leads his spectators to a pit housing the Freak. Upon seeing the latter, a woman in the audience screams in horror. The barker continues his story: "Friends, she was once a beautiful woman. A royal prince shot himself for love of her. She was known as the Peacock of the Air." She is Cleopatra, the former circus trapeze artist who (we see in flashbacks) has attracted the attention of the dwarf Hans, arousing the jealousy of Frieda, to whom Hans is engaged. Essentially the film revolves around three couples: Cleopatra and her true lover Hercules, the circus strongman; Hans and Frieda; and Phroso the clown and Venus the seal trainer.

The Freaks are mocked by other circus performers. To cushion themselves against such ridicule, the Freaks have established a strong sense of community, which is illustrated when they all gather for the birth of the Bearded Lady's baby. To Frieda's dismay, Cleopatra begins pursuing Hans. In a private moment, two of Hans' fellow Freaks, an armless woman (Martha Morris) and a dwarf (Angelo Rossitto), discuss the Cleopatra-Hans relationship; their conversation takes a dark turn:

> ARMLESS WOMAN: Cleopatra ain't one of us. Why, we're just filthy things to her. She'd spit on Hans if he wasn't givin' her presents.
> DWARF: Let her try it. Let her try doing something to one of us.
> ARMLESS WOMAN: You're right. Let her try doing anything to one of us.

Frieda tries to convince Hans of the reality of Cleopatra's true feelings toward him: "To me, you're a man. But to her, you're only something to laugh at. The whole circus — they make fun of you and her." "Let them laugh," says Hans. "The swine. I love her. They can't hurt me." "But," Frieda replies, "they hurt me." Frieda then tries the direct approach, appealing to Cleopatra not to marry Hans. During their encounter, Frieda discloses that Hans has inherited a fortune — a fact Hans wanted kept secret until after he and Frieda had left the circus. Now in possession of this knowledge, Cleopatra devises a scheme to murder Hans and get his inheritance. At their wedding feast, she slips poison into a bottle of wine, persuading Hans to drink it. When the Freaks pass a champagne glass among themselves, an act signifying their acceptance of Cleopatra as one of them, the latter is revolted by the scene. When the glass is passed to her last, she screams, "You dirty slimy freaks...! Get out of here...! You filth!" Hercules places Hans on Cleopatra's shoulders, then begins tooting a horn as the party breaks up.

The Freaks of Tod Browning's 1932 film rose up against those they felt mocked and disdained them. Similarly, outbreaks of popular rebellion, such as the bonus marchers who came to Washington that same year and others who collectively rose up against the sufferings of the Depression, provoked fears within the status quo of revolution (MGM/Photofest).

The next morning, Hans is diagnosed with a case of ptomaine poisoning. The Freaks now realize that Cleopatra and Hercules poisoned him in hopes of getting their hands on his money. On a stormy, rainy night the Freaks take their revenge. Hercules tries to kill Venus, who had threatened to turn him into the authorities for his part in the murder plot, but is felled by a knife thrown by one of the Freaks. Our last view of Cleopatra shows her fleeing her circus wagon, the Freaks in hot pursuit. The film then returns to the opening sequence with the barker. We now discover Cleopatra's fate once the Freaks had finished with her: The once haughty Peacock of the Air is now a Freak herself, a mutilated, squawking "chicken woman." The film then concludes with Hans, now a retired, wealthy man residing in a mansion, complete with a butler, reunited with Frieda. The little people, once derided by the big people, now reside at the top level of society!

Reviewing the film's Los Angeles debut, Louella O. Parsons enthused: "For pure sensationalism, *Freaks* tops any picture yet produced.... In *Freaks* there are monstrosities such as never before have been known. If you are normal go and see them yourself, if not, well, use your own judgment...."[49] Parsons' review, however, wasn't enough to keep the film from bombing in L.A. Nor did it fare well in Chicago. However, in other venues (Cincinnati, Buffalo, Boston, Cleveland, Houston, St. Paul, Omaha), *Freaks* did exceptional business. Just the same, this regional success failed to offset the film's failure in major markets like Los Angeles, where it died, and San Francisco, where it was never shown.[50]

The deficient box office performance of *Freaks* was only one of the woes besetting the film. It generated a backlash among various groups who viewed it as emblematic of all that was wrong with Hollywood. In David J. Skal's words:

> The country was going through a very, very difficult period in the early Depression, and then, as now, people are always looking for scapegoats. Hollywood was a convenient scapegoat for a lot of civic groups ... religious groups and women's groups.... There was a growing backlash against the kind of pictures Hollywood was putting out — gangster pictures especially, horror movies. And *Freaks* was a particular lightning rod for these groups. They felt it was a new low in Hollywood depravity, that it was an extremely cruel and exploitative film.[51]

Desperately seeking to recoup its losses in the *Freaks* debacle, MGM sought to convince the public that the film was compassionate toward its subjects:

> A LANDMARK IN SCREEN DARING!
>
> The inside story of the making of a picture that was debated for four years — the picture that is a challenge to the world!
>
> At every story conference the question was brought up "Do we are tell the real truth on the screen? Do we dare hold up the mirror to nature in all its grim reality? Do we dare produce FREAKS?"
>
> WHAT ABOUT ABNORMAL PEOPLE? THEY HAVE THEIR LIVES, TOO!
>
> What about the Siamese twins — have they no right to love? The pinheads, the half-man, half-woman, the dwarfs! They have the same passions, joys, sorrows, laughter as normal human beings. Is such a subject untouchable? While we hesitated, a great story, thoroughly planned, waited the word to go ahead. Finally TOD BROWNING cut the Gordian knot of indecision....

Such sentiment was dismissed by *Motion Picture Daily*. "The picture is unkind and brutal," the paper insisted, and couldn't simultaneously exploit the Freaks and feign sympathy for them.[52]

MGM held back on debuting *Freaks* in New York until July; the ostensible reason for this strategy was to keep the film from the important national media until after it had been seen nationwide. The studio's decision may also have been motivated by the fact that two other, more successful, MGM releases — *Grand Hotel* and *Red-Headed Woman* — were playing New York by then.[53] One scene in particular — Cleopatra introducing poison into Hans' champagne — raised the ire of the New York Board of Censors as it might educate viewers in how to commit a crime. Compared to classic gangster films, horror films raised hackles, explains David J. Skal, "on a truly primal level." He continues:

> Much of the censorship backlash in the early Depression era was based on strange assumptions about eugenics and evolution. The weak-minded classes, quote-unquote, were frankly believed to be genetically inferior, easily subject to anti-social suggestion. Ideas like this were shockingly common in 1930s America, and it's difficult today to fully comprehend how anxious average Americans were about the disintegration of the economy and the crumbling of basic social and scientific assumptions. The Depression itself seemed to be a kind of evolutionary devolution.[54]

Freaks was withdrawn from distribution after its New York engagement was completed. In Great Britain, which banned the film right from the start, *Freaks* would remain unseen for thirty years.[55] Discomfitted by the entire affair, MGM boss Louis B. Mayer went on to sell the notorious film to Dwain Esper on a 25-year distribution deal for $50,000. After finding an audience on the underground exploitation circuit, the film finally hit the big time when it played a successful engagement at the 1962 Cannes Festival Repertory, and ultimately found itself on home video and DVD.

The controversy the film aroused aside, *Freaks* is a microcosm of America during the worst year of the Great Depression. Essentially it is the story of the little people (average Americans) vs. the big people (the rich and businessmen). The film makes it clear that the big people, personified by Cleopatra and Hercules, scorn the Freaks. Such a disdainful attitude was reflected in the real-life social outlook of some business tycoons during the Depression. The economic crisis toppled the businessman from his exalted perch in American society to one of ill repute. Two titans in particular, Charles Mitchell and Samuel Insull, came in for sharp rebuke. Mitchell's National City Bank furnished its speculating officers with interest-free loans, the bill for which was ultimately footed by the bank's stockholders. Insull's utility empire collapsed, ruining thousands of small investors.[56] In contrasting the two classes of people in *Freaks*, Thomas Doherty characterizes "the strong and the beautiful" (by implication the wealthy) as "ignoble and cruel," and "the deformed and repulsive honorable and kind"[57] (and one such "deformed" individual, though paralyzed is a more accurate description, was about to be elected president of the United States).

Doherty further notes that the dangers Dracula, the Frankenstein Monster, Mr. Hyde, and Dr. Mirakle's ape man posed to society were more easily surmounted and provided more audience enjoyment "than the collective danger posed by mobs of monsters.... Like the downtrodden masses, tribes of the misshapen and mutated exist on the fringes of mainstream culture and threaten to overturn it."[58] Away from the movie theater, real-world events in 1932 suggested that America was on the brink of revolution. On March 7, 1932, nearly a month after *Freaks'* Los Angeles premiere, approximately 3000 people rallied in Detroit, Michigan, for a Communist-instigated procession to the Ford plant in Dearborn to submit numerous demands to management. When the marchers reached Dearborn, they met police resistance. After being tear-gassed when they refused to leave, the marchers retaliated by throwing stones and pieces of frozen dirt. Firemen stepped in, hosing the throng, followed by a renewed police barrage — this time combing tear gas and bullets, fatally wounding a protestor and scattering the multitude to a nearby field, where the police salvo resumed, resulting in three additional fatalities and fifty others gravely wounded. The shooting had been instigated by those commanded by business leaders. The editor of the Amalgamated Clothing Workers' *Advance* declared, "The outrageous shooting at defenseless, peaceably marching unemployed workers in front of Henry Ford's Dearborn plants best shows that the masters won't wait till the slaves will take matters into their own hands."[59]

Another assemblage of Depression victims provoked another violent response from the established order a short time later when 20,000 World War I veterans descended on Washington to ask Congress to pay them a bonus for wartime service, not scheduled for payment until 1945. The presence of this "Bonus Expeditionary Force" in Washington made governmental dignitaries increasingly edgy. Congress rejected their request for early payment of the bonus and, when some of the "bonus marchers" had a run-in with the police, President Hoover authorized the Army to disperse the veterans. Commanded by Army chief of staff, General Douglas MacArthur, the military destroyed the veterans' encampment, then dispersed the veterans and their families into Maryland. Conclusive proof to the contrary, MacArthur asserted that the veterans, "a mob ... animated by the essence of revolution," had been on the verge of taking over the government.[60] MacArthur exceeded his orders, yet his Commander-in-Chief, Herbert Hoover, was faulted for the Bonus Army debacle, dooming any hope he had of winning a second term in 1932. Discussing the incident with an adviser, FDR said, "This elects me."[61]

Elsewhere, Communist-led unemployed individuals conducted hunger marches. In Iowa, a farm-holiday campaign, founded by an ex–Populist named Milo Reno, threatened to halt all food shipments to cities unless prices for their products were increased. Though the protests dwindled as the winter of 1932 loomed — possibly due to the weather and possibly due to the impending "new deal"— the nation remained edgy.[62]

What was certain was that Tod Browning's time of glory in Hollywood was over. Though he would work another eight years, the failure of *Freaks* meant he would never have the free hand he earlier had to make the kind of films that interested him. Two factors contributed to his downfall. The first, and most significant, was that *Freaks* bombed at the box office, failing to recover the investment in it. Second was Browning's inability to master sound films — a handicap that prompted David J. Skal to wonder if *Freaks* would have been a greater success had it been done as a silent film which was the initial plan. This option, had it been followed, would have had two advantages: It would have solved the freaks' problem in reading dialogue, and the use of intertitles in a silent film to clarify the action for audiences, along with continual musical accompaniment, would have greatly diminished the film's shock for viewers.[63] After directing *Miracles for Sale* (1939), Browning retired from filmmaking to his California home and died at 80, thirty years after *Freaks* signaled the passing of his reign in Hollywood.[64]

The Perfect Representative Monster for the Unemployed: White Zombie *(1932)*

Another horror classic of 1932, *White Zombie,* emanated not from one of the major studios but from Hollywood's "poverty row."[65] The foundations of motion picture zombies were found, not in the minds of screenwriters, but in reality — in the genuine practices of Haiti that received study by legitimate anthropological observers and theologians. When Africans were first introduced to Haiti in 1510, their native superstitions accompanied them; these beliefs had originated from more than thirty different regions of Africa. Combined with Spanish Catholicism, these superstitions gave rise to voodooism. One of the strangest aspects of voodooism is creating a zombie:

> On occasion an apparent death is felt not to be a real death, but rather the simulacre of death brought about by the machinations of a sorcerer. If poison has not been administered ... or if the body was not stabbed, after the funeral the sorcerer recovers the body, which, deprived of its soul, works for him as a zombie, only returning to the grave when the time decreed by God for his natural death is reached.... Though the concept had been presented in recent years with unjustifiable sensationalism to the reading public, it is indisputably a living one.[66]

Essentially a zombie was the walking dead, incapable of doing anything more but walking. Because it couldn't think and lacked its own will, including independent moral judgments, a zombie was nothing more than a slave implementing the will of its master. For black slaves, who could only expect a life of perpetual servitude, the idea that such an existence would continue after death as a zombie was too appalling to contemplate. The precise origin of belief in zombies is uncertain. The term zombie, according to some, initially meant some kind of African nature spirit or god and it was in the new world that it became associated with the walking dead. Some even believed that voodoo priests, owing to their familiarity with drugs, could actually create a kind of genuine zombie — living men who were so extremely dazed by drugs that they possessed no consciousness of their environs, appeared insensitive to pain, and carried out whatever orders the priest issued. "Just what drugs might create such an effect we do not know, but it is possible that some narcotics, plus an intense belief in the power of the voodoo priest, might turn a living man into the very image of a zombie."[67]

It was this monster who became the perfect representative for masses of unemployed during the Depression.[68]

Zombies had been part of popular culture long before the debut of *White Zombie* on the nation's movie screens. Voodoo and zombies were found in novels, short stories, the theater, popular music, and early motion pictures — the latter including *Voodoo Fires* (1913), *Ghost of the Twisted Oak* (1915), *Unconquered* (1917), and *The Witching Eyes* (1929). It remained for William B. Seabrook to produce the definitive study of zombiism in *The Magic Island* (1929), a work that became to the subject what Shelley's *Frankenstein* became to man-made monsters and Stoker's *Dracula* to vampires. Seabrook was the first important writer of the English language to publish the word zombie as meaning the living dead. Moreover, Seabrook asserted: "The attempted rational explanation I gave of how the zombie may actually exist without being supernatural is recognized in the Haitian code and accepted by ethnologists as probably correct." "On this point," writes Gary D. Rhodes, "Seabrook is apparently accurate, as no prior texts seem to suggest the nonsupernatural explanations that he does." To bolster the plausibility of his arguments, Seabrook specified Article 249 of the Haitian Penal Code — a proviso that in fact was part of the code during the 1920s:

> Also shall be qualified as attempted murder the employment which may be made against any person of substances which, without causing actual death, produce a lethargic coma more or less prolonged. If, after the administering of such substance, the person has been buried, the act shall be considered murder no matter what result follows.

In the wake of *The Magic Island*'s success, the first significant entertainment vehicle to draw upon Seabrook's book was *Zombie*, a play written by Kenneth Webb, the protagonists of which were Sylvia and Jack Clayton, American plantation owners on the edge of the Haitian jungles.

When Clayton dies, Pedro, a foreman, returns him to life as a zombie to acquire the family wealth. The young Dr. Thurlow, whom Sylvia has flirted with, and Professor Wallace set out to discover the identities of the zombie masters. The play features a scene in which a horde of zombies shuffle across the stage in a half-live, half-dead manner. A twist ending reveals that the zombie lord is actually Professor Wallace. After an unsuccessful run in New York, the play enjoyed a better engagement in Chicago.[69]

Just as *Zombie* was inspired by Seabrook's work, so did Webb's play inspire the Halperin brothers to do a movie about zombies. The February 20, 1932, issue of *Motion Picture Herald* reported that negotiations were in progress and that the play would presently become a motion picture. Then writer Garnett Weston produced a script quite unlike Webb's play. According to Bela Lugosi's biographer Arthur Lennig, when Webb learned of the Halperins' project, he sued for copyright infringement on the grounds that the film diminished the commercial possibilities of his play. Years after Lennig's account, Rhodes could find no evidence supporting this story but did not rule out the possibility of an out-of-court settlement, or that the discussions regarding such a resolution persuaded the Halperins to revise their film's title from *Zombie* to *White Zombie*.[70]

Pared to its basics, the film is a fairy tale. A young man and his lady are to be married. A jealous suitor has other ideas, and seeks the assistance of a malevolent wizard to thwart the intended nuptials and have the bride for himself. The wizard casts a spell over the bride and takes her to his castle. There, the suitor sees the consequences of his actions and is overcome with remorse. But a new complication has arisen: The wizard desires the woman for himself and enslaves the suitor to prevent the latter from interfering. Meanwhile the bride's original love, guided by voices and a wise older friend, reaches the wizard's castle, where the sorcerer is finally defeated, and the bride freed from her thrall and reunited with her true love.

At the film opens, two young lovers, Neil and Madeline (John Harron and Madge Bellamy), are conveyed by carriage to the Haitian plantation of Beaumont, who has offered his estate as the site of their wedding. As the carriage continues on its journey, it comes upon a funeral for a man being laid to rest in the middle of the road. The reason for the latter, the coach drive explains, is to prevent the deceased's body from being purloined. As the carriage resumes its journey, we see the image of a pair of eyes superimposed over the scene as though the evil they exude pervades the land. The eyes belong to zombie master "Murder" Legendre (Lugosi), the latter standing by the road as the carriage driver stops to ask for directions to the Beaumont estate. Legendre leans into the carriage, staring at Madeline, removing her scarf. Legendre is accompanied by his zombie legion, prompting the coachman to make a panic-stricken departure. When they arrive at Beaumont's residence, Neil asks the driver why they rode so fast.

"We might have been caught," says the driver, who explains that the men they saw were "dead bodies.... Zombies, the living dead. Corpses taken from their graves, or made to work in sugar mills, in fields at night."

Madeline met Beaumont during the sea voyage to Haiti, then introduced him to Neil in Port-au-Prince. Beaumont convinced them to have their wedding at his residence, and promised Neil he would send the latter to New York as his agent. After happily greeting his guests, Beaumont (Robert Frazer) departs for a meeting with Legendre. Entering a carriage, he is shocked to find that its driver is one of Legendre's zombies. Beaumont is taken to Legendre's sugar mill, where the zombies mindlessly dump sugar cane into a thrashing machine. (In this sense they resemble oppressed workers.) When one of the zombies loses his balance, he silently plunges to his death in the machine below while his fellow automatons, unconcerned, attend to their business.

Beaumont, clearly stunned by what he sees, meets Legendre but declines the latter's handshake. Legendre has just returned from a journey collecting men for his mills: "They work faithfully. They are not worried about long hours.[71] You could make good use of men like mine on your plantations." That isn't the reason for Beaumont's visit: He wants Madeline for himself and seeks Legendre's help to realize this. Legendre says he has looked into her eyes: "She is deep in love but not with you." There is a way for Beaumont to have her but "the cost is heavy." Beaumont agrees to Legendre's terms, The price: transform Madeline into a zombie herself. The thought of this horrifies Beaumont but he reluctantly accepts a drug from Legendre that will effect the transformation. "Keep it," Legendre tells him. "You may change your mind.... There is no other way."

When the time for Neil and Madeline's wedding comes, Beaumont gives the bride away, pleading with her to go away with him. She declines and, as a farewell gift to her, Beaumont gives her a flower — one containing the potion. Outside Beaumont's estate, Legendre fashions a wax figure, covering it with the scarf he took from Madeline. Using the doll, he puts Madeline under his spell; she faints during her wedding dinner and is buried in a crypt. While a grief-stricken Neil gets drunk, Beaumont and Legendre, aided by the latter's zombie servants, disinter Madeline's coffin from the mausoleum. Neil enters the mausoleum after they've left and lets out a cry of anguish when he finds that the coffin is gone.

Once in Legendre's manor, the now zombified Madeline plays the piano. When Beaumont tries to talk to her, giving her a necklace, there's no response. Remorseful over his actions, Beaumont wants to restore her to life. Legendre, now having his own plans for Madeline and seeking to forestall interference on Beaumont's part, gives the latter wine tainted with his zombie potion and has his zombie murder Beaumont's manservant. Later, as Beaumont struggles to resist the effects of the potion, he tries to touch Legendre's hand. Recalling how Beaumont declined his earlier handshake, Legendre says, "You refused to shake hands once. I remember. Well, well, we understand each other better now."

Aided by a missionary, Neil finds Legendre's residence. Entering the great room where Legendre and Beaumont are, he collapses from fever. Now having a fiendish inspiration, Legendre summons Madeline, ordering her to plunge a knife into Neil's throat. When she hesitates to carry out the command, Legendre unleashes the full might of his power on her but the missionary thwarts her. Neil then pursues Madeline to a cliff above the sea, sitting her down. Legendre then summons his zombies to deal with them.

"Who are you?" Neil demands, "and what are they?'

"To you, my friend," Legendre replies, "they are the angels of death."

Cornered by the zombies, Neil shoots them to no avail. The missionary then appears, knocking Legendre unconscious. Neil flees to safety as, one by one, the zombies fall to their deaths from the cliff. Madeline momentarily rouses from her trance but reverts back when Legendre regains consciousness. He then tosses a gas pellet — presumably containing the zombie potion — at Neil and the missionary. Just then, Beaumont appears, tossing Legendre over the cliff, then following him to his own demise. With this, Madeline finally emerges from her trance, reunited with Neil.

Originally slated to play the Rialto Theater in New York beginning August 4, 1932, *White Zombie* instead premiered at the Rivoli Theater the morning of July 28. The chain to which that latter movie palace belonged to intended close it down in mid–July owing to what one publication termed a "declared product shortage." When the chain had second thoughts and ran two films during the second half of July, a need for additional product emerged that helped bring *White Zombie* and sustain the life of the Rivoli. Despite the negative reaction on the part of the New York critics, audiences flocked to the Rivoli. One reviewer took note of two young women in the audience the day the film premiered:

> When we caught the picture ... two girls sat alongside us ... [T]hey were intelligent girls as their whispered remarks proved.... "What a macabre situation" ... "But it's intriguing" ... said the other.... "It's enthralling" replied the first ... now, girls who talk like that are not dumb ... they know what they like ... and so these two sat bent forward with taut nerves ... and when it was all over ... they relaxed with sighs of complete satisfaction ... they had been thoroughly entertained.

The preeminent newspaper columnist of the day, Walter Winchell, took notice of other audience reactions to the film:

> That *White Zombie* movie is too spooky ... [T]he two women who fainted at the other midnight performance weren't "plants" either—they went out cold when the shudders were plentiful.... This type of flicker does bring some girls to their senses, at any rate.... Nearly every couple were in a clinch when the ghosts went gay.... And, after all, most of the lads who take their dolls to the midnight shows do not always go just to see the picture.

The same weekend of *White Zombie*'s New York debut also saw it open in Washington, D.C., Baltimore, and Kansas City. The film enjoyed great success in Washington, though week one of its three-week run there was the best. The Baltimore and Kansas City engagements, while only one week in both venues, were also profitable. Ironically, the film's D.C. engagement occurred simultaneously with the routing of the "bonus marchers" from the capital, the latter producing what *Variety* termed an "'[e]xcitement incident' that even brought many sightseers to town." While attendance problems bedeviled numerous theaters during that time, the theater featuring *White Zombie* in Washington didn't think the Bonus Army affair in any way affected attendance. Nor did the incident have any seeming impact on attendance in Baltimore. When the film opened in Seattle that fall, newspaper advertisements cautioned prospective viewers, "Only the BRAVE dare see it." The audience that came to Seattle's Music Box Theater, where *White Zombie* was playing the evening of November 8, 1932, the date of that year's presidential election, were most likely motivated not so much by a need to display their fortitude but by the theater's pledge to promulgate the election results.[72]

In its depiction of the relationship between the zombies and their master, *White Zombie* is a study of labor-management dynamics in the Great Depression. Not only is "Murder" Legendre a practioneer of the black arts,

Bela Lugosi's zombie legions in *White Zombie* (1932) were the perfect metaphor for the unemployed. Moreover, the film illustrated that no one, whatever their social standing, was immune to zombiism, as when the wealthy Beaumont (Robert Frazer, center) falls victim to the zombie spell of Lugosi (left) (UA/Photofest).

he is a business mogul — the owner of a sugar mill employing downtrodden laborers in the form of zombies — and he is completely indifferent to the latter's dignity and welfare. Legendre clearly belongs in the ranks of real-life businessmen Charles Mitchell and Samuel Insull who exploited others in pursuit of their interests, and who undoubtedly believed that their position in life gave them license to treat others any way they desired. The zombies themselves are completely dehumanized, their lives lacking dignity, individuality, and respect. And, just as polio demonstrated that it could ravage anyone, their social position notwithstanding (as evidenced by Franklin D. Roosevelt), the film demonstrated that, likewise, zombiism isn't merely an affliction of the lower classes but a malady that respects no socioeconomic strata: It equally affects the middle class (Madeline) and the well-to-do (Beaumont). Similarly, the real-life Depression cut across all economic levels — though in the case of reality, the majority of Depression victims, like the majority of zombies in the Halperins' film, belonged to society's lower classes.

Another illustration of the travails of American labor in *White Zombie* occurs when Legendre explains that his zombies are faithful workers, unconcerned about long hours. At the time of the film's release, the union movement, which had been treated with hostility by the federal government in the 1920s, was, owing to economic discontent, taking a more active role, advocating (among other things) regulated work hours and overtime pay; workers, including those in the movie business, were more apt to seek redress of grievances through strikes. Some newspapers drew a parallel between zombies and labor unrest. The New Orleans *Times-Picayune* argued that "the zombie system is the kind of thing that increases unemployment," while zombiism, in the words of the *St. Louis Post*, could "provide employment for a vast army [of 'laboring classes'] which has already passed beyond the need of work." As to whether the film was a denunciation of capitalism, film historian Gary D. Rhodes answers affirmatively, believing the zombies' situation closely parallels that of the American worker, especially those suffering from the Depression. Yet, Rhodes continues, the paramount issue of *White Zombie* isn't the worker analogy but sexual greed; Rhodes does not agree with another historian's notion that the film was a "Marxist" critique. Further evidence that the sufferings of Depression-era workers is not the film's primary point of concern is the fact that, at no time during the film do the zombies revolt against Legendre's dominance. The closest that comes is at the conclusion when Beaumont, still struggling against the effects of Legendre's zombie potion, rouses himself long enough to push the sorcerer to his death over the edge of the edge of the cliff his castle stands on.

One final issue is the depiction of blacks in *White Zombie*. One of the "catchlines" recommended to theaters to promote the film read: "They knew that this was taking place among the blacks, but when this fiend practiced it on a white girl ... all hell broke loose." Most of the studio materials and publicity, however, did not play the race card. Apparently the film made it plain that its title — *White Zombie* — signifies Madeline's innocence, chastity, and especially her status as a bride. It is true that Hollywood films of the time reflected prevailing American attitudes toward race, yet the principle malefactor of *White Zombie* is Caucasian. Additionally, the role of the carriage driver at the start of the film, played by black American actor-composer Clarence Muse, reflects the film's positive attitude toward blacks. Though cast as a servant, Muse in no way appears as debased and serves an essential role in the film: explaining to everyone — his fellow on-screen character and the viewing audience — what zombies are. His credentials as a serious actor and composer contributed to the esteem that audiences of the day felt toward his character in *White Zombie*. Perhaps when he subsequently recalled the problems the black American actor confronted in the entertainment field, he held favorable memories of the character he enacted in *White Zombie*:

> [W]hat of this new character which cries for self-expression? The Negro actor is willing to depict him. The black audience, comparatively small in number, applauds loudly for him, but with no avail. When the white audience sees him, it smiles and seems to say, "That is good, but when will he sing and dance? That is what we want to see and hear." The Negro actor is truly perplexed. What will he do?

In Gary D. Rhodes' words, Muse's character in *White Zombie* "did not leave most viewers in 1932 (or later) expecting humor or song or dance. If anything, his role suggests the production's modicum of sympathy to the situation of serious black actors."[73]

"Are We Not Men?": Land of Lost Souls *(1933)*

With films such as *Dr. Jekyll and Mr. Hyde*, *Murders in the Rue Morgue*, *Freaks*, and *White Zombie*, 1932 was a busy year for the horror genre. Yet by year's end some studios felt that the horror boom had run its course. Indicative of this belief was a notice that appeared in *Variety* two months before Paramount unveiled its latest horror offering:

> Admittedly a horror picture, Paramount is trying to find a selling angle for *Island of Lost Souls* that will eliminate reference to it as such. With the cycle of blood and thunder deemed passed, studio is afraid *Lost Souls* will do a dive unless the creepy angle is eliminated.[74]

Such a pronouncement would be proven premature.

Island of Lost Souls had is genesis in H. G. Wells' 1896 work *The Island of Dr. Moreau*; the latter was rooted in its author's efforts to conquer his own working class origins. He once described himself in the third person, "a child of change ... still enormously aware of and eager to understand and express, the process of adaptation...." The principle character of *Dr. Moreau* is a disgraced practioneer of vivisection who now presides over a South Pacific island populated by a collection of grotesqueries of his own making. Into this milieu comes a shipwrecked sailor, Edward Prendick, who is astonished by the appearance of its indigenous residents: They appear *both* animal and human. Employing advanced methods of vivisection, Moreau has transformed the island's animal inhabitants into semi-humans. Moreau's Beast Folk have their own primitive society and language. In addition to creating them in his "House of Pain," Moreau utilizes hypnosis to enhance their mental capacities and eliminates their natural instincts with some form of education. Despite his achievements, Moreau faces an obstacle: "The stubborn beast flesh" grows back. Despite his prohibition against drinking blood, the Beast Folk resume hunting. They rebel, and Moreau is killed by his own creation: a half-human puma. After staying on the island for a considerable time, watching Moreau's creations revert to their normal selves, Prendick returns to London, only now his experience on Moreau's island has left him unable to regard humans as truly human.

Directed by Erle C. Kenton, the film opens with a freighter, the *Covena*, rescuing a man floating at sea. The man, Edward Parker (Richard Arlen), is a survivor from another vessel, the *Lady Vain*, that went down. He has the *Covena* send a message to his fiancée Ruth in Apia that he's fine. Fully recovered from his ordeal, Parker goes topside for a breath of fresh air and discovers that the *Covena* is carrying a cargo of various wild animals bound for "Dr. Moreau's island," which lacks both a name and a listing on the charts. When the ship's captain, whose been drinking, slugs a crew member for bringing food for the dogs on deck, Parker punches the captain himself, then discovers the man he's helped has a curious physical feature: a hairy, animal-like ear. Moreover, he possesses an odd face and animal-like fangs. Later, when the *Covena* rendezvouses with Dr. Moreau's boat and unloads its beastly cargo, the *Covena*'s captain throws Parker overboard onto Moreau's vessel, stranding him with the doctor, then sails away. The crew aboard Moreau's vessel is equally strange: hairy, primitive-looking men.

Upon reaching his island, Moreau (Charles Laughton) guides Parker to his house. Along the way, they encounter more odd-looking characters, all of whom Moreau keeps in line by cracking his whip. "Strange—looking natives you have here," Parker observes.

Moreau wastes little time putting his newest scheme into action. He has brought Parker to his island to meet Lota, an exotic-looking woman — the only one there. While Moreau discreetly watches, Parker tries to get to know the lady better. Moreau is then called away by an assistant. Shortly thereafter, a scream is heard emanating from what the island inhabitants call "The House of Pain." Rushing to investigate the disturbance, Parker discovers Moreau and his assistant experimenting on a man. "They're vivisecting a human being," Parker says. "They're cutting a living man to pieces. Now I know about his natives — they're his victims." Trying to flee with Lota, Parker runs off into the jungle where they discover a large gathering of Moreau's "natives" encamped. Before the natives can do anything to Parker and Lota, they are interrupted by Moreau banging a gong and cracking his whip.

"What is the law?" Moreau asks.

"Not to run on all fours," replies the group's spokesman, the Sayer of the Law (Bela Lugosi). "That is the law. Are we not men?"

"Are we not men?" reply the Beast-Men in unison.

"What is the law?'

"Not to eat meat. That is the law...."

"What is the law?"

"Not to spill blood. That is the law...."

Moreau appears in this scene, as he does throughout the film, wearing a white plantation suit, resembling an overseer surveying his charges. Film historian Thomas Doherty writes that the scene of the Beast Men in the jungle, gathered around a bonfire, resembles "hoboes in a Hooverville of mutant man-beasts."[75] The ceremony concludes with the Sayer of the Law addressing Moreau as if the latter were a god:

"*His* is the hand that makes! *His* is the hand that heals." He concludes: "*His* is the House of *Paaa-iin*."

The Beast-Men repeat the line: "His is the House of Paaa-iin."

In contrasting Laughton's portrayal of Moreau with Lugosi's mad scientist persona, Arthur Lennig wrote:

> Dr. Moreau could easily have been portrayed as one of those Continental scientists who grandiloquently and passionately carry out their mad dreams. Laughton plays the role far differently. His Dr. Moreau is a logical, albeit cruel, scientist with overtones of the sexual deviant. There is something slimy and unhealthy about him.... With his little tuft of beard, thin mustache, and soft, almost infantile face, he is an excellent example of what Hannah Arendt described as "the banality of evil." ... Moreau is not in the mode of the Promethean scientists of Lugosi's type. Lugosi was much more old-fashioned, an obsessed experimenter, part poet, part madman, part scientist, but by no means a grotesque case history out of Krafft-Ebing. Lugosi is the mad scientist

we would like to envision. Laughton is more the type he might actually be. Laughton soft-pedals many of his lines and with his sardonic humor, nonchalance, and casualness gives them a kind of menace even more disturbing than Lugosi's. When Laughton says, "Mr. Parker, do you know what it means to feel like God?" his gentle manner make the presumption even more sinister and hateful. Most reviewers favored Laughton's approach, and he received a good amount of praise, though the film itself was liked less well.[76]

Laughton's biographer Charles Higham saw another dimension to Laughton's portrayal of Moreau, feeling that Laughton's interpretation went further than H. G. Wells' conception: "a perversion of a British Colonial administrator and at the same time a symbol of Colonial repressiveness."[77]

After dismissing the assembly, Moreau takes Parker to the House of Pain, his laboratory, all the while explaining the history of his work: how he began experimenting on plants in London years earlier, speeding up the evolutionary process, progressing in his work to Man himself. Along the way, he was forced out of London in disgrace. He has, he says, "wiped out hundreds of years of evolution." His experiments have reached the stage where he has transformed animals into men. The "natives" on his island all were once animals before he tinkered with them. Moreau's purpose in introducing Parker to Lota is to see if she will mate with him. Toward that end, Moreau wrecks the schooner on which Parker was to have left the island, preventing his departure.

In Apia, Ruth Thomas (Leila Hyams), Parker's fiancée, hooks up with Captain Donahue, who takes her aboard his ship and sets out for Moreau's island. Back on the island, Lota tries to seduce Parker. When the latter discovers that she is one of Moreau's creations, he confronts Moreau, from whom he learns that he intended to mate the two of them. Captain Donahue delivers Ruth to the island, where she is reunited with her missing lover. Moreau persuades the newcomers to remain for the night. When one of the Beast-Men tries to enter Ruth's room, she screams, bringing Parker to her assistance. Apprised of Moreau's activities by Parker, Donahue sets off to get help from his crew aboard his ship but is murdered en route by one of the mutants, acting on Moreau's instructions. The other Beast-Men, upon learning that Moreau ordered a murder (a violation of Moreau's own moral code), rise up in revolt against him. Watching them setting fire to their encampment with torches, audience members were perhaps reminded of the recent unrest as discontented Depression victims rose up against their plight.

Confronting the now mutinous creatures he has created, Moreau demands, "What is the law?"

"Law no more," replies the Sayer of the Law.

None of Moreau's furious whip-cracking can save him now: The defiant Beast-Men advance on him.

"Have you forgotten the House of Pain?" Moreau asks. The mob momentarily halts at this. Then the Sawyer of the Law speaks up: "You made us in the House of Pain. You made us *things*. Not men, not beasts, part-man, part-beast-things."

A full-scale rebellion is now underway. Like the people who bought into the promises of material success and prosperity during the Roaring '20s, only to see those assurances evaporate in the Depression, Moreau's Beast-Men, now feeling betrayed by his violation of his own law, pursue him into his laboratory, where they subject him to the same treatment he inflicted on them. Parker, Ruth, Lota, and Moreau's assistant Montgomery

The Beast-Men revolt against their master, Dr. Moreau (Charles Laughton) in *Island of Lost Souls* (1933). Dr. Moreau had broken his promise to his creations, leaving them feeling betrayed — much like those who believed 1920s promises of success, only to be wiped out by the Depression (Paramount Pictures/Photofest).

flee. As they depart, Lota is killed while struggling with a Beast-Man. As the others row away from the island in a boat, a burning fire is visible in the background, signaling the demise of Moreau's mad creation.

Debuting in New York City on January 11, 1933, *Island of Lost Souls* was ballyhooed as a super-shocker, with the emphasis on the Panther Woman. Reviewing the film in the *New York Herald-Tribune*, Richard Watts, Jr., opined:

> With most of the Neanderthal extras in Hollywood made-up to represent some of Boris Karloff's wilder dreams, the new film at the Rialto has a certain nightmare, or, more accurately, hangover quality.... More and more does it seem that Mr. Laughton was wasting his time on the stage; that he should have been rescuing motion pictures for us long before this.... Never having encountered a Panther Woman, I cannot say how accurate Miss Kathleen Burke's impersonation is, but it must be said for her portrayal of the wistful half-woman that it possesses a certain bewildered, sad-eyed quality which manages to be rather touching....[78]

Kenton's film succeeded in offending both religious and political sensibilities. The church faulted it because Moreau dared to take upon himself the Divine's right to create life. The established political order looked askance at the film, seeing, in the rebellion of the Beast-Men, Moreau's murder, and the toppling of the natural order, the real-life threats to its existence posed by the discontented masses of people in the Depression. That fear wasn't limited solely to American shores either. When *Island of Lost Souls* made its Australian debut, it bore the specification "N.E.N."— meaning it wasn't to be shown to the natives, lest the aborigines begin asking, "Are we not men?"[79] Some foreign audiences never got the opportunity to see it in the first place: It was banned in Lativa, the Netherlands, India, South Africa, Germany, Tasmania, Holland, New Zealand, and Singapore.[80]

American censors' attitudes toward the film were mixed. In 1932, before its initial American release, the Studio Relations Committee's Jason Joy cautioned Paramount's B. P. Schulberg about the risk of "injecting the idea of crossing animals with humans" and advised that the film "should be abandoned, for I am sure you would never be allowed to suggest that sort of thing on screen." Aware that Joy's admonition lacked force, Schulberg and Paramount proceeded with production of the film. By 1935, when the studio sought a Code seal for reissuance of the film, the Production Code Association, headed by Joseph Breen, was in force and Breen vetoed Paramount's appeal. Not until 1941 would the film finally win approval—

only after conforming with Breen's stipulations to "eliminate from the picture the suggestion that Moreau considers himself on a par with God as creator, and reduce him to the status of a scientist conducting bio-anthropological experiments; remove any suggestion that Moreau attempts to mate the beast girl with a human being; [and] remove any suggestion that he encourages the mating of a beast man with a human being." [81]

Island of Lost Souls had a rougher time of it in England. None other than H. G. Wells, whose own story inspired the film, disavowed the latter, and was overjoyed when it was banned on the grounds that its theme was unnatural. "Of course it's against nature," cracked Elsa Lanchester. "So's Mickey Mouse." The British prohibition remained in force a quarter-century until it was rescinded in 1958 — and even then, three scenes had to edited.[82]

The common theme binding each of the aforementioned films was the exploitation of the powerless by the powerful — an argument amplified by the fact that these films were released during the nadir of the Great Depression, the period between 1932 and Roosevelt's inauguration in March 1933. Dr. Jekyll (as Mr. Hyde) and Dr. Mirakle both exploited women of the lower-class — in both cases prostitutes. Tod Browning's circus Freaks rose up against the big people they felt disdained them and who also abused one of their own — pulling one of their big tormentors down to their level. Similarly, Dr. Moreau's Beast-Men rebelled against their creator, one who had promised them a better life if they followed his "law," and then violated his own decree, rendering his edicts meaningless. Zombie master "Murder" Legendre used his mindless automatons to operate his cane mills and enslaved others, whatever their social class, into his zombie legions. It was a dark time and, with the old, discredited regime thrown out in 1932, and a new one about to take power, everyone waited to see what direction the nation would now take.

3

The Banking Crisis (*King Kong*) and the Fascist Alternative (*The Invisible Man*)

For a pair of reasons, the banking crisis of early 1933 was significant. Historically, it marked both the nadir of the Great Depression and the beginning of the New Deal's crusade to restore the American economy to health. It was also a time when some Americans advocated turning power over to a strongman to guide the nation out of its ills, even if doing so meant abandoning traditional democratic methods. Pop-culturally, the year was dominated in the fantasy-horror genre by two films, *King Kong* and *The Invisible Man*, both of which reflected the historical currents of the time. Kidnapped from his native Skull Island and taken to New York City to be exploited as a commercial attraction, King Kong erupted in rage at his captors, trashing America's financial capital to the vicarious delight of those victimized by the Depression and who saw New York as the embodiment of everything vile and objectionable about cities. This sentiment doubtless received reinforcement from the fact that *Kong* was released in the midst of the bank closures. *The Invisible Man*'s central character undoubtedly resonated with those individuals who longed for the kind of leader who seized power and wielded it ruthlessly.

King Kong *(1933)*

Late in the afternoon of March 2, 1933, two days before his scheduled installation as president of the United States, Franklin Delano

Roosevelt and his party left the president-elect's 65th Street townhouse in New York to begin the final leg of his journey to Washington. Owing to a recent assassination attempt in Miami, Roosevelt departed New York under heavy security. The wailing of the sirens of the motorcycles escorting FDR's motorcade attracted the attention of onlookers; those of whom who recognized FDR cheered and waved to him.[1] Taking a ferryboat ride across the Hudson River, Roosevelt then boarded a train that would convey him to the capital. Reading that morning's newspapers in bed, FDR learned the effect the banking crisis sweeping the nation was having: Half the states had declared bank holidays, with more certain to come.[2] The crisis had begun the preceding month when depositors, lacking confidence in banks, withdrew their money, precipitating a panic whereby banks shut down, declaring bankruptcy. In mid–February, Michigan's governor briefly closed all his state's banks. The crisis spread: By March 1, when Roosevelt

The crowd lining up outside New York's Radio City Music Hall on March 2, 1933, for the debut of *King Kong* provides clear evidence that the banking crisis then sweeping the nation in no way dampened enthusiasm for the giant simian's initial appearance in the Big Apple (RKO/Photofest).

left his Hyde Park, New York, residence to take up his presidential duties, bank holidays were in effect in seventeen states and the president-elect was informed that "in the view of J. P. Morgan & Co., the emergency could not be greater."[3]

The same day that Roosevelt left New York, other crowds were lining up to see what one filmmaker has dubbed the *Jurassic Park* of its time. The film was a huge success: Not even the new president's bank holiday, which took effect shortly after its New York debut, could dampen its popularity, as its releasing studio proudly noted in *Motion Picture Herald*: "With no money last week *King Kong* played to 189,402 paid admissions."[5] "It took you," explained movie special effects legend Ray Harryhausen, "from the mundane world of the Depression and brought you into the most outrageous fantasy that's ever been put on the screen."[6] Noting that its New York debut was during the absolute nadir of the Great Depression, film historian Rudy Behlmer said that people, "even though they were broke, ... would pay their money to get in and see it because it was the great escape of all times."[7] Long after its premiere, it would continue to reap honors: It was twice honored by the American Film Institute, first in 1975 as one of the fifty best American movies of all time and, second, in 1998, when the AFI ranked it 45th among the 100 Greatest American films of all time. In between it was added to the National Film Registry of the Library of Congress in 1991.[8]

To moviegoers of the 1930s, *King Kong* was one of the most outstanding films of that era. One of them, future film historian David Zinman, recalled: "One rainy afternoon..., I plunked down a dime at the third-run Lakeland Theatre (nicknamed "the Dump") in Brooklyn. I can still remember crouching low in my seat when the massive Kong made his first frightening appearance, beating a tattoo on his chest."[9]

King Kong was essentially the creation of three men — two of whom, Merian C. Cooper and Ernest B. Schoedsack, began as documentary filmmakers. The initial inspiration for *Kong* came to Cooper while he and Schoedsack were filming on location in Africa for Paramount's *The Four Feathers* (1929). Becoming interested in the habits of gorillas, Cooper dreamed up the notion of a gigantic gorilla rampaging in the cities of the modern world. He added other elements to his idea: His gargantuan simian would tangle with a Komodo dragon (the latter in the news at the time because two of them had died in captivity after being brought to New York's Bronx Zoo); the film would end with the gorilla fighting atop the Empire State Building. As part of his job reorganizing RKO Studios, Cooper had to decide which projects the old administration had initiated should go forward; one of them, an animated adventure, *Creation*, dealing with the development of life on Earth, featured special effects work by Willis O'Brien. Impressed by the latter's work, Cooper scrapped his original plans to film *Kong* on location in favor of a studio production.

Encouraged by RKO's vice president in charge of production David O. Selznick, O'Brien and Cooper shot a one-reel test for the studio's stockholders. The test reel passed muster with the stockholders, and the production was green-lighted. Edgar Wallace, who prepared the initial screenplay, died during the film's development — though his name was listed in the completed film's credits. The final screenplay was completed by James Creelman and Ruth Rose, the latter Ernest Schoedsack's wife. The majority of *King Kong's* final production cost — $650,000 — was spent on special effects.[10]

Against the backdrop of the banking crisis, *King Kong* debuted in New York on March 2, 1933. Within the space of a week, the film had drawn 180,000 people in the two venues where it was playing: Radio City Music Hall and the New Roxy theatre. In the former, "constant exclamations issued" forth, noted one critic.[11]

The film opens with an "ancient Arabian Proverb":
And the prophet said:

> "And lo, the beast looked
> upon the face of beauty. And
> It stayed its hand from killing.
> And from that day, it was as
> one dead."

The "ancient Arabian Proverb" was in reality Cooper's creation.[12] It wouldn't be the last time that Hollywood fabricated a "celebrated" piece of verse for inclusion in a horror film.

The scene now shifts to New York harbor, where a ship, the *Venture*, commandeered by film photographer Carl Denham, is docked, waiting to sail. Weston, a theatrical agent, comes aboard to tell Denham that he can't secure the services of an actress to appear in Denham's latest film. This isn't the only obstacle Denham confronts: The fire marshal will be coming aboard to examine the explosives he has stored aboard — enough to obliterate the harbor.

Taking matters into his own hands, Denham ventures into New York himself to find his leading lady, meeting a destitute former actress, Ann Darrow (Fay Wray), whom he persuades to appear in his film. When we first see Darrow, she almost purloins an apple from a fruit stand, so great is her hunger; this is "a preview," in film historian Thomas Doherty's words, "of her role as the seductive Eve in the garden of a primeval Adam," one who will lure Kong to his ultimate demise.[13] After paying for the fruit Ann tried to steal, Denham takes her to a drugstore — coffee shop, where he makes his pitch to her to be in his film. "She is unemployed and her complete destitution generates its opposite, voiced by Denham: a dream of fortune, riches versus rags. The Depression details of privation anchor and call forth, so to speak, the Depression fantasy of wealth and fame."[14]

Ann is soon aboard the *Venture* and the latter has set sail. First mate Jack Driscoll (Bruce Cabot) initially takes umbrage to her presence but it's clear he's falling in love with her. Ultimately, Denham apprises Driscoll and the ship's captain of their destination: an uncharted island, the inhabitants of which maintain a great wall to keep out something known as Kong — "neither beast nor man. Something monstrous, all powerful. Still living, still holding that island in a grip of deadly fear.... There's something on that island that no white man has ever seen." Denham's objective is to photograph this mysterious being.

"Suppose it doesn't like having its picture taken?" Driscoll asks.

"Now you know why I brought along those cases of gas bombs," Denham replies.

The *Venture* finally reaches its objective: an island with a mountain dubbed Skull Mountain as it's shaped like a skull. Once the ship drops anchor, a shore party, including Ann, goes ashore and almost immediately discovers a native ceremony in progress, featuring a woman about to be sacrificed and men (wearing gorilla suits) dancing and chanting "Kong." The natives, like the Transylvanian villagers of *Dracula*, are downtrodden people in thrall to a far superior being — be it a giant gorilla, a vampire, or, by implication, an upper-class tycoon. Discovering they have visitors, the natives are displeased at their intrusion, believing their ceremony has been marred because the outsiders have witnessed it. However, upon seeing Ann, the witch doctor offers to trade six of his women for her as a gift to Kong. Refusing the offer, the shore party leaves. That night, a group of natives row out to the *Venture* and kidnap Ann. Discovering her absence, the crew arm themselves and set out to rescue her.

Back on the island, the natives open the massive gate at the wall, tie Ann to a pair of columns as their sacrifice, then leave her to her fate. The wait isn't long: An animal roar emanates from the jungle, then the source of the sound, King Kong, a giant gorilla, appears. Intrigued by Ann, he carries her off with him back into the jungle — just as the rescue party from the *Venture* arrives. Leaving some of the crew to guard the gate, Denham, Driscoll, and the others set off in pursuit of Ann. What they encounter is a world inhabited by prehistoric beasts. Leaving Ann in a tree, Kong disposes of her would-be deliverers, save for Denham and Driscoll, by rolling them off a ravine-spanning log into the abyss. Kong then has to save Ann from being eaten by a Tyrannosaurus Rex, killing the latter by snapping his jaw.

Denham meets up with Driscoll, the latter telling Denham to return for more gas bombs while he follows Kong. With Driscoll close behind, Kong returns to his lair — a cave in the mountain. Once again, he has to fight for Ann's life when she's menaced by a snake-like elasmosaurus. Taken to a cliff, Ann faints; picking her up, Kong undresses her, sniffing her garments, then playing with her. Where critics, scholars, and audiences saw this scene as intentionally erotic in nature, O'Brien and Cooper saw it quite differently, O'Brien, who devised the scene, saw Kong as treating Ann as an object of beauty and her disrobement by Kong the same as removing the petals from a flower. Cooper viewed the scene as a playful, comical one.[15]

When Driscoll knocks over a rock while climbing up the cliff, Kong leaves Ann to investigate. In his absence, Ann is attacked yet again, this time by a pterodactyl that tries to snatch her away. Kong dispatches this latest threat to Ann's safety but, during the fight, Driscoll finally catches up with Ann and the two go over the cliff's edge and climb down a vine. When Kong begins pulling the vine up. Ann and Driscoll drop to the water below, then flee back through the jungle, an enraged Kong hot on their trail. They make their way back to the natives' village. Joined by the natives, Denham and the *Venture*'s crew struggle to prevent Kong from breaking through the gate. The effort proves futile: Kong breaks through, rampaging through the village before being felled by one of Denham's gas bombs.

Ever the showman, Denham scraps his original plans to make a movie in favor of bringing Kong back to Broadway as the "Eighth Wonder of the World." On opening night a huge crowd flocks to the theater to see Kong.

3. The Banking Crisis and the Fascist Alternative 81

Addressing the audience from the stage, Denham says, "He was a king and a god in the world he knew. But now he comes to civilization merely a captive, a show to gratify your curiosity. Ladies and gentlemen, look at Kong, the Eighth Wonder of the World." The curtain raises, revealing Kong, bound in manacles on a platform, to the astonished audience. After introducing Ann and Driscoll, Denham summons the press to photograph the couple with Kong. Thinking the photographers are attacking Ann, Kong breaks free. Finding Ann, he carries her off and rampages through New York. Here, Kong becomes a symbol of Depression-era moviegoers' sense of impotence in the face of the economic crisis, "a one-ape revolution, momentarily venting the pent-up fury and indignation of a frustrated audience, their feelings of powerlessness relieved in an orgy of power, as if indulging infantile flights of pandemonium were their only option."[16]

King Kong makes his last stand atop the Empire State Building. Kong's rampage through New York City personified a resentment many felt toward America's financial capital (RKO Radio Pictures Inc./Photofest).

Ultimately Kong climbs to the top of the very symbol of New York — the Empire State Building — where he makes his final stand. At Driscoll's suggestion, airplanes are dispatched to shoot him down. Putting Ann out of harm's way, Kong does battle with his attackers, downing one of the planes. Still he's no match for them: Riddled with machine gun bullets, a stranger in a strange land, Kong plunges to his death in the street below, in Doherty's words, "like the stock market, the nation, flat on its back."[17] "Well, Denham," a police officer on the scene says, "the airplanes got him." Shaking his head, Denham has the last word: "Oh, no, it wasn't the airplanes. It was beauty killed the beast."[18]

During the first four days of its New York engagement, *King Kong* earned $89,931. The turnout was so enormous it became necessary to have ten screenings daily. The total number of seats in Radio City Music Hall and the New Roxy combined (ten thousand) wasn't sufficient, Rothafel explained. *Kong*'s official Hollywood debut followed on March 24 at Grauman's Chinese Theater. "This is a Grauman opening in the full sense of the word," exclaimed Louella Parsons: In addition to the spotlights and celebrity interviews that characterize such events, the full-sized head and shoulders of Kong were on display. Inside, a stage show preceding the film featured a fifty-voice African choral ensemble and a dance company, comprised of black girls, performed "The Dance to the Sacred Ape" and several other musical numbers.[19] The debut was a smash as Sid Grauman informed Cooper: "Never saw greater enthusiasm for any picture in my experience of presenting premieres. First time in the history of any picture where applause so frequent and spontaneous. Audience applauded at least twenty times tonight."[20]

April 10, 1933, marked *Kong*'s nationwide debut, followed by its international debut in London on Easter Sunday. It became a universal sensation — except in Nazi Germany, where propaganda minister Joseph Goebbels prohibited it from playing, perhaps because Kong, in the Nazi mind, signified the violation of the sexual purity of Aryan womanhood.[21]

The Nazis weren't the only ones to discern symbolic meanings in *King Kong*. European Communists saw the image of Karl Marx in Kong's shattering of the gates shielding him from the island's inhabitants (when, in reality, his violent behavior was motivated solely by his desire to recapture Ann Darrow). One French critic, who evidently confused *Kong* screenwriter Ruth Rose with Rose La Rose or Gypsy Rose Lee, believed the film's sexual elements stemmed from the "fact" that it was authored in part by "a former strip-teaser." Another school of thought saw Kong as a symbol of racial repression: He was black so as to denote the black experience in America; like Kong, blacks were transported to America, bound in chains, to be exploited by whites.[22] Subscribing to this view, Thomas Doherty notes that when Kong is revealed on stage to the New York audience, he is shown "standing with his arms outstretched above him, in chains, on a pedestal, evoking nothing so much as an African slave on an auction block, just off-loaded from his" oceanic crossing.[23]

Another concept, rooted in the Freudian school, contended that audiences, battered by the Depression, found "proxy gratification" in Kong's rampage through New York.[24] This latter view was reflected in the cycle of "shyster" films Hollywood turned out in the early '30s and the real-life ambivalence Americans felt toward New York. The stars of "shyster" films were shady lawyers, politicians, and newspapermen who lived and worked in the urban environment, and the logical place for such unsavory types was America's greatest metropolis — and financial heart — New York. This anti–New York sentiment predated the Depression. The words of *The Nation,* published the year of the Wall Street Crash, summed up the popular feelings the city engendered: "New York is not popular in the United States at large. Other places are a little jealous and a bit afraid of it. But it is the city to which, if possible, all Americans come some time before they die." Still, *The Nation* observed, it was the "Mecca and the model of the continent." The issue of whether New York was "American" was a hot topic in popular magazines. "The American who settles in New York," asserted Ford Maddox Ford, "becomes at once an ex–American." It was a city that best epitomized American dynamism but was also populated by the unethical and the immigrants whom native Americans viewed as a threat to their racial purity and employment opportunities. (This sentiment was expressed by a character in the 1932 novel *State Fair:* "It's God's greatest gift to mankind except for the dirt, Tammany, dagos and subways.") These conflicting views were ready-made for Hollywood to exploit. Andrew Bergman described Hollywood's New York:

> This city could be identified as follows: opening shot of lower Manhattan's skyline (boats steaming past in the harbor) or Broadway, electric in the night; to shots of society people (long gowns, tails, silk hats) promenading after the theatre. They stepped into limousines or honking taxicabs manned by men in caps and sped off to a nightclub or penthouse. The nightclub was smoky and peopled by women with blond hair who did fast dancing and sat on the laps of men with

mustaches. They laughed a lot. The penthouse overlooked a section of skyline (squares of lighted windows painted on the backdrops) and had a balcony on which stood corrupt lawyers with Anglo-Saxon names, politicians with Irish names, and women with shiny shoulders and low-cut evening gowns.

Deals were made. Standing on the sidewalk below were men with pads, pencils, and snap-brim hats who told other men holding cameras to "Get ready, here he comes." These people were newspapermen, who "phoned in" to "the chief" (a man they hated but loved) and make a great many wisecracks.[25]

Film exhibitors weren't above emphasizing the anti–New York theme to pack audiences in to see *King Kong*. After advising exhibitors to combine the romance between Fay Wray and Bruce Cabot with the "thrill angle" as a lure, Roland Viner of the Morris Theatre in Illinois added a final suggestion: "And don't let them forget that the beast charges through New York City."[26]

King Kong was also a warning against the dangers of upward mobility. Noting a similarity between *Kong* and the classic gangster films of the era, film historian Noel Carroll observes that when the gangsters "don ritzy airs, replete with laughable *nouveau riche* manners," they're doomed. Similarly, when King Kong leaves his native island habitat for the modern, urban wilderness, he is unprepared to confront the latter, and is inevitably marked for destruction. "Life in the modern jungle, exactly because it is a jungle, is precarious, even for a Kong — a piece of perennial American folk wisdom distilled to a higher proof by the experience of the Depression."[27] Striving to advance beyond one's present station in life to a higher strata could be risky: There were perils on the road to the top.

Rejecting such interpretations of the film's meaning, others (writers Orville Goldner and George E. Turner and Merian C. Cooper himself) contended that *King Kong* was merely an entertaining adventure story — nothing more. Writer Ray Morton offers another explanation: *Kong*'s enduring hold on people's imaginations

> can best be explained by the fact that it is a breathtaking work of pure cinema — a stellar example of the twentieth century's most powerful art form. As exciting as it is, the story would not have the impact it does had it been realized as a novel or a stage play or even as a comic book (it has been translated into all of these forms, with diminished results). It is only through the cinema's unique and alchemic mixture of image, movement, and sound that Merian C. Cooper's strange and fantastic tale can come roaring to life and fulfill its incredible potential to amaze, to terrify, and, ultimately, to move. At its core, *King Kong* is a supreme example of the power and the magic of the movies.[28]

Fay Wray herself offered a simpler, more direct analysis: "Of course, this picture was a special one.... It was unique. You can't compare it really with anything else."[29]

The Invisible Man *(1933)*

"So first of all, let me assert my firm belief that the only thing we have to fear is fear itself— nameless, unreasoning, unjustified terror which paralyzes needed efforts to convert retreat into advance.... We are stricken by no plague of locusts.... Plenty is at our doorstep, but a generous use of it languishes in the very sight of the supply.... This nation is asking for action, and action now."[30]

Thus spoke President Franklin Delano Roosevelt at his inauguration on March 4, 1933. He would submit a program for economic recovery to Congress, but should Congress fail to act and the Depression continue, "I shall not evade the clear course of duty that will then confront me. I shall ask the Congress for the one remaining instrument to meet the crisis — broad Executive power to wage a war against the emergency, as great as the power that would be given to me if we were in fact invaded by a foreign foe."[31]

This passage elicited the greatest applause on the part of the throng present for the inaugural ceremony than any other words Roosevelt uttered that day. Listening to the speech, the new first lady, Eleanor Roosevelt, shuddered at the implications her husband's declaration concerning war powers carried. Years later she recalled that during this time she told FDR of her wish that America have a beneficent dictator who could force the adoption of reforms, to which her husband replied that no one could count upon a dictator remaining benevolent. An editorial in the *Il Giornale d'Italia* of Mussolini's Italy declared: "President Roosevelt's words are clear and need no comment to make even the deaf hear that not only Europe but the whole world feels the need of executive authority capable of acting with full power of cutting short the purposeless chatter of legislative assemblies. This method of government may well be defined as Fascist."[32] Some months after Roosevelt's installation, another dictator lauded his performance: "I have sympathy with President Roosevelt," declared Adolf Hitler, "because he marches straight to his objective over Congress, over lobbies, over stubborn bureaucracies."[33]

In the coverage of Roosevelt's inaugural oration, the majority of newspapers, *The New York Times* among them, emphasized the martial undertones emanating from the speech — giving the impression that there existed ample justification for fear. The atmosphere in Washington, in the words of one commentator, was comparable to "a beleaguered capital in wartime."

For the first time since the Civil War, armed men patrolled the entrances to federal buildings, while machine gunners were stationed on rooftops. "Editors knew that the world war, ... had concentrated great power in the hands of Woodrow Wilson's government." Roosevelt apparently was "proposing the same thing."[34]

In view of the crisis confronting the United States, there were those who were prepared to discard the democratic process in favor of more authoritarian methods. Indicative of this sentiment was a resolution, endorsed by the American Legion in September 1931, that the Depression couldn't be "promptly and efficiently met by existing political methods." An organization, the "American Facist [sic] Association and Order of Black Shirts," had been spawned in Atlanta; in its wake there came the Silver Shirts, White Shirts, Khaki Shirts, the Minute Men, and the American Nationalists. "A secret clique of reserve army officers was reported ready to act if the new president proved ineffective."[35] Retired General Smedley Butler, who had officiated as a pallbearer at Lon Chaney's funeral in 1930, disclosed the he had been offered money by a New York bond salesman to prepare a coup against Roosevelt should the latter be unable to meet the crisis. Though Butler aired this fantastic scheme, no treason charges were filed.[36]

Columbia University president Nicholas Murray Butler told his students that authoritarian governments yielded "men of far greater intelligence, far stronger character, and far more courage that the system of elections" — a declaration that, considering the credentials of the one uttering it, no one disputed. Governor Landon of Kansas declared, "Even the iron hand of a national dictator is in preference to a paralytic stroke." New York Congressman Hamilton Fish, Jr., who had already said, "If we don't give it [dictatorship] under the existing system, the people will change the system," informed president-elect Roosevelt that he and his fellow Republicans were prepared to "give you any power you may need." Al Smith believed that the Constitution should be wrapped up and put "on the shelf" until the Depression was past. *Vanity Fair* cried: "Appoint a dictator!" Walter Lippmann wanted to give Roosevelt full authority at the expense of the Legislative Branch; "the danger," in his words, "is not that we shall lose our liberties, but that we shall not be able to act with the necessary speed and comprehensiveness," while Republican Senator David A. Reed was far blunter: "If this country ever needs a Mussolini, it needs one now."[37]

The banking crisis threatened to become violent, and by inaugural weekend, the police in almost every American city were preparing to confront outraged depositors, some of whom were certain to be armed. The sheet number of banks was such that not even the United States Army, National Guard and Reserve units included, might have sufficient manpower to handle the crisis. If such were the case, should Roosevelt create an army of veterans to impose martial law? The initial radio speech of FDR's presidency, delivered at the end of his first full day in office, March 5, was to an American Legion convention. As disclosed by Jonathan Alter, a draft of FDR's remarks contained an extraordinary passage: "As new commander-in-chief under the oath to which you are still bound I reserve to myself the right to command you in any phase of the situation which now confronts us." "The speech draft prepared for FDR," Alter writes, "brought to mind Mussolini addressing his black-shirt followers, many of whom were demobilized veterans who joined Il Duce's private army."[38]

Roosevelt never uttered that passage.[39] America didn't follow the example of Italy and Germany and adopt fascism as the remedy for the Depression. Roosevelt intended to utilize the democratic process to solve the nation's problems. He greatly feared the likes of Huey Long. The latter had backed FDR for the Democratic nomination in 1932, believing that Roosevelt shared his desire to distribute the nation's wealth. In reality, Roosevelt feared that if the Depression wasn't soon alleviated, the American people would abandon democracy in favor of extremists like Long, whom FDR equated with General Douglas MacArthur as the two most dangerous men in America.[40]

The desire for power was the theme of Universal's adaptation of H. G. Wells' 1897 novel *The Invisible Man*. By the time of the film's release in late 1933, the panic that had gripped America earlier in the year and culminated with Roosevelt's inauguration, owing to FDR's fulfillment of his inaugural pledge of "action and action now," had faded. The film can thus be read two ways — as a vicarious wish fulfillment for the attainment of power in the midst of the Depression and a cautionary tale regarding the realization of that goal. Either way, it became a classic of Hollywood horror.

The notion of invisibility did not originate with Wells' story, having appeared with Plato and then sustained in philosophy, fantasy, and folklore. What set Wells' tale apart from its predecessors was that Wells set his story within a scientific framework: The cause of Wells' protagonist's invisibility is scientifically induced. The hero, an erstwhile medical student, was expelled from medical school because of his unorthodox experiments with animals. He then began studying physics and light and optical density — all culminating in his discovery of the secret of invisibility. He has yet to find a way to become visible again, and intends to initiate a reign of terror. For Wells, a committed socialist, science fiction afforded him a platform from which he could address social problems and social change. David J. Skal has noted: "The interesting thing about Wells' original story is that ... the Invisible Man was not really a mad scientist, although he certainly became that in Hollywood. In the novel he speaks more like a political revolutionary who wants to tear down the existing social order because he's so totally alienated from it by his invisible state. He's not an unreasonable man but he is caught in an unreasonable situation."[41]

Others have expressed a similar view. Noting that the status quo is unwilling to embrace advancement and change, Don G. Smith explains that ambivalence characterized Wells' portrayal of the villagers in both *The Invisible Man* and his earlier story *The Wonderful Visit*: "[Wells] is fond of their humorous simplicity on one level, but he loathes their stubborn ignorance and lack of vision on another." Smith continues that Wells' invisible protagonist becomes a sympathetic character on account of the vulnerable aspects he shares with the common people he loathes, yet that understanding disappears when Griffin appreciates that the key to progress is suffering, hence the rationale for his proposed reign of terror. "Finally," Smith notes, "*The Invisible Man* is another Wellsian critique of society in the tradition of Saint-Simon, a 'scientific romance'" intended to usher in "an age of world socialism. A reign of terror might be necessary to ensure human progress and save mankind from democracy. Though Wells professed a disbelief in the possibility of invisibility, the point is that science must be the foundation on which the future is constructed by Carlyle's great men and captains of industry."[42] The notion that a reign of terror might be required to guarantee progress and rescue humanity from the "perils" of democracy echoed the sentiments of those who felt that the democratic process was inadequate to counter the Great Depression and would have to be scrapped in favor of fascism. Conversely, the belief in science and the "captains of industry" had been discredited by the Depression.

Finally, there is the view, expressed in the 1980s by Frank McConnell, that Wells' story was at odds with the "realistic" novel, where the protagonist would succeed within the status quo. To be successful, one would have to be visible making his way up the social ladder, noticed by others. Griffin's discovery of invisibility, by contrast, proves a mixed "blessing": It literally renders him unseen, an outcast from society, yet endows him with great power to manipulate that same society.[43]

Directed by James Whale and starring Claude Rains in the title role, *The Invisible Man* opens on a snowy, windy night, introducing us to a mysterious figure (Rains) trudging through the snow to the English village of Iping, where he takes lodging at an inn. The lodger's appearance is quite odd: bundled up against the cold in a hat, scarf, and overcoat, his face and eyes completely obscured by bandages and goggles. His arrival creates a stir among the patrons at the inn: "If you ask me," opines one, "he's a criminal flying from justice.... You be careful and lock your money up." When Mrs. Hall (Una O'Connor), the innkeeper's wife, delivers his mustard for his dinner to him, she finds the lower portion of his face uncovered — only there's nothing to see. "Bandages right up to the top of his head, all around his ears," she tells the others.

"Any blood?" one of them inquires.

"No, no blood. Looks like some kind of 'orrible accident."

"Bumped his head on the prison wall gettin' over," says another patron.

The absence of the Invisible Man, whose real name is Jack Griffin, has upset his fiancée Flora (Gloria Stuart), who hasn't heard from him in nearly a month. Her father Dr. Cranley (Henry Travers) tells her not to worry as he (Griffin) is completing "a difficult experiment" and that "it's a good thing to go away" given the circumstances. Kemp (William Harrigan), Dr. Cranley's assistant, is less sympathetic to Flora's concerns about Griffin, telling her the latter "meddled in things men should leave alone.... He worked in secret, ... kept a lot of stuff locked in a big cupboard in his laboratory. He never opened that cupboard until he'd barred the door and drawn the blinds. Straightforward scientists have no need for barred doors and drawn blinds." When Kemp, whose in love with Flora himself, tries to tell her how he feels about her, she screams, "Oh, leave me alone!" and breaks down in tears.

Griffin has set up a makeshift laboratory in his room at the inn, experimenting with chemicals. "There must be a way back," he says aloud to himself. When Mrs. Hall tries to serve him lunch, he angrily shoves her out. Fed up with this and with Griffin's delinquency in paying his rent, she orders her husband to evict Griffin. When Griffin assaults Hall, the police are summoned. A constable and some of the lodgers and townspeople go to Griffin's room to arrest him. "You're *crazy* to know who I am, aren't you?" Griffin defiantly tells them. "All right, I'll show you!" Laughing maniacally, he undresses in the presence of his would-be captors, revealing that he's completely invisible. Stripped down to his shirt, he leads them on a merry chase through the room.

"Put the handcuffs on," a member of the posse tells the constable.

"How can I handcuff a bloomin' shirt?" the latter rejoins.

During all this, the Invisible Man explains the secret of his invisibility: "A few chemicals mixed together, that's all. And flesh and blood and bone just fade away. A little of this [the invisibility formula] injected under the skin of the arm every day for a month. An invisible man can rule the world! Nobody will see him come. Nobody will see him go. He can hear every secret. He can rob and wreck and kill!"

Overpowering his pursuers, Griffin then runs out of the inn and proceeds to create mayhem: stealing a bicycle and a man's hat; he throws a rock through a window, saying, "We do our part." (This latter bit of dialogue was meant to be a takeoff on the New Deal agency the National Recovery Administration — NRA — the motto of which was: "We do our part.")[44]

Searching with Kemp for clues to Griffin's experiment, Dr. Cranley discovers a list of chemicals Griffin left behind, one of which, monocane, in Cranley's words, "is a terrible drug.... It's never used now...." Manufactured from a flower native to India, monocane "draws color from everything it touches. Years ago they tried it for bleaching cloth. They gave it up because it destroyed the material.... It does something else.... It was tried out on some poor animal — a dog, I believe. It was injected under the skin, and it turned the dog dead-white — like a marble statue ... and it also sent it raving mad.... I only pray to God that Griffin hasn't been meddling with this ghastly stuff." Telling Kemp he's going to notify the police of Griffin's disappearance, he also instructs him not to tell anyone else about it.

That night Kemp hears a radio account describing the strange events in Iping — just as the Invisible Man himself enters his house, shutting off the radio, and ordering him to provide him clothing, lest he be killed. Once he's properly dressed, Griffin tells Kemp of the "great, wonderful day" when he achieved his breakthrough in invisibility, then left for a little village to complete his experiment and find the antidote to the invisibility drug. The latter's psychotic effects have clearly taken over Griffin's mind: When the people of Iping wouldn't let him complete his experiments in peace, he had to teach them a lesson. What had begun as a simple experiment has become something far more sinister in Griffin's mind: "The drugs I took seemed to light up my brain. Suddenly I realized the power I held. The power to rule, to make the world grovel at my feet. We'll soon put the world right now, Kemp. You and I." Griffin needs Kemp as his "visible partner" to help him "in the little things." He then outlines his plans: "We'll begin with a reign of terror — a few murders here and there. Murders of great men, murders of little men — just to show we make no distinction. We might even wreck a train or two. Just these fingers around a signalman's throat."

Where *Dracula* and *Frankenstein* introduced American moviegoers to the Gothic, supernatural horror film, *The Invisible Man* is significant in that he was one of the first scientists to both declare himself greater than ordinary people and enjoy such a distinction, seeing no reason why he shouldn't dominate the world. Such an attitude toward possessing power had been hinted at in earlier horror films: "Audiences relished the supernatural abilities of Dracula and Im-ho-tep, the ruthlessness of Dr. Mirakle, the brilliance of Henry Frankenstein and Henry Jekyll, and the physical force of the Frankenstein Monster and Mr. Hyde," wrote Paul Jensen "[Audiences] were fascinated by these characters' independence and isolation, by their willingness to venture into the Forbidden and the Unknown." Yet, despite all of the preceding, their ambitions were finite in scope, "and few verbalized a desire for power."

What set Jack Griffin apart from these other characters was that he was the total personification of the Superman aspect — one found in Wells' story and one that, owing to screenwriter R. C. Sherriff's dialogue and Rains' energetic performance, is greatly augmented in the film. "In this regard," writes Jensen, "*The Murderer Invisible* [a 1931 novel by Philip Wylie and similar to Wells' story] may have influenced the script, for Wylie's novel does deal directly with its invisible character's megalomania, as when he declares, 'Power has always been denied me. My compensation will come — and it will not be the power of Wealth — wholly — not power over a few thousand employees — it will be power over leaders — the power over a nation — and at last the power over the world." For those rendered powerless by the Depression, such an almighty figure who disregarded the status quo in favor of more direct action — by they a movie character (Jack Griffin; Little Caesar) or a real-life figure (FDR) — was clearly irresistible — a strong man capable of bringing order out of chaos. However, "This fascination faded in the late 1930s and early 1940s, as the Depression receded and reports from Germany revealed some of the realistic results of putting the Superman philosophy into practice."[45]

After forcing Kemp to drive him back to Iping to retrieve his notebooks, Griffin kills a police inspector who believed the invisible man story a hoax. Later, while dining at Kemp's residence, Griffin advises him on some pointers in dealing with his invisibility: "I must always remain in hiding for an hour after meals. The food is visible inside me until it is digested. I can only work on fine, clear days. If I work in the rain, the water can be seen on my head and shoulders. In a fog, you can see me like a bubble. In smoky cities, the soot settles on me until you can see a dark outline. You must always be near at hand to wipe off my feet. Even dirt

The Invisible Man (Claude Rains) boasts of his plans for power to Gloria Stuart. Such visions struck a responsive chord with those rendered powerless by the Great Depression (Universal Pictures/Photofest).

between my fingernails would give me away. It is difficult, at first, to walk down stairs. We are so accustomed to watching our feet. But these are trivial difficulties. We shall find ways of defeating everything."

While the Invisible Man sleeps at Kemp's home, the authorities set out to apprehend him. Kemp phones Dr. Cranley, telling him Griffin is there. Flora overhears their conversation and insists on seeing Griffin. Kemp also calls on the police. When Flora and her father arrive at Kemp's, Flora sees Griffin alone. When she tells him her father will help him find a cure, he scoffs: "You think he can help me? He's got the brain of a tapeworm, a maggot beside mine. Don't you see what it means? Power! Power to rule! To make the world grovel at my feet! ... Power to walk into the gold vaults of the nations, into the secrets of kings, into the Holy of Holies; power to make multitudes run, squealing in terror at the touch of my little invisible finger. Even the moon's frightened of me. Frightened to death. The whole world's frightened to death." It is now evident that Griffin is past the point of redemption and must be brought to heel whatever the means.

Just then the police arrive, surrounding the house, linking hands, and closing in. Realizing that Kemp betrayed him, Griffin vanishes — but not before warning Kemp he'll kill him at ten the following evening. In the interim he embarks upon his reign of terror — further thwarting his pursuers, derailing a passenger train, and robbing a bank, tossing the purloined funds to passersby — a sight that undoubtedly resonated with movie audiences of the day, given the Depression. Despite the best efforts of the police to protect Kemp, the latter is murdered on schedule by Griffin, who arranges his death in an automobile accident.

Griffin now takes refuge in a farmer's barn. The farmer discovers him sleeping there and notifies the police, who set fire to the barn, driving the invisible man out into the snow. Leaving his footprints in the snow, he is mortally wounded by police gunfire. Reunited with Flora at the hospital, he dies, the effect of the invisibility drug dying with him. As the closing scene of the film plays out, he finally becomes visible. As he expires, Griffin, echoing the words Kemp had earlier used to describe his unorthodox scientific behavior to Flora, says he intruded in those things that man has no business with. This confession, explains Michael Sevastakis, "is a standard reply from the repentant villain-heroes of these films. Some film antagonists experience remorse over their crimes, and unlike their literary counterparts, do not die fighting." Griffin's cinematic remorse differs markedly from his demise in the pages of Wells' story, where he dies unrepentantly at the hands of men who crush him to death. By contrast, the invisible man's death on film was necessitated by a precept that films of this type had to conform to: "Even madmen like Whale's Griffin are made to realize in their final moments that what they have done was wrong."[46]

Though he was happy with the film for the most part, Wells himself had one objection: the use of monocane and its transformation of the invisible man into an invisible demoniac. For his part, film historian Don G. Smith felt the movie "would have been more philosophically provocative" if screenwriter Sherriff adhered "more closely to Wells' conception of Griffin as a great mind hounded by little people such as Kemp and the country bumpkins," which would have raised the issue of how such an intellect would have handled such unsophisticated commoners. As Sherriff presented it, Griffin's downfall resulted from a derangement over which he was powerless. Though he characterized Sherriff's concept as "certainly not bad," Smith nonetheless concludes that "it just could have been better had he challenged his audience rather than pandered to it. Griffin's final words, 'I meddled in things that man must leave alone,' is most un–Wellsian and equates goodness with lack of imagination and mediocrity."[47]

Sevastakis and Smith's analyses both suggest that the invisible man's brief flirtation with absolute power came with a price, one he had to pay for with his life, realizing too late the folly of his actions. In the real world the temptation of absolute power such as wielded by Griffin was great to those who viewed such might in the hands of a strong man as the remedy to the nation's ills in 1933. However, unlike Germany, Roosevelt had no intention of setting up a fascist regime in America to meet the crisis of the Great Depression. And, as the New Deal alleviated but by no means cured Depression woes the sense of crisis abated and the American democratic system remained intact.

And, where Roosevelt proved the right tonic for America in 1933, so, too, did *The Invisible Man* do for Universal that year, alleviating the studio's financial woes much as *Dracula* had done the same in 1931.[48]

4

Fade Out and Revival: From the Depression to the Eve of War (1935–1941)

The horror film continued to be a winner for Universal. The studio's biggest money-maker for 1934, *The Black Cat,* featured the initial onscreen pairing of Hollywood's reigning masters of terror — Boris Karloff and Bela Lugosi. The horror genre had played a vital role in sustaining the studio during the darkest years of the Great Depression. Now Universal's improved profit situation — it had turned a profit of $200,000 for 1934 — along with the overall economic comeback and steadily improving market conditions prompted Junior Laemmle to rekindle his ambitions to produce A-level films geared toward the first-run market. The fact that Universal was ill-equipped to realize that goal didn't hinder Junior in the least; to his mind, taking the plunge into the first-run market was critical. Toward that end he began building up two other genres, the musical and the woman's picture, with the intention of making them as successful as the horror genre had been.

Concurrently Laemmle also expanded A-class horror production — doing so without hiking production costs, even when primary studio personnel like director James Whale and writer John Balderston were employed, as was the case with Universal's best horror film of the decade, *Bride of Frankenstein.* The latter, moreover, evolved from what it may initially have been intended to be — just another sequel aimed at exploiting its predecessor's success — into an offbeat love story, the real star of which, despite the return of Colin Clive and Boris Karloff to their former roles from the original *Frankenstein*, was Elsa Lanchester, who had the distinction of playing both the "bride" of the sequel's title and Mary Shelley in the opening scene of the new film. Lanchester's bride's revulsion toward her intended spouse added a new dimension to the horror genre — that of black comedy.

Another hit for Universal lay completely outside the horror genre. *Imitation of Life,* directed by John Stahl, earned the studio its first Academy Award nomination for Best Picture since *All Quiet on the Western Front* in 1930.

The success of both *Imitation of Life* and *Bride of Frankenstein*, along with Universal's improved profit status, greatly enhanced the Laemmles' confidence, and seemed to vindicate Junior's ambition to make the studio a player in the first-run market. He began planning a half-dozen prestige ventures for 1935, the majority of which would receive his personal guidance. The two most significant films on this list, *Magnificent Obsession* and *Show Boat*, with the latter a remake, were entrusted, respectively, to Stahl and James Whale.[1]

Ultimately this decision would bode ill for the Laemmles' fortunes at Universal as well as contribute to the demise of the first horror cycle at the movies.

WereWolf of London *and* Dracula's Daughter *(1935–1936)*

Of all the classic monsters that made their screen debuts during the formative years of the horror cycle, there was one omission — the werewolf. Early cinema paid scant attention to the werewolf. What films there were on this subject were rooted in American Indian lore or presented "werewolf" characters that were human rather than supernatural beings. At the time the terms "vampire" and "werewolf or wolf" denoted, not supernatural entities, but, respectively a woman who charmed money out of her paramours and a man devoid of ethics in business or romantic interests.[2] Among literary works, the nearest to a lycanthropic *Dracula* and *Frankenstein* was Guy Endore's 1933 novel, *The Werewolf of Paris*. Yet when Universal decided to add the werewolf to its roster of cinematic monsters, it chose not to adapt Endore's work nor utilize the author in preparing the film. The resulting product, *WereWolf of London,* failed to establish the definitive pop culture image of the werewolf—most likely because the film's star, Henry Hull, refused to submit to the lengthy amount of time necessary to apply the required makeup, forcing the fabrication of a revised makeup that resulted in an extra fee being paid to Universal's makeup wizard Jack Pierce.[3] The screenplay was written by John Colton, "a world-weary homosexual playwright-scenarist," who had adapted Somerset Maugham's *Miss Sadie Thompson* into the Broadway triumph *Rain.* Colton, who was partial toward lower-class people, situated the monster's attacks in the tawdry environments that he himself haunted.[4] The lead role of the werewolf went to veteran stage and movie actor Henry Hull, whose first film for the Laemmles was the adaptation of Dickens' *Great Expectations,* in which he played the role of Magwitch, *Werewolf of London* was his first starring role for Universal.[5]

As the film begins, Dr. Wilfred Glendon (Hull), accompanied by his friend Hugh Renwick (Clark Williams), is leading an expedition in Tibet to find a specimen of the *mariphasa lupina lumina,* a plant that blooms only under moonlight. Their superstitious Tibetan coolies, thinking the valley they seek is inhabited by demons, are reluctant to continue on. At the sight of a man astride a camel, they flee. The stranger turns out to be a holy man. Told of their mission in Tibet by Glendon and Renwick, the Father cautions them, "There are some things it is better not to bother with." He has never been into that valley, and has never known a man to return from it. Despite the warning, Glendon and Renwick proceed on to the mysterious valley.

Upon arriving at their destination, Glendon and Renwick both begin experiencing strange phenomena: Renwick can't move his feet while Glendon is struck by an unseen presence. Renwick falls behind while Glendon proceeds alone, discovering the prize he's come for. As he digs the plant out of the soil, a mysterious, beastly figure lunges at him from the surrounding rocks. Glendon drives his assailant off and secures the flower but not before being severely bitten in the arm by the attacker.

Returning to England with his specimen, Glendon tries to make it bloom in his London laboratory with a giant lamp, the light of which is meant to simulate moonlight. At a party at Glendon's residence, his wife Lisa (Valerie Hobson) is reacquainted with an old friend, Paul Ames (Lester Matthews). Also present is Professor Yogami (Warner Oland of Charlie Chan fame), a botanist like Glendon, who congratulates the latter on his collection of plants. Asked by Glendon if they've met before, Yogami replies, "In Tibet, once. But only for a moment, in the dark." Like Glendon, Yogami has been seeking the *mariphasa*. He explains that it is an antidote for werewolfry, or lycanthrophobia, as it is known medically. "The werewolf," Yogami continues, "is neither man nor wolf, but a satanic creature with the worst qualities of both.... In workaday, modern London today, ... there are two cases of werewolfry known to me," both of which owe their affliction to the bite of another werewolf. At these words, Yogami touches Glendon's arm — the one the beast attacked. We now know that Yogami is the werewolf whom Glendon encountered in Tibet. Before taking his leave, Yogami warns that the two afflicted with the lycanthropic curse are doomed, save for the *mariphasa* plant.

Later, while working in his lab, Glendon succeeds in getting one of his *mariphasa* buds to bloom under the lamp but, at the same time, observes hair growing on the back of his right hand. Cutting the *mariphasa* bud, he injects its fluid into his hand, whereupon the hair growth vanishes. Shortly afterward, Yogami returns, asking for two *mariphasa* blossoms. The plant, he explains, in not a cure for werewolfry, merely a short-term antidote. When Glendon denies the request, Yogami departs but not before imparting a warning: "The werewolf instinctively seeks to kill the thing it loves best." That night an intruder enters Glendon's laboratory, stealing two *mariphasa* buds. Glendon himself then experiences the werewolf transformation. After hurrying to the lab and finding the buds gone, he dons a scarf, cap, and overcoat and ventures forth into the night. Glendon initially tries to attack Lisa's aunt Ettie Coombes (Spring Byington) in her bedroom. When she screams, he flees into the London streets, where he murders a prostitute.

The following night, prevented from taking a moonlight ride with Lisa and Paul because of his condition, and unable to persuade Lisa to return home before the moon rises, Glendon seeks refuge in a working-class lodging. Asked by the landlady if he's single, he replies, "Singularly single, madam. More single than I ever realized is possible for a human being to be." Glendon's latter remarks demonstrate how his wolfish affliction has changed his social outlook: It has brought him down to a level on a par with everyone else. Here social and class distinctions are meaningless. In the same manner zombiism did in *White Zombie* and, in real life, polio with Roosevelt, so does lycanthrophobia with Glendon. And, in the same way Roosevelt's paralysis did for him, lycanthrophobia opens Glendon's eyes to the realities of life for those beyond the privileged.

4. Fade Out and Revival   99

Tainted by the werewolf curse, Dr. Wilfred Glendon (Henry Hull), an upper-class scientist, seeks sanctuary in a lower-class boarding house in *WereWolf of London* (1935) (Universal Pictures/Photofest).

Shown to his boarding house quarters, Glendon locks himself in, praying for divine intervention to forestall his fate. His entreaty is unheeded: The transformation once more occurs, and he jumps through the window for another night of mayhem. His next victim is a woman keeping a rendezvous with a married zookeeper at the zoological gardens.

Yogami, his *mariphasa* buds now spent, appeals to Scotland Yard to secure Glendon's specimen of the plant and learn how to nurture it in England, otherwise "there'll be an epidemic that will turn London into a shambles." Glendon, in the meantime, returns to his lab, only to discover that the remaining *mariphasa* bud in his possession hasn't bloomed. Desperate, he goes to Falden Abbey, a manor where he courted Lisa years before, and has himself locked inside a long deserted room, instructing that he be confined there until dawn. Again his precautions are futile: Becoming the wolf man, he escapes and attacks Lisa, only to be driven off by Ames. The latter realizes that the beast was Glendon and convinces Scotland Yard to investigate. As Ames and the inspector are leaving for the Glendon residence where Lisa is hiding out with Ettie Coombes, word comes of another murder — this time a chambermaid in Dr. Yogami's hotel room.

Glendon returns to his lab just in time to find the *mariphasa* has bloomed but, before he can cut it off to administer the antidote, Yogami, who has sneaked into the lab at the same time, gets to it. In the ensuing scuffle between the two, Glendon becomes the werewolf and kills Yogami. Having eliminated Yogami, Glendon goes in pursuit of Lisa and Ettie, knocking out Ames in the process. Lisa tries to reason with her husband. Before he can harm her, Scotland Yard arrives and shoots Glendon. Dying, he says, "Thanks for the bullet.... In a few moments now, I shall know why all of this had to be. Lisa, goodbye.... I'm sorry I couldn't have made you happier." In death, Glendon returns to human form, the werewolf curse dying with him. Script writer Colton would have given the film a sunnier finale in a scene that never made it to the finished product: Mrs. Moncaster (Zeffie Tilbury), who resides at the boarding house where Glendon sought sanctuary, is acclaimed as "the lady that lodged the werewolf"; however her photo session is marred by fellow lodger Mrs. Whack (Ethel Griffies), who contends she initially took Glendon in, hence *she* warrants the glory as well as six bottles of gin — courtesy of the local pub.[6]

By then, however, humor alone wasn't sufficient to overcome Universal's problems. A pair of crises — one domestic, the other foreign — were simmering for the studio.

Junior Laemmle's decision to hand the musical *Show Boat* to his top horror director James Whale would prove to be a grave error on Junior's part — the worst of his career. But at the time he made it, it seemed quite logical. The first-run market was on a roll in 1935, and Laemmle's desire to be in on that action was so great, he was blind to the reality that Universal was incapable of pursuing such a course. Several issues came into play here. The studio possibly could manage one or a pair of expensive melodramas per annum, but a blockbuster musical was a different matter entirely. There was also the matter of whether to let Universal's most important horror director, Whale, leave the studio's in-house specialty for other genres, and at a time when virtuoso cameraman-turned-director Karl Freund had left for MGM, which wanted to set up its own horror division. The absence of these talents left the Universal horror film in the hands of low-grade talent, precisely at the time it was reaching its commercial and artistic pinnacle. Finally, Laemmle's choice to produce *Show Boat* was an error, as the studio couldn't afford to wreak havoc with its management system and forfeit its studio head and production chief. Without Laemmle at the helm, Universal was on a collision course with disaster.

The studio's financial status was such that it couldn't wait for *Magnificent Obsession* to turn a profit and rescue them. Universal's total box-office profits had fallen far below expectations, and the combination of preproduction costs on *Show Boat* and location problems on what was to be a disaster for the studio, *Sutter's Gold,* had taken a great bite out of the studio's cash reserves. In the case of *Show Boat,* the costs of sets and props had been considerable and, when filming began, the salaries for the film's actors and director Whale would burn up more cash.

At a meeting with his father Carl in December, Junior defended his strategy, arguing that inexpensive productions would provide funding for operative expenses while the expensive high-risk films would allow Universal a piece of the action in the profitable first-run market. Concurring with his son's line of reasoning, the elder Laemmle obtained a loan of $750,000 from Standard Capital Corporation, a Wall Street firm specializing in rescuing financially troubled companies. The loan specified that, in the event Laemmle failed to repay it within ninety days, Standard Capital's chief, J. Cheever Cowdin, possessed an exclusive option to take control of Universal by means of stock purchases of $5.5 million.[7]

An additional conundrum for the studio, originating abroad, spelled potential disaster for the future of the current horror cycle. A trio of American horror films, all released in 1935, raised the ire of those Britons concerned about the effect these films were having on their children.[8]

Bride of Frankenstein had its British debut on June 27, 1935, with the Duke and Duchess of Kent and Elsa Lanchester among those in attendance. Critical reaction to the film was positive. *Bride*'s general release to the British movie-going public was scheduled for September 30. However, less than two weeks before the slated release date, the ax fell. "It was officially announced that *Bride of Frankenstein* will not be publicly screened in Birmingham," announced the British publication *Kinematograph Weekly* in its September 19 issue. "This is the outcome of a private viewing of the film at the Gaumont Palace attended by members of the Public Entertainment Committee." The decision provoked an angry response in the form of a letter to the *Birmingham Daily Mail,* the author of which expressed the sentiment of those displeased with film censorship: "With all due respect to the Committee and its ban on *Bride of Frankenstein,* one wonders how much longer the Birmingham citizen will put up with being smacked and put to bed. Why should I have to go outside the city to see *Bride of Frankenstein,* a picture passed by the British Board of Film Censors and has been shown with great success in London?" Apparently the letter-writer was unaware of the fact that in order to secure clearance to be shown, numerous scenes were deleted.

One reason *Bride of Frankenstein* may have run afoul of the British censors was its theme of Frankenstein on a par with God was found objectionable. The film encountered scant disapproval in London. Confronting the censorship matter, the London County Council in early October 1935 declared, "No film shall be exhibited which has not been passed by the Board"— a proclamation that, nonetheless, failed to deter the provinces from proscribing films that had already received Board clearance.

Bride of Frankenstein again engendered controversy when the following month the Caernarvonshire Stage Play Committee took up the matter of allowing the film to be exhibited. For local cinema owners, the main issue was the financial investment of promoting a movie that was subsequently enjoined from viewing — something the chairman concurred was a poor business procedure. Yet, when Universal offered a print of the film so the committee could screen it before making a decision, the committee rejected it.[9]

Bride of Frankenstein wasn't the only Universal production giving Britons fits. *The Raven,* another Karloff-Lugosi vehicle using a Poe title, presented Lugosi as an insane plastic surgeon afflicted with an extreme Poe fixation and Karloff as an escaped convict who wants a facial renovation. This Lugosi does by disfiguring his appearance, making him look even worse. There is a method to Lugosi's madness: He believes that the more gruesome Karloff looks, the meaner he'll become, serving the crazed surgeon's purposes in a story replete with mangling, sexual obsession, and a basement chamber of horrors right out of Poe.

Such cinematic fare may well have prompted *The London Times* to wonder, editorially, what purpose movie horror served. While acknowledging that Elizabethan theatre was no stranger to horror, *The Times* pointed out that even their most gruesome tales were redeemed by poetry. Where was poetry to be found in Hollywood? Why were science and medicine being depicted in service of ghastly ends? Seldom did a film doctor utilize his skill toward life-saving ends. "The favorite purpose of an operation on the screen is either disfigurement or the creation of a monster...." The fact that filmdom's mad doctors were so immaculate in their techniques made them more frightening than supernatural menaces.[10]

A third American horror film to outrage British guardians of decency—and another Bela Lugosi vehicle—was MGM's *Mark of the Vampire*, which reunited Lugosi with his old *Dracula* director, Tod Browning. A remake of Browning's earlier *London After Midnight*, this latest production featured Lugosi as Count Mora, who seemingly became a vampire after committing incest with his daughter, which culminated in a murder-suicide. The film ultimately reveals that Lugosi's "vampire" was in fact fictitious in nature and was involved in a police inquiry. Even before the film was submitted to the Hollywood censors for review, all traces of incest were deleted, hence the bullet hole that Lugosi's Mora wore in his right temple wasn't explained. The Breen Office did find one fault with the production, hence the following recommendation to MGM: "There should be no suggestion that the Baron is guarding against leaving fingerprints."[11]

The common thread binding *Bride of Frankenstein, The Raven,* and *Mark of the Vampire* as objects of wrath to Britons, specifically British parents, was deviant sex and the thought that their children were being exposed to this when they viewed these films. Taking their case to the County Councils of London, Essex, Surrey, and Middlesex, the parents insisted that entertainment they believed injurious to their offspring's moral character be discontinued. The British anti–horror drive took other forms: local movements proliferated in major counties from Scotland to Wales; newspaper editorials berated those theater owners who didn't voluntarily boycott horror films. "Parents petitioned the councils to take immediate action to curtail the showing of such unwholesome films, while civic organizations banded together to focus pressure on the one government bureau" sufficiently empowered "to make their demands a reality: the British Board of Film Censors."[12]

While *Bride of Frankenstein* experienced censor wrath in Great Britain, in America its success mandated a sequel to the film, that along with the original *Frankenstein,* helped ignite the horror boom: *Dracula*. Released in 1936, *Dracula's Daughter* begins where the original film ended five years earlier. Two London bobbies discover Renfield's lifeless body in Carfax Abbey, where Von Helsing (Edward Van Sloan reprising his role as the vampire hunter with his character's name changed from "Van Helsing") had just staked the Transylvanian in his coffin. Arrested and taken to the Scotland Yard office of Sir Basil Humphrey (Gilbert Emery), Von Helsing recounts his tale to the skeptical Sir Basil, who dismisses it as "utterly mad." Asked if he has retained someone for his defense, Von Helsing names, not a lawyer, but a psychiatrist — Jeffrey Garth.

That evening, at the jail where the bodies of Dracula and Renfield are being kept, a mysterious figure, a woman clad from head to foot in black, save for her eyes, appears, asking to see the bodies. Unable to bribe the sergeant on duty, she hypnotizes him with the large ring she wears. When the authorities return to the jail, they find the sergeant unconscious and Dracula's body missing from its box.

The body has been taken by Countess Maria Zaleska, Dracula's daughter (Gloria Holden), and her manservant Sandor (Irving Pichel). Cremating her father's body, Countess Zaleska then says a ritual of exorcism over it, believing that her father's demise will release her from the vampire curse she shared with him. Not only does she want to destroy her father's curse, she wants to eliminate his "influence" over her from beyond the grave. Back in her London residence the following evening, however, she discovers that her dream of living the life of a normal woman is still just that — a dream. "Sandor, look at me," she asks her servant. "What do you see in my eyes?" "Death," he replies. He then helps her into her cape and hypnotic ring, whereupon she ventures into the London night, claiming a male victim, then returns to her coffin.

Called back to London from his hunting holiday, Dr. Garth (Otto Krueger), though initially as skeptical of Von Helsing's defense of his action as Scotland Yard, agrees to help his former teacher: "I don't know how. I haven't the faintest idea where to start. But I'll stake my reputation against the facts. If there's a way to clear you, I'll do it." One wonders where Harker, Mina, and Dr. Seward, who were all witnesses to Dracula's depredations in the first film, and thus far more credible witnesses in Von Helsing's behalf, are now.[13]

Von Helsing and Dracula are the primary topic of discussion at a party Garth attends. Another attendee is Countess Zaleska herself. When Garth says the murder charge won't hold up as Dracula's body hasn't been found, another guest chimes in, "Maybe one of his vampire friends flew in and spirited him away!"— a statement quite close to the truth. Garth believes Von Helsing has taken his research into vampirism too literally.

Countess Zaleska asks Garth if the two of them might discuss the subject privately. Garth agrees. When they meet, she asks, "Do you believe that the dead can influence the living...? Could you conceive of a super–human mentality influencing someone from the other side of death? ... There is such a one.... Something that reaches out from beyond the grave and fills me with horrible impulses." She wants Dr. Garth to use her brain

The sadness of her vampiric existence clouds the face of the title character (Gloria Holden) in *Dracula's Daughter* (Universal Pictures/Photofest).

and will, not as the evil force has, but to release her from its grip. The answer, Garth replies, lies within herself, in her strength: "The next time you feel this influence, don't avoid it. Meet it, fight it, score the first victory."

After Garth leaves, Countess Zaleska goes to her studio to paint, sending Sandor out into the streets to find a model. He returns with Lili (Nan Grey), a penniless streetwalker. As Lili prepares to pose for the countess, the latter's vampiric cravings overcome her and she attacks the defenseless girl. The notion that Countess Zaleska sought release from her father's vampiric heritage made her unique in the annals of vampirism at the time.[14] Her plight once again demonstrates that membership in the aristocracy, such as she holds, is no guarantee of happiness. One could find a real-life counterpart in misery in Woolworth heiress Barbara Hutton, whose failed marriages to European aristocrats during the 1930s earned her the designation "poor little rich girl."[15]

Hospitalized, Lili becomes Dr. Garth's patient. He diagnosis her condition, not as amnesia as originally thought, but posthypnosis. The presence of marks on her neck prompts him to consult Von Helsing, who concludes that one of Dracula's victims-turned-vampire is the culprit: Garth intends to administer the Letelier test to Lili to learn the truth of her condition. When Von Helsing tells him that a vampire casts no reflection in a mirror, an alarm goes off in Garth's mind: There were no mirrors in Countess Zaleska's residence when he visited her there.

Before he can treat Lili, Garth is visited by the countess, who informs him she's leaving London that night. Her situation is hopeless, and she wants Garth to accompany her. The doctor, suspecting she is a vampire, tells her to remain until he returns and not to plan on leaving London. To make certain Garth does follow her, the countess and Sandor kidnap Garth's assistant, Janet Blake (Marguerite Churchill).

When Garth tries to bring Lili out of her trance, the shock of remembering what happened to her proves fatal to Lili. Now certain that Countess Zaleska is responsible, Garth finds her missing and sets out in pursuit. Ultimately tracking her down to her artist's studio, he learns her real identity from her and that she is holding Janet hostage to force him to return to her native land with her. Informed that Janet is with the countess, Scotland Yard issues a special broadcast to the public, seeking its help in finding her. Upon learning that Dracula's daughter is returning to Transylvania, Garth hops aboard a plane in pursuit.

4. Fade Out and Revival

In Transylvania, in the vicinity of Castle Dracula, the villagers happily celebrate a wedding as the daylight hours fade. However, the howling of a wolf cuts short the festivities. Upon seeing a light in the castle, the villagers assume that the dreaded Dracula has returned and scurry for cover. Similarly, Americans who overwhelmingly returned Roosevelt to office in 1936, the year *Dracula's Daughter* was released, were to discover their own real-life economic woes still weren't over when, the following year, the economy slumped into a recession. Garth arrives and proceeds to the castle, where Countess Zaleska and Sandor have taken up residence. Dracula's three wives, whom the count left there while he moved to England, are nowhere to be seen, which leads one to wonder what happened to them. As Garth has now become the cynosure of the countess' attention, she reneges on her promise to Sandor to confer eternal life upon the latter. When Garth approaches the castle, the jealous Sandor shoots an arrow at him and misses. Finding Janet under Countess Zaleska's spell, Garth consents to stay in Transylvania as a vampire with the countess in exchange for Janet's life. Just as the countess begins working her spell on Garth, Sandor fires another arrow — this time hitting Countess Zaleska herself in the heart and freeing Janet from the vampire's control. Just as Sandor is about to take aim with a third arrow, he is shot dead by a policeman accompanying Sir Basil and Von Helsing. As the latter pair scrutinize the body of Countess Zaleska, Sir Basil remarks, "The woman is beautiful."

"She was beautiful when she died a hundred years ago," replies Von Helsing.

Variety raved about the film but *Dracula's Daughter* came too late to alleviate Universal's financial crisis under the Laemmles' watch.[16] In late December 1935, in the immediate aftermath of Standard Capital's loan to the studio, the outlook was brighter. *Magnificent Obsession* debuted during the holiday season, while the rushes from *Show Boat* were fantastic. Presently, however, that bright picture faded into gloom. *Sutter's Gold* was in the postproduction phase, and any possibility that it would enjoy even nominal success appeared doubtful. Nor were things any better on the *Show Boat* front: It was evident that such a film wasn't director James Whale's forte. He was working slowly and his operating expenses were astronomical. Not even Junior Laemmle's personal involvement with the project could expedite production. *Show Boat*'s costs greatly exceeded a million dollars, with the overruns rapidly devouring the receipts *Magnificent Obsession* was earning. Any chance that Whale's film could wrap up production by mid–February for an immediate release to the theaters now seemed gone. As filming continued into March, the sole option remaining for the Laemmles was that Standard Capital's J. Cheever Cowdin would make another deal or choose not to utilize his option.[17]

It proved to be a forlorn hope: on March 14, 1936, four days after filming on *Dracula's Daughter* was wrapped up, Standard Capital exercised its option, purchasing eighty percent of Universal's common stock, thus ringing down the curtain on the Laemmle era — both at Universal and in Hollywood. Universal's new president was an old Laemmle acquaintance, Robert H. Cochrane. Given a cash settlement of $1.5 million, Uncle Carl was "promoted" to chairman of the board, while Junior was replaced by former RKO administrator Charles R. Rogers. After failing to set up his son as an independent, the elder Laemmle died in 1939. His own Hollywood career over, Junior died forty years to the day after his father died, September 24, 1979. He was interred in the family mausoleum with his father.[18]

As Universal's new vice-president in charge of production, Rogers was a stern taskmaster. The man who helped deliver the "New Universal" (as it was called) from financial ruin, Joe Pasternak, formerly a Universal production head in Central Europe, was responsible for the 1937 smash *Three Smart Girls,* which not only redeemed the company financially, but made a star of an adolescent soprano, Deanna Durbin. The success of Durbin and another maturescent film star, Mickey Rooney, indicated a changed mood among moviegoers, one that extolled a sunny climate in place of the gloomy tone that characterized the films of the early Depression era. Citing Durbin and Rooney, Thomas Schatz noted:

> They embodied the movies' capacity for wish fulfillment and naive optimism, a capacity that seemed to intensify throughout the 1930s. It was fueled by myriad forces, from the PCA (Production Code Administration) and Legion of Decency (with their efforts to legislate an innocent and upbeat world view) to the Depression and the Dust Bowl, which uprooted families and changed the American landscape, and seemed to demand a palliative in our collective fictions that couldn't be found in our lives. A good many Hollywood movies of the era expressed a longing for simpler times and celebrated simpler folk. Will Rogers was Hollywood's biggest star in 1934, and after his untimely death, Shirley Temple held that special spot for four straight years. Hollywood's top filmmakers were Frank Capra and John Ford, who also evoked a way of life that was fading or had already vanished for most Americans — except on movie screens.[19]

In this new Hollywood landscape, there was no place for horror films. In the wake of the New Universal's advent, *Variety* in its May 6, 1936, edition announced:

> Universal is ringing curfew on horror picture production for at least a year, following release of *Dracula's Daughter,* just completed. Latter will be released on current season's schedule, with no chiller pictures contemplated for 1936–37 release. Reason attributed by U for abandonment of horror cycle is that European countries, especially England, are prejudiced against this type of product. Despite heavy local consumption of its chillers, U is taking heed to warning from abroad. Universal has for a long time had virtual monopoly on this type of production, with unusual success at the box office. Studio's London rep has cautioned production exec to scrutinize carefully all so-called chiller productions, to avoid any possible conflict with British censorship.[20]

The pressure exerted by the British anti–horror backlash was ultimately too much for the London City Council to ignore; the elders prepared a petition requesting the issuance of an official decree on horror films suggesting that in addition to their two existing categories of film (U, Universal exhibition, and A, Adults only), there should be a third category, 'H,' passed as 'horrific,' i.e., for public presentation when no children under 16 years of age are present." Indeed, the London Council screened many of Hollywood's best features sent for viewing by British audiences, reporting the results of such screenings directly to the Board of Film Censors, accompanied by a recommendation that "films of this character are suitable for exhibition to children under no circumstances."

A nationwide reaction against horror films erupted after the London City Council's decision. The main focus of British ire was concentrated on the Karloff-Lugosi vehicle *The Raven,* which conservative Britons judged to be the most vile type of the lot. The British Board of Film Censors' decision, retroactive to January 1, 1937, advocated a total and indefinite termination to the import of horror films until all such fare of that genre made since 1929 had been scrutinized and reclassified in line with their appropriate ranking. "The immediate effect of this ruling on the American horror film," wrote Robert Cremer, "was catastrophic. British distribution represented roughly 40 percent of the income from overseas distribution. Without that prized market, producers found horror films" too daring a gamble to make. The British ban killed the production of horror fare, signaling the end of the horror cycle Universal had started in 1931 with *Dracula* and *Frankenstein.*[21]

As the 1930s entered its last years, horror films were in limbo, their future quite uncertain. Presently they would make a comeback and, when they did, the United States and the world would be confronting a crisis far graver than the Depression — one the Depression itself had contributed to — and, like the Depression, would leave its own unique mark on the horror film.

The Horror Revival Amid the March to War (1938–1941)

The horror blackout in Hollywood in no way extended to other pop culture media. The novels *Dracula* and *Frankenstein* were still available to the reading public; horror fans could also satisfy their taste for the macabre with such publications as *Weird Tales*. Radio offered *The Witch's Tale* between 1936 and 1938. Orson Welles' famed *Mercury Theater on the Air* featured an adaptation of *Dracula*, broadcast July 1, 1938. A residue of interest in horror film characters was the catalyst for an article in the May–June 1938 edition of *Cinema Progress*. Entitled "Cold Chills and Cold Cash," the article was devoted to the career of Lon Chaney, Sr., and the triumph of Lugosi's *Dracula* and Karloff's *Frankenstein*. This was followed, shortly thereafter, by another article, this time in *The New York Times*, covering the huge volume of fan mail sent to Hollywood bearing a drawing or diagram as the sole means of ascertaining which performer was the intended recipient. "Sometimes the amateur draftsmen try to convey their meaning by a snarling, ghoulish face," the article explained. "When this happens, office workers have to gamble on whether to send it to Boris Karloff, Claude Rains, or Bela Lugosi."[22]

Even before the *Cinema Progress* and *New York Times* coverage, a sequence of events had been set in motion that would resurrect the horror film, putting it back on the Hollywood map.

The first had begun as 1937 was passing into antiquity, when Robert Cochrane resigned as Universal Studios' president, to be replaced by Nate J. Blumberg, formerly of RKO. *Film Daily* noted Blumberg's "frequent trips to the studios and burning the midnight oil in New York"; moreover, his examination of Universal's financial records for the Charles R. Rogers era did not reflect well on Rogers: During that time the studio had lost in excess of $3,000,000. On May 19, 1938, Rogers "resigned" as vice-president in charge of production, though he walked away with a $297,000 "contract" and retained a seat on the company's directorate. Rogers went so far as to take out a full-page ad, complete with portrait, in the 1939 *Film Daily Yearbook*. Rogers' replacement, Cliff Work, came to Universal from the job of RKO's divisional chief in San Francisco, where he oversaw the Golden Gate Theatre. Work, Blumberg, and the producers now searched for a way to make Universal a profit-generating enterprise.

The second event, and the one that really catalyzed the horror revival, occurred August 5, 1938: With bankruptcy looming on its horizon, the Regina Theatre in Los Angeles sought financial salvation by running a horror triple hitter — *Dracula, Frankenstein,* and *The Son of Kong,* the latter the sequel to the megahit *King Kong.* Overnight, the gruesome trio became an attraction. Regina manager Emil Ullman kept his establishment open 21 hours a day, while police had to keep the crowds flocking to the theatre in line; the last of the multitude left at 3:00 A.M. Among those in attendance was *Dracula* and *Frankenstein* star Dwight Frye, who brought his seven-year-old son with him. Dwight Jr. later remembered:

> My father took me alone, just the two of us ... my mother later told me that she thought he had devilment in his mind. He was hoping I'd come home terrified out of my skull and apparently I came home and started criticizing the films for not having been terrified at all! From what I am told he was very disappointed that the films hadn't scared the pants off me....[23]

The size of the throngs converging on the Regina clearly indicated one thing: The fan base for horror wasn't restricted to a mere cult following but was far more mainstream than anyone in the movie business realized. When the theatre ran a cartoon between the second and third features, the audience was quite unrestrained in expressing its disapproval: They had come to see monsters — and nothing else! The show attracted fans from as far away as San Diego, Stockton, and Fresno. For Ullman, it was the financial miracle he had been seeking, one which earned a $3,000 gross. Naturally, the Regina's success didn't go unnoticed by Universal, which printed 500 additional copies of *Dracula* and *Frankenstein* for other theaters yearning to cash in on the new interest in horror. Within two weeks, the studio turned out new publicity materials "that took up Ullman's challenge to audiences to 'see them together.'"[24]

Another to reap the benefits of the horror revival with Ullman was Bela Lugosi, whose career had nosedived in the wake of the horror ban. Lugosi himself witnessed the revival firsthand: "One day I drive past and see my name and big lines of people all around," he said in a newspaper interview that fall. "I wonder what is giving away to people — maybe bacon or vegetables. But it is the comeback of horror, and I come back." Three weeks into the Regina's horror spectacular, Ullman hired Bela to make live appearances with the films. Other horror films — *WereWolf of London, The Raven, King Kong*— were brought out of storage.[25]

From Los Angeles, the double bill horror revival which the Regina originated spread across America to astounding success. Everywhere they played — Cincinnati, Indianapolis, Manhattan — the diabolical pair of *Dracula* and *Frankenstein* was a hit. *Variety* called attention to the fact that "other reissues, excepting old Valentinos, have been duds in New York." The same publication also observed that when the same pair of films had played separately in Philadelphia only a short while earlier, both hadn't been as successful; as to why the two films did better as a team, *Variety* remained silent. Another dual revival, this one featuring *King Kong* and Boris Karloff's *The Ghoul,* was another success.[26]

The horror revival did not go unnoticed across the Atlantic, in the country where the popular aversion to the American output of horror had been responsible for the horror blackout in Hollywood. Writing to the PCA's Joseph Breen in November 1938, J. Brooke Wilkinson, secretary of the British Board of Film Censors, expressed concern regarding Universal's wish to get back into the horror business. This time, Hollywood turned a deaf ear to British anxieties, initiating a second horror cycle at the movies.[27]

Universal hastened to enter the fray with a second sequel to its most successful monster hit. Released in January 1939, *Son of Frankenstein* was a major success, playing a vital role in restoring horror films to life. In *Photoplay*'s words: "Boris Karloff (the original Monster of 1931), Bela Lugosi (of *Dracula*) and Basil Rathbone work together with an awesome effect of terror.... Prepare for nightmares."[28] Taking place a quarter-century after the death of Henry Frankenstein (the film identifies him as Heinrich von Frankenstein), *Son of Frankenstein* opens with the arrival of the late Frankenstein's son Wolf, along with his wife and son, to occupy the family castle. The newcomers must contend with the distrust of the villagers, the latter having never absolved Wolf's father for the misdeeds his creation perpetrated, and believing that the Monster still lives. As the new tenants converge upon their dwelling aboard a train, the viewer sees them in their passenger compartment; outside, rushing past their window, is a lifeless, desolate landscape, reminiscent of a battlefield after the carnage has ceased — symbolic of the last war, as if the train is conveying its passengers back to Europe on the verge of the new war that was about to erupt.[29]

Combing their new abode after their arrival, Wolf finds his father's records, then encounters Ygor, who was sentenced to death for body snatching, yet survived his execution by hanging, which left him with a broken neck. Now in a cataleptic state induced by a lightning strike, the Monster previously served as Ygor's instrument of revenge, murdering the members of the jury who had sent him to the gallows. Now determined to restore his father's creation to full strength, Wolf fails to comprehend that it will again become Ygor's tool. Believing the Monster's revival is in the offing, Inspector Krogh (Lionel Atwill) keeps a constant eye on Wolf. Krogh has a special reason for his action, one that permanently altered the course of his life, as he explains to the son of Frankenstein:

> The most vivid recollection of my life. I was but a child at the time — about the age of your own son, Herr Baron. The Monster had escaped and was ravaging the countryside — killing, maiming, terrorizing. One night he burst into our house. My father took a gun and fired at him, but the savage brute sent him crashing to a corner. Then he grabbed me by the arm.... One doesn't easily forget, Herr Baron, an arm torn out by the roots!

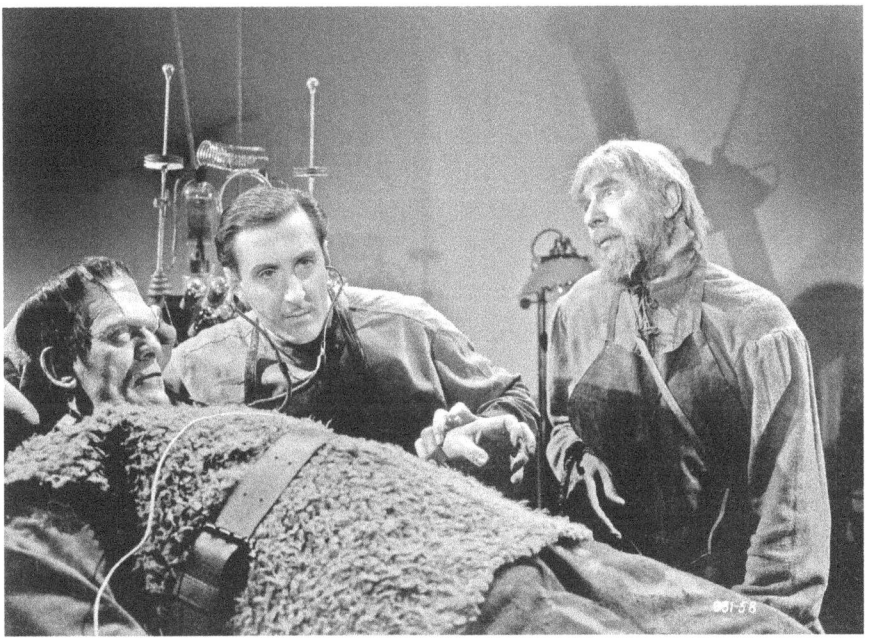

Boris Karloff, Basil Rathbone, and Bela Lugosi in *Son of Frankenstein*, the film that signaled the return of the horror genre in 1939 (Universal Pictures/Photofest).

Maimed for life as a result of his injury and forced to use an artificial arm as a result, Krogh had to abandon his dream of a military career, reducing him to the position of commander of the local police force. "He certainly acts like a general," opined Gregory William Mank of Atwill's performance as the one-armed policeman. "One would almost suspect he's lampooning General Douglas MacArthur," an ironic commentary on Mank's part as Atwill, in real life, was then the husband of MacArthur's first wife, Louise Cromwell![30] After three additional murders, and the Monster's abduction of Wolf's son, the scientist kills Ygor, then sends the Monster plunging into a boiling sulfur pit.

Opening its New York run at the Rivoli Theatre on January 28, 1939, *Son of Frankenstein* again proved a winner, going on to shatter box office records, the complaints of guardians of motion picture decency notwithstanding. Even in England, despite the dreaded "H" classification, the film continued its success. Along with W.C. Fields — Edgar Bergen — Charlie McCarthy's *You Can't Cheat an Honest Man,* Deanna Durbin's *Three Smart Girls Grow Up,* and Bing Crosby's *East Side of Heaven, Son of Frankenstein* helped Universal earn a $1,000,000 profit for 1939, an occurrence that for Universal, considering its financial history, was a singular achievement! A new horror cycle at the movies had begun.[31]

For Karloff, *Son of Frankenstein* would be the last time he would play the Monster on the big screen. He already divined what the future held for his most celebrated character:

> The reason I played the Monster only in the first three films was because I could (and I was right as it turned out) see the handwriting on the wall as to which way the stories were going ... that they would go downhill. There was not much left in the character of the Monster to be developed; we had reached his limits. I saw that from here on he would become rather an oafish prop, so to speak, in the last act, or something like that, without any great stature, and I didn't see any point in going on.[32]

The primary reason for the decline in quality of subsequent Frankenstein films at Universal can be attributed to the lesson *Son of Frankenstein* imprinted on Universal: Never begin production on a film without a completed script. Owing to the expensive subsequent productions of directors Rowland V. Lee and Joe May, the team of Blumberg and Work likely decided to replace such elaborately produced, exorbitant projects as *Son of Frankenstein* with B films that could be turned out like assembly line product, within schedule and budget: *The Invisible Man Returns* (1940), *The Invisible Woman* (1940), *The Mummy's Hand* (1940), *Black Friday*

(1940), *Man Made Monster* (1941).[33] In light of this, an explanation for the lack of quality in the post–Karloff Frankenstein films is clear. Commenting on the series from the perspective of the 1960s, horror film historian Drake Douglas wrote:

> The Monster became a clumsy automaton, incapable of swift movement, walking slowly and heavily with outstretched arms reaching for his victim. Through most of his later films, he lay in a coma, to be revived only for his destruction at the film's end. He was immensely powerful; but his slowed movements and delayed reactions made escape not too difficult, and thus much of the horror was gone, also diminished by alteration in facial appearance. Where Karloff's monster was a nightmare with its sunken, shadowed cheeks, thin, cruel lips and hate-blazing eyes, the later monster had chubby cheeks and dead eyes and the face of a mindless somnambulist rather than a vibrantly living, evil creature. Karloff's monster was a being of deadly cunning; the beast of Lugosi and Strange seemed to have lost all power of thought as well as he had of speech.[34]

All of that lay in the future; the more immediate question at hand was why the horror film was now in vogue once more? A contemporary view, offered by Rowland V. Lee as he was in the midst of directing *Son of Frankenstein*, maintained that such fare invariably remained topical "for the same reason that a murder or kidnapping or a major accident or a great catastrophe is always front page news."[35] The most recent catastrophe to unsettle Americans had been the Munich crisis during the fall of 1938 and the possibility that it would trigger another war in Europe. In a pictorial article on *Son of Frankenstein*, *Look* magazine noted:

> Movie producers attribute the public's current thirst for terror to the war scares of unsettled Europe. Quick to take their cue, they have started a race to produce blood chillers on a more lavish and fantastic scale than they ever have attempted before.
> Death rays, space ships, disintegration beams and other weirdly lethal instruments are being built in every property shop. "Nightmares for everybody" is the Hollywood slogan for a more horrible 1939.[36]

Films weren't the only pop culture barometer of Americans' anxious mood. Less than three months before *Son of Frankenstein*'s release, on October 30, 1938, in the immediate wake of the Munich alarm, a nationwide panic was touched off by Orson Welles' *Mercury Theater on the Air*'s adaptation of H.G. Wells' *War of the Worlds* in which invaders from the planet Mars land on the Atlantic seaboard of the United States, utilizing "death rays" to annihilate everyone before them. That a mere entertainment broadcast was responsible for a case of real-life mass hysteria is attributable to the fact that the program was written and enacted in the form of a news broadcast, hence it was easy for listeners, who had followed radio coverage of the Munich crisis and failed to tune in to the *Mercury Theater* broadcast from its beginning, to believe that the Welles program was a legitimate newscast. "Nothing had ever demonstrated so conclusively the power of network radio; nothing more clearly revealed the apprehensive mood of the nation's people."[37]

Post-mortems on the reaction to the "Martian invasion" in the immediate aftermath of the Welles' broadcast and beyond clearly revealed the sense of foreboding gripping Americans that autumn of 1938. Surveys of those who ran in terror from their homes revealed a common feeling: "I felt the catastrophe was *an attack by the Germans....*" In turn the Nazis crowed, "How can a people which trembles before the attack of the Martians ... solve world problems?"[38] Writing about the *War of the Worlds* broadcast three days after it aired, newspaper columnist Heywood Broun opined: "I doubt if this sort of thing would have happened four or five months ago. The course of world history had affected national psychology. Jitters have come home to roost. We have just gone through a laboratory demonstration of the fact that the peace of Munich hangs heavy over our heads, like a thundercloud."[39] A contemporary study of the panic induced by the broadcast, written by Hadley Cantril and published in 1940, attributed the hysteria to the Depression, which had left numerous Americans in a perpetual condition where they were incapable of understanding what was happening to them. After nearly a decade, the Depression and unemployment remained. Why didn't the experts devise a remedy for the economic crisis? Cantril observed that "a mysterious invasion fitted the pattern of the mysterious events of the decade.... The war scare had left many persons in a complete state of bewilderment. They did not know what the trouble was all about or why the United States should be so concerned. The complex ideological, class, and national antagonisms responsible for the crisis were by no means fully comprehended. The situation was painfully serious and distressingly confused.... The Martian invasion was just another event reported over the radio."[40]

With the threat of another, more technologically advanced war than the last looming, Americans paused to celebrate, not the dark images of science and technology as conveyed by popular culture, but rather its wonders at the New York World's Fair of 1939–1940.[41] The fair's initial season, beginning April 30, 1939, had as its theme, "The World of Tomorrow." The fair's symbolic structures, a 610-foot-high "Trylon" (a three-sided pylon) and a "Perisphere" (globe) 180 feet in diameter, reflected, in one historian's words, "an architectural theme of clean, streamlined modernity." For twenty cents, a visitor to the Perisphere rode an escalator 120 feet up to a rotating platform and, from the latter, beheld the futuristic Democracity. Designed on a radial platform, it featured vast homes occupying enormous tree-dotted lots and wide streets radiating from the center to a rim accommodating sanitary industries and government offices. Next, the visitor might have taken in the numerous corporate industrial exhibits, sponsored by the railroad industry, Eastman Kodak, American Telephone and Telegraph, General Electric, and Ford and Goodrich. The biggest of all was General Motors' Futurama which presented GM's conception of what the city of the future would be like in 1960. Among the international pavilions at the fair were those representing authoritarian nations — Russia and Italy. Conspicuous by its absence was Europe's predominant scientific and technological power, Germany.[42]

A little over four months after the fair's opening, at 2:40 in the morning of September 1, 1939, in Washington, D.C., President Roosevelt received a phone call from his ambassador in Paris.

"This is Bill Bullitt, Mr. President."

"Yes, Bill."

"Tony Biddle has just got through from Warsaw, Mr. President. Several German divisions are deep in Polish territory, and fighting is heavy. Tony said there were reports of bombers over the city. Then he was cut off...."

"Well, Bill," FDR replied, "it's come at last. God help us all." Shortly afterward, Roosevelt called his secretary of state, Cordell Hull.

"Cordell," he said, "Bullitt has just been on the phone. The Germans have invaded Poland."[43]

In a combined air and land offensive, Germany rapidly overwhelmed Polish defenses. France, which could have rescued Poland by mounting an offensive that would have necessitated the dispatch of major German units to the Western front, instead remained behind the Maginot Line. Presently the Soviet Union invaded Poland and took part in the Polish tragedy. At the end of October, the World's Fair closed for the season, but not before it put on a Halloween spectacular that in retrospect seemed to symbolize the spirit of the moment: With the aid of project light, the "Perisphere" was recast in the image of a smirking jack-o'-lantern, becoming, in Skal's description, "quite likely the biggest display of a mocking death's-head in human history, superimposed on a symbol of pure rationality," on the brink of history's greatest war.[44] When the fair's second season began the following May, just as Germany initiated an offensive against France and the low countries, its theme of "The World of Tomorrow" had been replaced by a new one: "For Peace and Freedom." By then, the world confronted two, paradoxical visions of the future: the peaceful, scientific utopia the fair imagined, or the brutal, militaristic, dictatorial reality that had engulfed Europe.

"For Europe," writes historian Alonzo L. Hamby, "Warsaw seemed more probable. Americans continued to hope for the world of Flushing Meadows"—site of the World's Fair.[45]

By the time the fair's second season opened, Hollywood had already begun turning out a new cycle of mad science films. Just as the genre had mirrored the social anxieties of the Great Depression, in which the powerful had exploited the weak, so now would it do the same during World War II, presenting mad scientists who employed their expertise, not to advance the wonders of science for humanity's benefit, but to achieve their own twisted objectives at humanity's expense.

In Universal's *The Phantom Creeps,* a 12-part serial that began playing in August 1939,[46] Bela Lugosi, his career back on track now that the horror ban had been lifted, played Dr. Alex Zorka, the discoverer of a mysterious, meteorite-born substance, who intends to sell his find to a foreign government in exchange for millions. When the American government tries to foil his plans, Zorka escapes and fakes his own death. Zorka's ambitions change, however, when his wife is killed in a plane crash: His primary objective now becomes revenge against those he believes forced him into hiding. The source of Zorka's power is a meteorite he retrieved from Africa, where it fell long ago. Now in possession of it, Zorka feels he has the perfect right to use it for however he chooses — even if that includes conquering the world! After Zorka instructs his henchman Monk (Jack C. Smith) in the handling and care of the container housing the meteorite and departs, Monk tries to steal the box in order to profit from its treasure himself—only to fall into the hands of federal agents. Despite Monk's warning not to, one of his captors opens the box just as their car passes a high voltage tower. The vehicle begins slowing down and the towers lining the road begin exploding, forcing the car off the road. Monk retrieves the container but, when he is wounded in the arm, is forced to leave it.

Monk's disloyalty to Zorka almost costs him his life at the hands of

Zorka's robot but the doctor spares him when he (Monk) shows him his wounded arm. Using his invisibility device, Zorka retrieves the meteorite container from another scientist's lab and flees. Owing to Monk's treachery, Zorka must relocate his headquarters. However, two members of Zorka's old spy ring steal the meteorite box themselves. When the espionage ring's boss tries to escape with the meteorite, Zorka once more turns himself invisible, hops a ride aboard the spies' car, and eventually commandeers the car himself, recovering the meteorite. The spies themselves are nabbed by the government.

Escaping back to his lab, Zorka makes final preparations to implement his scheme of revenge. As he does so, a detachment of federal troops move in on his residence. Zorka sends his robot against them but the mechanical man explodes during the battle. Escaping their would-be captors, Zorka and Monk steal a plane and take flight. Once airborne, Zorka begins bombing everything in sight in the air, on the ground, and at sea. Surrounded by squadrons of planes sent to stop his barrage, Zorka orders Monk to dive their plane into the sea. Monk refuses, forcing Zorka to overpower him, sending their plane out of control, plunging both men to a watery death.

Far more sinister than Lugosi's Dr. Zorka is Albert Dekker's Dr. Thorkel in Paramount's 1940 Technicolor release *Dr. Cyclops*. A renowned biologist who has been toiling in the Amazon jungle for two years, Thorkel sends for three scientists to help assist him because of an eye malady that hinders his work. Ultimately four people wind up journeying to Thorkel's encampment — the fourth traveler being the owner of the mules used to transport Thorkel's guests and who insisted upon accompanying the party. Apparently Thorkel merely required his visitors' help for a brief moment; much to their displeasure, he bids them farewell almost as soon as they arrive. Thorkel remains secretive about the nature of his work. The initial clue as to his activities is provided when we see that he has reduced a horse in size. This isn't the only miniature animal on the premises — Dr. Bulfinch (Charles Halton), the leader of the visiting delegation, discovers the bones of what he believes he is a new species of life, a midget pig that grows to a length of four inches at maturity. Upon learning that his guests are remaining, Thorkel warns them that should they stay another hour, they do so at their own peril.

Presently the Bulfinch party makes another discovery: Their host possesses radium ore. Thorkel lures his guests into an experimental chamber,

The "little people" (Victor Kilian, Charles Halton, Janice Logan, Thomas Coley, Frank Yaconelli) confront the mad scientist (Albert Dekker) who reduced them in size in Paramount's *Dr. Cyclops* (1940) (Paramount Pictures/Photofest).

where he imprisons them, then activates the mechanism which diminishes them in size to tiny, doll-like figures. In the wake of their miniaturization, Bulfinch is the first to speak, posing a question that, no doubt, many victims of Hitler's crimes were then asking: "Why does Providence permit the existence of such a monstrosity?" David J. Skal has noted that Thorkel's all-consuming interest in his work blinds him to the fact that Bulfinch and the others resent becoming guinea pigs in Thorkel's experiments and being shrunk in size.[47] Likewise Hitler likely believed that advancing his concept of a "master race" at the expense of Jews and others he deemed unacceptable was benefiting mankind. Now that the problem that prompted Thorkel to send for the scientists in the first place has been identified, the now insane scientist, again in a Hitler-like fashion, announces, "Now I can control life absolutely."

With this declaration, Thorkel falls asleep, permitting the little people an opportunity to escape. The film now takes on an almost comedic tone as the tiny humans encounter to them gigantic chickens, a cat, and a dog — the latter belonging to Thorkel's assistant Pedro. The bizarre situation elicits a profound query from Pedro: "He is my dog. But who is Pedro?" The fun and games soon end: While examining Bulfinch, Thorkel discovers that the former is returning to his normal size. To prevent this, he smothers Bulfinch with a wet cotton swab. The others take flight into the jungle, trying to escape in a canoe, only to be foiled by Thorkel who has followed them with Pedro's dog. Pedro himself is killed by Thorkel while he lures the dog away from the others. When Thorkel sets fire to the grass in which the little people are hiding, the latter take shelter in a case he brought with him.

Unaware he has the tiny captives with him, Thorkel returns to his lab. Escaping from his case when Thorkel steps out, they rig a shotgun to slay Thorkel when he returns for another snooze. When the mad scientist instead slumbers at his desk, the little people steal his glasses. Thorkel cannot see well enough to find them. He ultimately pursues them to the ore shaft behind his house; falling off the board holding him, Thorkel is finally overcome when one of the little people knocks loose the chain he clings to, sending Thorkel to his death in the shaft below. When the effects of Thorkel's miniaturization device dissipate, the little people return to normal size.

Hitlerian dreams of global domination also motivated Dr. Paul Rigas, the equally demented scientist in Universal's pre-war take on mad science,

Man Made Monster, released in 1941. The role of the bogeyman scientist, Dr. Rigas, was filled by the actor who earned a special niche in classic horror's hall of fame as the genre's greatest mad doctor — Lionel Atwill. *Man Made Monster* marked the horror debut of an actor born Creighton Chaney but who would achieve fame as Universal's preeminent horror star of the 1940s as Lon Chaney, Jr. The younger Chaney, son of the "Man of a Thousand Faces," candidly admitted his lack of his father's genius for makeup, thus he spent his early film career appearing in serials, westerns, and B-movies. Reminiscing about that formative era proved painful for Chaney, Jr. "I was in a new picture practically every two weeks, always a heavy," he recalled. "I'll swear I spoke the line 'So you won't talk, eh?' at least 50 times. I'd rather not think about the times I had to say, 'Don't shoot him now. I have a better plan.'" The turning point in his career came in 1939 when he won the role of the towering, feeble-minded Lennie in a stage adaptation of John Steinbeck's *Of Mice and Men.* For Chaney, opening night was a stunning success: he received 13 curtain calls. He repeated his triumph in the film version of the story, appearing with Burgess Meredith.[48]

Man Made Monster opens on a rainy night as a spending bus crashes into an electrical tower. The accident claims the lives of the driver and every passenger aboard — save one: "Dynamo Dan" (as he is billed) McCormick, a carnival performer who amazes audiences with electrical magic. One man interested in McCormick's abilities, Dr. John Lawrence (Samuel S. Hinds), an electrobiologist, asks him to drop by for a visit. Working with Lawrence is Dr. Rigas, whose grand obsession is to prove that men can be electrically controlled, spawning "a race of superior men ... men whose only wants were electricity." Expounding on his theory, Rigas presents a concept that would have fit in with Hitler's "master race" theory:

> You know as well as I do that half the people in the world are doomed to a life of mediocrity. Born to become idiots, millstones around the neck of progress. Men who have to be fed, watched, looked over, and taken care of by a superior intelligence. My theory is to make these people of more use to the world. By successive treatments, their bodies can be so electrilized that they are no longer subject to the pains and frailties of ordinary mankind.

Rigas' disdain for the moral concerns his theory presents was echoed in real life by the comments of Enrico Fermi, who worked on the wartime atomic bomb effort at Los Alamos, New Mexico. Before he viewed the destructive power of the test blast at Alamogordo, an event that greatly unsettled him, Fermi cavalierly dismissed the possibility that utilization of the bomb might rise to ethical dilemmas, reportedly saying at one point, "Don't bother me with your conscientious scruples. After all, the thing's superb physics." Moreover, before the test detonation occurred, he supposedly speculated with his fellow scientists whether the bomb might kindle the atmosphere and annihilate the world.[49] Fermi's subsequent second-thoughts would have never have occurred to Drs. Rigas and Thorkel.

Leaving the hospital after a mere night's stay, McCormick goes to see Lawrence, who believes McCormick's survival is due to the latter's experiments with electricity which have conferred an immunity on him. Such protection, Lawrence believes, holds the key to preventing death by electrocution; unlocking the secret of McCormick's electrical invulnerability would have obvious benefits in saving countess lives. McCormick consents to help Lawrence, and is housed in Lawrence's residence. With Lawrence away at a scientific convention, Dr. Rigas begins experimenting on McCormick, administering daily dozens of electricity that ultimately transform the unsuspecting carnival performer into an electricity addict. Finally Rigas gives McCormick a full charge that produces a glowing electrical monster who has to be insulated by wearing a rubber suit. In words that would make any dictator proud, Rigas gloats at his creation:

> There he stands — the shell of a man — electrically alive. Every impulse controlled by me.... Think of an army of such creatures. Doing the work of the world, fighting its battles.... The worker of the future — controlled by a superior intelligence!

When Lawrence tries to call a halt to Rigas' plans, the latter orders McCormick to prevent him; the newly created electrical man kills Lawrence, then, following Rigas' command, takes the rap for Lawrence's death.

The conflicting scientific agendas Drs. Lawrence and Rigas have regarding their respective intentions toward Dan McCormick clearly personify the paradoxical images of scientific progress and the application of such advances that confronted Americans on the eve of their involvement in World War II. Dr. Lawrence's goal of utilizing Dan's immunity to electricity for the benefit of humanity reflected the World's Fair's vision of a scientific utopia ("The World of Tomorrow"), whereas Dr. Rigas sought to use Dan's gift as the key to creating an army of electrified zombies —

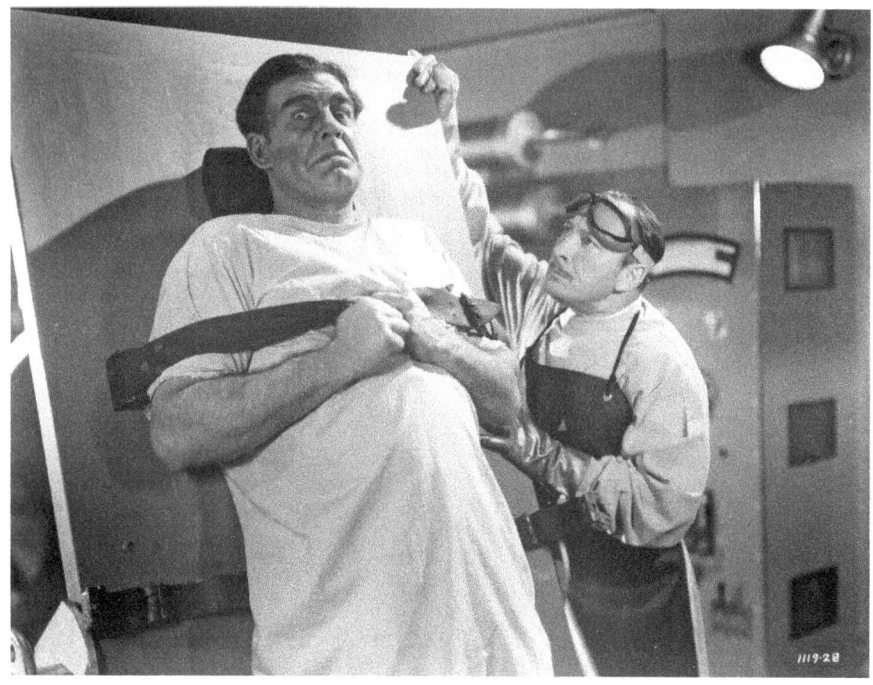

Another pre-war mad science film, *Man Made Monster* (1941) found Dan McCormick (Lon Chaney, Jr.) falling prey to the unscrupulous Dr. Rigas (Lionel Atwill) (Universal Pictures/Photofest).

(the Hitlerian vision). Caught in the middle is the very image of supreme innocence — Dan McCormick, who trustingly accepts Lawrence's invitation to help humanity, unaware that Rigas will pervert that offer, transforming McCormick into a destructive monstrosity. Likewise, America was about to lose its innocence in war, then emerge from that war both sanctified and tarnished — sanctified in that it led the forces of righteousness to victory over the forces of darkness, then utilized its technological and scientific resources in the postwar restoration of both its allies and enemies; tarnished in that it failed to accord the rescue of Jewish victims of Hitler's barbarism the same priority it did the military vanquishment of the Nazis and Japanese, and that it applied its scientific know-how to creating the most destructive weapon in history and, in so doing, giving the world a power that could both revolutionize and destroy it.

Tried and convicted of Lawrence's death, McCormick is sentenced to die in the electric chair. However, when the time comes for the prison officials to carry out the sentence, McCormick withstands the electricity and escapes from the prison, walking through the countryside, shuffling like the Frankenstein Monster, wreaking havoc as he goes. He returns to the lab just as Rigas is about to subject Lawrence's niece June (Anne Nagel) to the same treatment he gave McCormick. His face contorted with hate, McCormick electrocutes Rigas. Donning his protective attire, he frees June, then in the best movie monster tradition, carries her off into the night. Walking up to a barbed wire fence, he releases June, then tries to proceed through the fence; catching himself on it, his electrical life-force ebbs away, ending his torment. In what has been described as "a nice dose of pre–World War II idealism," June then prevails upon her newspaper reporter boyfriend to destroy Rigas' notes, forever preventing the secret of Dan McCormick's transformation into a monster from being publicized.

"Wrapped" at Universal on December 14, 1940, *Man Made Monster* debuted the following March at New York's Rialto Theatre. Reviewing the film, *Variety* termed it "a shocker that's in the groove for horror fans. It makes no pretense of being anything but a freakish chiller, going directly to the point and proving mighty successful.... Young Chaney looks like he is on his way ... backed up by Lionel Atwill in one of his better characterizations...."[50] For both Lon Chaney, Jr., and director George Waggner, *Man Made Monster* was a stepping stone to greater things: Chaney won an exclusive long-term contract from Universal, while Waggner won a seven-year contract from the same studio.[51] Before year's end, the same duo would reteam for another, greater horror collaboration — one that would arrive just in time for America's entry into World War II.

5

The War Years, Part I: The Saga of the Wolf Man (1941–1945)

The White House switchboard operator set up a conference call with the three wire services at 2:30 P.M. Eastern Standard Time on Sunday, December 7, 1941. White House press secretary Steve Early then issued a news release that news tickers nationwide almost instantaneously rapped out: "White House says Japs attack Pearl Harbor."[1] Most Californians received word of the Japanese strike in Hawaii while they were returning home from church, Nebraskans as they were preparing for dinner, and New Yorkers when WOR interrupted its coverage of the Giant-Dodger football game from the Polo Grounds.[2]

At twelve noon the next day, President Roosevelt left the White House to address Congress:

"Yesterday, December 7, 1941 — a date which will live in infamy — the United States of America was suddenly and deliberately attacked by naval and air forces of the empire of Japan.... I ask that the Congress declare that since the unprovoked and dastardly attack by Japan on Sunday, December 7, 1941, a state of war has existed between the United States and the Japanese Empire." Thirty-three minutes after Roosevelt concluded his remarks, both houses of Congress granted FDR's request for a declaration of war — one which he signed shortly after four that afternoon.[3] In a fireside chat to the nation on the evening of December 9, Roosevelt told his fellow countrymen, "We are now in this war. We are all in it — all the way.

Every single man, woman, and child is a partner in the most tremendous undertaking of our American history. We must share together the bad news and the good news, the defeats and the victories — the changing fortunes of war."[4]

Speaking to the German Reichstag on December 11, Adolf Hitler branded Roosevelt "the main culprit of this war" and a creature of the Jews, then disclosed that he had arranged for the American charge d'affaires to be given his passport.[5] Summoning the American representative to his office that same day, German Foreign Minister Joachim von Ribbentrop read the American Leland Morris a dispatch, then bellowed, "*Ihr Präsident hat diesen Krieg gewollt; jetzt hat er ihn*"— translation: "Your president has wanted this war; now he has it."[6] The United States responded in kind, declaring war on both Germany and Italy that very day.[7]

In the midst of these world-shaking events, Universal Studios on December 9, 1941, the day after the American declaration of war against Japan, unveiled its latest horror offering to the press — one which reunited George Waggner with the studio's rising horror star, Lon Chaney, Jr., and featured Claude Rains, Warren William, Ralph Bellamy, Patric Knowles, Bela Lugosi, Maria Ouspenskaya, and Evelyn Ankers. Written by Curt Siodmak, the film failed to impress its preview audience as *Motion Picture Herald* noted: "Previewed at the studio for a press and professional audience, which displayed no enthusiasm for the enterprise."[8]

The film in question was *The Wolf Man*, Universal's first cinematic exercise in lycanthropy since 1935's *WereWolf of London*. The *Hollywood Reporter's* review was more positive:

> *The Wolf Man* serves its horror straight. A very substantial cast undertakes to sell believably a tale of superstitious folklore.... Lon Chaney assumes the really terrifying makeup created by Jack P. Pierce and bears favorable comparison to his esteemed father. And he is pleasantly personable as the untransformed Larry....[9]

When the film began its New York run shortly before Christmas, *The New York Times* took a dim view:

> Nobody is going to go on believing in werewolves or Santa Clauses if the custodians of these legends don't tell them with a more convincing imaginative touch ... the wolf man is left without a paw to stand on.... [H]e looks a lot less terrifying and not nearly as funny as Mr. Disney's Big Bad Wolf.[10]

Variety gave the film a mixed review, calling it "a completely-knit tale of its kind, with good direction and performances by an above par assemblage of players, but dubious entertainment at this particular time."[11]

The critics aside, it was the movie-going public that rendered the final judgment on the quality of *The Wolf Man:* The film was a million-dollar winner for Universal, becoming the studio's biggest hit of the season as well as providing escapist entertainment for wartime audiences. It elevated Chaney to horror superstardom ("[T]he studio received more mail for me during that period than any other star," the actor recalled) and the werewolf to its rightful place as a pop culture icon.[12] Indeed, the Wolf Man was Hollywood's most successful horror figure of the war years.

The success of *The Wolf Man* owed not only to Chaney but to screenwriter Curt Siodmak, whose work on the film established the popular mythology of the werewolf in the public mind.[13] "Unlike *WereWolf of London,* which combined the werewolf legend with modern science, Siodmak temporarily forsook his science fiction proclivities and firmly rooted his story in European folklore."[14]

Born in Dresden, Saxony, Germany, Siodmak got his start as a published author at an early age: nine. He later explained that his literary career began as a means of escaping a melancholy childhood. Despite his writing talent and success, his father packed him off to engineering schools in Germany and Switzerland. By his early twenties, young Curt had forsaken an engineering career and was on his way to a successful career in the German film industry. Firmly established as an author and journalist, he frequently underwrote the independent film productions of his brother Robert and Billy Wilder. One of the Siodmak brothers' initial film productions, *People on Sunday* was shot on expired film with non-actors and without a budget. Despite these handicaps, the film achieved critical success. Forced to flee Germany with the advent of Hitler, Siodmak worked in the British and French film industries until the spread of Naziism again forced him out, this time to America. From that time forward, his experiences as a political refugee would greatly influence his life and career.[15] Even after coming to America, Siodmak's refugee problems continued: In his memoirs, he recalled a visit he received from the FBI after Pearl Harbor. Accompanying the two bureau agents was a copious file about the writer. "I had the uncomfortable feeling that I was back in Germany, constantly watched by the Gestapo. Since I was not politically minded, I couldn't imagine what kind of information the FBI could have collected on me."

The real purpose of the meeting concerned "an older, rather mysterious German who lived on our street.... I told them that I had talked to that man only once and didn't even know his name. The next day that old German had disappeared from sight." Before the meeting ended, Siodmak's callers informed him he was under curfew and had to be home every night by eight o'clock. "Just because I still had a brown German passport, and not a blue American one, I was a suspected enemy of my new country."[16]

In his introduction to the published version of his *Wolf Man* screenplay, Siodmak provided this account of how he got the assignment to write the film from George Waggner:

"We have a title," said George.

> The title comes from a story written for Boris Karloff, ten years earlier but he cannot play in that picture, since he is busy on another one. The title is *The Wolf Man*. We have Claude Rains under contract for one more picture. Also Lon Chaney, Jr., Madame Ouspenskaya, Evelyn Ankers, who is gifted with a terrifying scream, Ralph Bellamy, Warren William, and Bela Lugosi. Of course Bela would like to play the Wolf Man. His Hungarian accent is right for Dracula, but not for the Wolf Man. Since we have Claude, the tale might play in England. We are limited in funds, as usual, and I will get from the front office $180,000 for the production. That's why you can't have a raise. Confidentially, get your raise at another studio, and we'll match it. We shoot in ten weeks. And don't talk to me until you've finished the screenplay. I want your ideas, and not mine. Good-bye.[17]

Siodmak originally conceived the Wolf Man character as an American dispatched to Scotland to install a telescope in a castle. Chaney's broad American accent, in Siodmak's opinion, disqualified him from playing the role of an Englishman. Moreover, "for an American innocent, and certainly not a mystic, to be afflicted with wolf madness was more horrifying to me than the change George Waggner made: making him the son of a Scottish nobleman...." Finally, Siodmak didn't want audiences to view the werewolf's face, save for when Chaney beheld his appearance in a mirror or in water. Yet Waggner altered that concept as well, "maybe rightly so. The public doesn't like mysticism, especially since there are no ghosts in America. They all live in Europe, preferably in England."[18]

Coming as it did at the start of the American involvement in World War II, *The Wolf Man* presented another example of Hollywood's "Europe," one combining elements of America, England, and the Continent, much the same way World War I had, and which this latest conflict was repeating. "The Europe of American horror movies," noted David J. Skal, "was a nearly surreal pastiche of accents, architecture, and costumes, like the scrambled impressions of a soldier/tourist on a whirlwind tour of duty." This anomalous atmosphere was augmented by setting the film in contemporary Great Britain, which, in real life, was directly experiencing the horrors of war. In Hollywood's never-never land version of Britain, war was out of sight and mind; its greatest menace came, not from Nazi Germany, but rather the lycanthropic threat.[19]

After eighteen years away from his family, Lawrence Talbot (Chaney) returns to his ancestral estate in Wales. His elder brother John was killed in a hunting accident, prompting Larry's return and his reunion with his father, Sir John Talbot (Claude Rains). The latter, an award-winning scientist, asks Larry's help in installing a newly arrived component for his telescope. Once the installation is completed, Larry sneaks a peek through the instrument at the village, casting his eye on Gwen Conliffe (Evelyn Ankers), daughter of the antique shop owner, as she prepares herself for another day's work. Visiting the shop, he tries to ingratiate himself to Gwen. While there, he buys a cane, one adorned with a wolf's head and a star — the pentagram, the sign of the werewolf. Larry is unfamiliar with the legend of the werewolf, so Gwen recites an old poem:

> Even a man who is pure in heart
> And says his prayers by night,
> May become a wolf when the wolfbane blooms,
> And the autumn moon is bright.

Like the "ancient Arabian proverb" that began *King Kong* eight years earlier, this famous verse, supposedly rooted in "gypsy folklore," was another motion picture contrivance — this time conceived in the imagination of Curt Siodmak: "That's how folk horror history is made."[20]

Gwen continues that every werewolf bears the mark of the pentagram as well as seeing it in the palm of his next victim's hand. Larry buys the cane from her, trying to persuade her to see him that evening. She declines. Just then, a traveling band of gypsies arrive in town.

Returning to the antique shop that evening, Larry finally convinces Gwen to accompany him to the gypsy camp to have their fortunes told. Gwen has arranged for a chaperon — Jenny Williams (Fay Helm). Together the trio proceed to the camp where they meet Bela the fortune-teller (Bela Lugosi), who reads Jenny's fortune first. The latter inadvertently brings some of the wolfbane she picked on the way to the camp with her into Bela's wagon; the branches' presence there produce an adverse reaction in the fortune-teller; he also bears the mark of the pentagram on his forehead. Asking for Jenny's hands, he sees the pentagram in her right hand. Panic-stricken, he orders Jenny out, telling her to return the following night. As she flees through the fog-shrouded, darkened forest, the howling of a wolf is heard, then Jenny's scream. Going to investigate, Larry finds a wolf mauling Jenny; fighting off the animal, Larry beats it to death with his newly purchased cane but not before he's bitten on the chest by the wolf. Wounded, Larry is taken home by Gwen and Maleva (Maria Ouspenskaya), Bela's mother.

Informed of Jenny's death, Captain Montford (Ralph Bellamy), head of the local police, goes to investigate. At the crime scene, he finds both her body and that of, not a wolf, but Bela whose skull has been crushed by a sharp instrument. They also find the instrument—Larry's cane, as well as wolf tracks. Questioned about Bela's death, Larry insists he killed a wolf. When he tries to show the authorities his chest wound, he discovers the injury has healed overnight. When Bela's body is brought to the mausoleum for burial, Maleva opens his coffin and recites a prayer over his body:

> The way you walked was thorny, through no fault of your own.
> But as the rain enters the soil, the river enters the sea, so tears run to a predestined end.
> Your suffering is over...,
> Now you will find peace.

The inspiration for Maleva's verse was the quality of *Harmatia*. "In ancient Greek tragedies," Curt Siodmak explained, to possess "*Harmatia* means that a person must suffer by the whim of the gods, though he has not committed a crime." This concept formed the crux of Siodmak's idea for the film: "We all have *Harmatia* in us, and suffer life's mishaps and pain without having been guilty of any misdeed. The world as we saw it was being drawn into wars. Life itself contains the curse of the Wolf Man: suffering without having been guilty, being subjected to fates, which are decided by the pleasure of the gods."[21]

As the film progresses, Larry has a strained meeting with Gwen's fiancé, Frank Andrews (Patric Knowles), the gamekeeper for Larry's father's estate. Frank cautions Gwen to stay away from Larry: "There's something very tragic about that man, and I'm sure that nothing but harm will come to you through him."

The tension between Larry and Frank seems to disappear that evening when they and Gwen meet up at a festival at the gypsy camp. Encouraged by Frank, Talbot fires a rifle at "pop-up" animal figures at a vendor's stand. When the wolf figure appears, he's unable to shoot it; when he finally fires, he misses. As Larry passes Maleva's wagon, the old gypsy woman beckons him inside, where she tells him that Bela was a werewolf, giving a Larry a pentagram which can break the evil spell. Agitated, Larry rises to leave, only to be stopped by Maleva's warning: "Whoever is bitten by a werewolf and lives, becomes a werewolf himself." She tells him to wear the pentagram charm over his heart and convinces him to show her his chest wound; seeing the pentagram there, she tells him to leave, then informs her fellow gypsies to break camp. Meeting up with Gwen, Larry gives her the pentagram, telling her to have it as a protection against him! Observing that the gypsies are leaving, he asks one what's going on: "There's a werewolf in camp!" is the reply.

Returning home, Larry feels an itch; removing his clothes, he discovers wolf hair growing on his legs and feet. Once the transformation is completed, Larry, now a werewolf, ventures forth into the night woods, killing his first victim, Richardson the gravedigger. Awakening in his bed the next morning, Talbot finds animal tracks on the floor of his room.

With the village on the brink of hysteria over the murders, Andrews and Montford set traps in the woods for the murderous beast. That evening Larry once again is seized by the werewolf curse. Prowling in the woods, he steps into one of the traps. Trying to break free, he falls unconscious. At this moment, Maleva happens to appear; as she says a prayer over him, he transforms back into his normal self. Fleeing into the village, he awakens Gwen, telling her he's going away. Gwen wants to go with him. When Larry sees the pentagram in her hand, he realizes Gwen is destined to be his next victim and hurries from the antique store.

Sir John, refusing to believe Larry's story that he is a werewolf, convinced his son is suffering a delusion, binds him to a chair in his room, then bolts the door shut. As Sir John leaves, Larry tells him to take the wolf's head cane. Sir John's efforts avail nothing: Larry again becomes the werewolf, attacking Gwen in the woods. Just as the Wolf Man attacks Gwen, Sir John appears; when the beast attacks him, he beats it to death with Larry's cane. Maleva now arrives, saying the same verse she recited over her son's body. As Sir John watches, Larry reverts to human form, leaving his father to mourn over him.

The Wolf Man elevated the werewolf to the status of pop culture icon, joining the ranks of Dracula, Frankenstein's Monster, and the Mummy in that exalted company. In many ways, the character was the perfect monster for World War II. David J. Skal believes that the Wolf Man and other devolved animal-men appearing in films of the era were metaphors for Nazi brutality. Similar films capitalizing on the devolution theme included *The Undying Monster* (1942), *Cry of the Werewolf* (1944), *The Ape Man* (1943), and *Return of the Ape Man* (1944).[22] For Siodmak, the Wolf Man's tragedy profoundly resonated in his own life, as he explained in an interview not long before his death:

> I am the Wolf Man. I was forced into a fate I didn't want: to be a Jew in Germany. I would not have chosen that as my fate. The swastika represents the moon. When the moon comes up, the man doesn't want to murder, but he knows he cannot escape it, the Wolf Man destiny. Something happens that you know is going to happen, but you cannot escape it, like being sent to a concentration camp.[23]

The star of four films during the war years, the Wolf Man (Lon Chaney, Jr., seen here in 1945's *House of Dracula*) represented screenwriter Curt Siodmak's experiences as a Jewish refugee from Nazi Germany — a man aware of his fate but powerless to alter it (Universal Pictures/Photofest).

Wolves also resonated with the man who sought to destroy Siodmak and his fellow Jews. Adolf Hitler, noted historian Robert G. L. Waite, was fascinated with them:

> As a boy he was well pleased with his first name, noting that it came from the old German "Athalwolf" — a compound of Athal ("noble") and Wolfa ("wolf"). And "noble wolf" he sought to remain. At the start of his political career he chose "Herr Wolf" as his pseudonym. His favorite dogs were Alsatians — in German *Wolfshunde*. One of [his dog] Blondie's pups, born toward the end of the war, he called "Wolf" and would allow no else to touch or feed it. He named his headquarters in France *Wolfsschlucht* (Wolf's Gulch). In the Ukraine his headquarters were *Werwolf* (Man Wolf), and in East Prussia *Wolfsschanze* (Wolf's Lair) — as he explained to a servant, "I am the Wolf and this is my den." He called his SS "My pack of wolves." Later he would recall with exaltation how in the early days of the movement his Storm Troopers pounced upon the opposition "like wolves" and were soon "covered with blood...."
> When he telephoned Winfred Wagner, he would say, "Conductor Wolf calling!" The secretary he kept longer than any other (more than 20 years) was Johanna Wolf. She recalled that while Hitler addressed all other secretaries for-

mally as "Frau" or "Fraulein," he invariably called her "Wolfin" (She-Wolf). One of his favorite tunes came from a Walt Disney movie. Often and absent-mindedly he whistled "Who's Afraid of the Big Bad Wolf?"—an animal, it will be recalled, who wanted to eat people up and blow their houses down.[24]

During the war years, Universal relegated its horror output to B level, factory status, a strategy designed to occupy the vacuum created by the major Hollywood studios' decision to emphasize prestige film production—an approach the majors adopted to harmonize production plans with the wartime American economy. The advantage to Universal in stressing B production lay in the fact that it enabled the studio to employ stars and manpower already contractually bound to the studio. In addition to the horror film, of which Chaney was now the principal star, Universal concentrated on Abbott and Costello comedies, which were so successful that they were literally the studio's financial saviors during the 1940s, and the Sherlock Holmes films teaming Basil Rathbone and Nigel Bruce as, respectively, the renowned detective and his companion in crime-solving, Dr. Watson. Universal updated the characters from their original Victorian London milieu to the World War II era—a move that had obvious money-saving advantages. Some of the entries in Universal's Holmes series—*The Scarlet Claw* and *The Pearl of Death*, both 1944 releases—amalgamated the mystery and horror genres. In addition to cutting production expenses, modernizing Holmes' adventures to wartime helped the American war effort.[25]

When it came to the artistic merits of Universal's B productions, those who made them appreciated that they weren't turning out *Gone with the Wind* and other cinematic masterpieces. Nor were the audiences for such fare highbrow types. Universal's B efforts, according to Reginald LeBorg, who directed many of them during this period, were aimed at "factory workers and blacks." "Angry and alienated, the monster characters," writes Skal, "had a clear appeal for the socially and economically marginalized." [A] large audience could be especially depended upon for each new installment of Universal's *Frankenstein* series, whose work-booted monster" had initially become popular with Depression-era moviegoers.[26]

The studios' next chapter in its Frankenstein series—and Lon Chaney, Jr.'s next horror assignment after *The Wolf Man*—began filming on December 15, 1941, eight days after Pearl Harbor, and wrapped slightly over schedule, on January 15, 1942. *The Ghost of Frankenstein* proved a gamble for Universal as it was the first of the series without Boris Karloff in the Monster role. With Chaney now occupying the Monster's work boots, the studio mounted a major publicity campaign in his behalf. The early reviews were laudatory but, when began the film playing New York City on April 3, 1942, *New York Times* film critic Bosley Crowther did not share the initial critics' enthusiasm:

> Don't look now, gentle reader, but Frankenstein's Monster is loose again.... Gorgons, hydras and chimera dire! Aren't there enough monsters loose in this world without that horrendous ruffian mauling and crushing actors?
> [T]he thought that he may yet return for further adventures with this body and Lugosi's sconce fills us with mortal terror. That is the most fearful prospect which the picture manages to convey.

The main reason for this and other, similar reviews the film garnered was the fact that true-life war horrors far surpassed those that Hollywood produced. "Still, with a grab bag of exploitation gimmicks for exhibitors, *The Ghost of Frankenstein* proved a hit — but as a *programmer*, not as lavish fantasy venture."[27]

As the action in *The Ghost of Frankenstein* progresses, Ludwig Frankenstein (Sir Cedric Hardwicke) intends to destroy the Monster but, after a "visit" from the ghost of his father, the Monster's creator, he decides to remove the Monster's original, criminal brain and replace it with a normal one. Ygor, the Monster's companion, again played by Bela Lugosi, desires that *his* brain be transplanted instead: "My brain in that body would make me a leader of men. We would rule the state, and even the whole country." Like Hitler, Ygor is a social outcast who aspires to power. The notion of Ygor as a would-be dictator was an integral element of an early draft of the film's script: Wolf von Frankenstein — Basil Rathbone's character from the earlier *Son of Frankenstein*—was back as the doctor, this time with a hunchbacked assistant, Theodor, who, with Ygor, plotted a power grab with other cripples and misfits to take over the village, with the Monster leading the coup.[28] In the final version of the film, in exchange for help from Ludwig's assistant Bohmer (Lionel Atwill) in installing his brain in the Monster's body, Ygor will reward the disgraced medico by making the latter head of that nation's medical commission. The Monster himself has his own choice of whose brain he should receive: that of a little girl who befriended him.

The operation is successful but Ludwig, who thought he'd replaced the Monster's old brain with that of his murdered assistant Dr. Kettering, is in for an unpleasant surprise: Ygor's brain now resides in the Monster's

Lon Chaney, Jr., steps into Karloff's role as the Monster, with Bela Lugosi reprising his role of Ygor in 1942's *The Ghost of Frankenstein*. Ygor's desire to have his brain transplanted into the Monster's body mirrored his dreams of attaining power (Universal Pictures/Photofest).

body: "I am Ygor. I have the strength of a hundred men. I cannot die. I cannot be destroyed. I, Ygor, will live forever!" He then orders Bohmer to fill the house with gas, killing all the townspeople who have obligatorily stormed Frankenstein's residence. The Monster's (Ygor's) maniacal dreams of glory, nevertheless, prove short-lived: He suddenly goes blind. Kettering's blood type is incompatible with Ygor's hence the new brain cannot feed the sensory nerves. Enraged, the now sightless Monster goes berserk, demolishing Ludwig's laboratory, setting the house afire.[29]

Despite the negative critical reviews, *The Ghost of Frankenstein* was a success. An article appearing in *The Saturday Evening Post* the year of the film's release stated that horror movies had an estimated 60 million aficionados. Horror films could even surpass more prestige fare: In Cincinnati, *Ghost* eclipsed films such as *Dumbo* at the box office.[30] One reason for the film's triumph undoubtedly was that it — and other horror productions—worked as escapist entertainment for a country at war. Such films, explained *The Saturday Evening Post*, "help people to get away from the horror of realism. A Chinese baby crying in the midst of a bomb-blasted station is heart-rending, but a monster strangling Sir Cedric Hardwicke is entertainment."[31] Universal's pressbook for *The Ghost of Frankenstein* even urged theater owners to exploit the war with a "Will the Nazi Frankenstein Monster Follow the Famous Legend and Destroy Its Makers" Contest:

> Cash in on the times with a patriotic contest calling for letters stating how and when entrants think the Frankenstein Monster created by the Axis and now endangering the world will turn on its Nazi makers just as the screen monster in *The Ghost of Frankenstein* turns and destroys its creator....
> Will the Nazi Frankenstein created by the Axis follow the tradition of the original legend and destroy its maker? Every American knows it will....
> The (paper) and (theater) are offering a Defense Bond and several books of Defense Stamps for the best letters telling (1) When you think the war Monster now loosed on the world will turn on its Axis makers and destroy them, and (2) How you think this will come about.
> Send your letters in care of the Contest Editor of the (paper)(,) then see *Ghost of Frankenstein* at the (theater) for the newest and latest thrilling story of this arch-monster.[32]

Frankenstein's creation, assembled from the parts of various cadavers, also served as a substitute means for the public to confront the trauma of combat-inflicted injuries without actually witnessing the ghastly realities of such injuries. During and after World War II, wrote Paul Fussell, the visual record of the fighting in no way depicted the true, gruesome nature of combat. In the popular photographic collections of the war published after the guns fell silent, no matter the severity of their injuries, Allied soldiers were shown physically intact, no evidence of amputation of any body parts evident, and displaying sunny dispositions. Under actual battlefield conditions, one could be treated to the spectacle of the scenery littered with the remnants of those individuals blown apart in combat. The type of carnage World War II produced was unprecedented in history. Facing the reality of death or the possibility of dying yourself, explains Skal, could and did result in madness. Fussell observed that starvation and thirst experienced by those held captive by the Japanese and fliers floating on rafts produced numerous instances of insanity, which drove its victims not only to drink their urine to alleviate their thirst but to resort to vampirism by biting their comrades' jugular veins for their blood. None of these unpleasant realities found their way into contemporary newsreels.

The Frankenstein films, by contrast, provided a symbolic treatment of amputation and limb restoration. Man-made monsters, whose injuries could easily be repaired, "were the perfect toy soldiers to battle semiconscious fears." This may well explain *The Ghost of Frankenstein*'s popular success, coming as it did early in the American participation in World War II, at which time American and Allied fortunes were at a low point. The Monster, with his ability to vanquish all that stood in his way, may have furnished an image for audiences to rally to at a juncture in the war when morale was low.[33]

If the Frankenstein Monster which, in the 1930s, had symbolized the downtrodden and impoverished, had now assumed a new role for wartime America — that of representative of the physical suffering and agony of war-related injuries — then the Wolf Man signified the other half of the coin: one who sought to quell "irrational, violent, European forces" symbolized by his own yearning to rid himself of his bestial impulses.[34] In 1943, Universal brought together its two reigning wartime screen ghouls for the "monster rally" *Frankenstein Meets the Wolf Man,* the first time the studio merged its scientific and Gothic fiends.[35] The film's origin lies in a perchance apocryphal yarn provided by the film's scenarist and Wolf Man originator, Curt Siodmak:

> In 1942, with the war raging, I was having lunch in Universal Studios' commissary when George Waggner ... passed me on his way to the executive table. I was sitting with Yvonne de Carlo..., perhaps the most beautiful woman I had even laid my eyes on, and Marie MacDonald..., whose legs were as shapely as those of Betty Grable. I wanted to show off my wit and said, "George, why don't we make a picture, *Frankenstein Wolfs the Meat-Man* — I mean, *Frankenstein Meets the Wolf Man.*" To "wolf" somebody had the connotation of sexual harassment.
>
> I laughed, Yvonne laughed, Mary laughed, but not George. He only looked at me quizzically and walked on.
>
> That was the time during the war when America's factories rolled out tanks, airplanes, and guns, but no automobiles for private use. I needed a different car, since my Buick had passed the retiring age.
>
> A young writer, who had been drafted, wanted to sell his Buick. I wanted to take advantage of that opportunity and asked George if I would get another job when I was through with *The Climax,* a screenplay that I wrote for him with Boris Karloff ... and Susanna Foster ... in the lead.
>
> I didn't have enough cash for that sports car, and for Henrietta [Siodmak's wife], a Swiss, to pay interest on borrowed money was an abhorrent idea. George stuck his head into my office every day, asking me whether I had bought the automobile. When I questioned him with "What's the assignment?" he only answered, "Buy the car."
>
> I found out, to my surprise, that it was easy to get a loan from the bank. They just kept the pink slip of ownership.

"Here is your assignment," George said. *"Frankenstein Meets the Wolf Man."*
"But it was a joke," I said.
"Not anymore," George said. "I give you two hours to find a brilliant idea."
He didn't say "to accept the assignment" or ask me "to make up my mind." He knew he had me over a barrel.[36]

Having no choice but to accept the assignment in order to replenish his finances, Siodmak now confronted the challenge of devising a central idea — or "weenie" as he called it — that would form the basis of his screenplay. He found his "weenie" in the fact that both monsters were already established characters.[37] Since the Wolf Man had been killed off in his first film, it became necessary to explain his resurrection in the new film. Siodmak resolved this issue by tossing out the rules governing the slaying of a werewolf from the original film, rendering the character immortal.[38] The Frankenstein Monster, who would be found frozen in ice in his latest screen appearance, would want to live forever. Once Siodmak had his "weenie"— one monster, the Wolf Man, wanted to die, while the other wanted immortality — he submitted it to Waggner, who accepted it, then set to work writing his script.

When it came to preparing *Frankenstein Meets the Wolf Man* for production, the initial plan was to have Lon Chaney, Jr., play both monsters, aided by stunt men and doubles. A pair of considerations vetoed that idea: It seemed too exorbitant and involved to have Chaney play both parts,[39] and Chaney, while normally professional when it came to his work, still had his capricious side. The final decision was to have Chaney merely play the Larry Talbot and Wolf Man roles. That decision, along with Karloff's absence and his own decision not to play the Monster ever again, left Bela Lugosi as the only remaining horror star big enough in public recognition to play the Monster. Despite the Hungarian's low standing with the top brass at Universal, the brain of Lugosi's Ygor had been implanted in the Monster's noggin at the conclusion of *The Ghost of Frankenstein*. Finally, the actor's financial situation was such that he was willing to accept whatever job offers came his way. This time Lugosi accepted the role that he had spurned at enormous cost to his career in 1931— that of the Frankenstein Monster. What made the situation different this time was that the new film was slated to pick up the threads of the last Frankenstein epic, with the Monster not only blind but speaking. The latter may have convinced Lugosi that the role was now a far more challenging one for him.[40]

Filming began October 12, 1942, and wrapped almost a month later

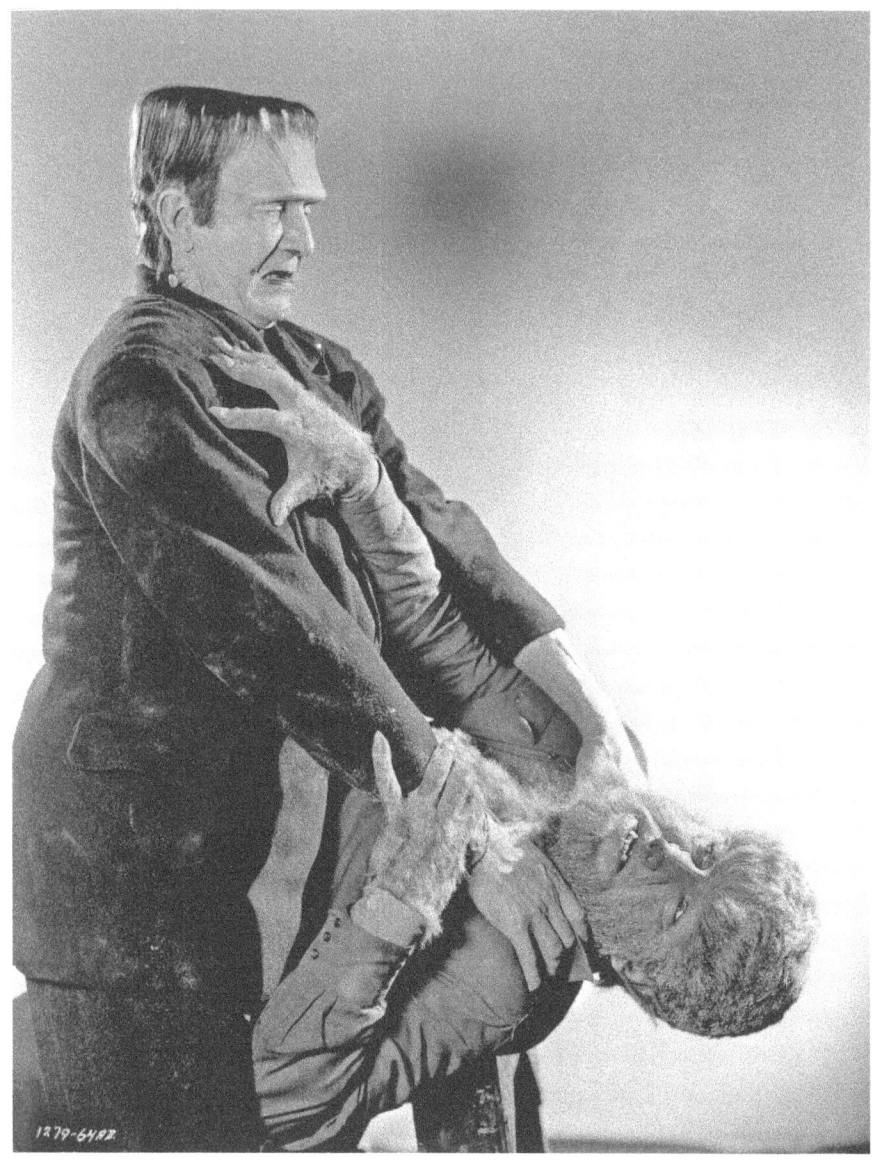

Finally playing the role he initially spurned at great cost to his career, Bela Lugosi was the Frankenstein Monster in Universal's initial wartime "monster rally," *Frankenstein Meets the Wolf Man* (1943) (Universal Pictures/Photofest).

on November 11. While working on the film, Lugosi established the American Hungarian Defense Federation in Los Angeles, which was able to confer $1,600 upon the Red Cross, purchase $65,000 in War Bonds in a single day, and completely outfit an ambulance for service abroad.[41] The film was well received at its Los Angeles preview February 18, 1943, with *Variety* calling it "a strong dish for the mass of customers who go for the bizarre, the weird, the creepy...," *The Hollywood Reporter* drew an unusual parallel between the film and the war: "Roosevelt meets Churchill at Casablanca, Yanks meet Japs at Guadalcanal — and yet these events will fade into insignificance to those seemingly inexhaustible legions of horror fans when they hear that *Frankenstein Meets the Wolf Man*. Yay, brother!"[42] War imagery also found its way into promotional campaigns for the film: Exhibitors were urged to emphasize the "mechanical" and "animal" details of the monsters' names in their lobby exhibits by representing the names in metal and fur, respectively. "'Metal and fur,'" wrote David J. Skal, "was an apt, if unintentional, comment on the contradictions of modern warfare; the spirit of the ancient berserker pitted against high industrial sublimation." An enormous lobby card, used to herald the film during its New York engagement, featured a timely exhortation: BUY WAR BONDS AND STAMPS.[43]

The film's opening sequence presents two grave robbers breaking into the Talbot family crypt for the purpose of purloining whatever valuables were buried on Lawrence Talbot's corpse. Upon opening Talbot's coffin, they find his body shrouded in wolfbane — a preventative measure to confine him in his final resting place, lest his wolfish self is revived. As fate would have it, the thieving duo chose to carry out their nefarious activities the night of the full moon. Almost immediately, Talbot returns to life, slaying one of the grave robbers while his partner high-tails it out of the crypt.

When we next see Talbot, he has somehow made his way from his hometown, Llanwelly, Wales, to another Welch community, Cardiff. Found unconscious in the street there, he is hospitalized for a skull fracture (undoubtedly resulting from the thrashing he received from his father in the original *Wolf Man*). When the full moon next shines in the night sky, Talbot transforms into his werewolf alter ego, escapes the hospital, and murders a constable on patrol. The next morning, upon being told that Lawrence Talbot has been dead four years, Talbot realizes that his lycanthropic condition prevents him from dying a normal death. Escaping the hospital again, he locates the gypsy camp of Maleva, asking her assistance in finding the peace of death. Unable to grant his request, Maleva agrees to take care of Talbot and lead him to the one man capable of alleviating his suffering — Dr. Frankenstein.

Traveling to Vasaria, Talbot and Maleva receive a hostile reception from the innkeeper, who tells them that Frankenstein is dead, then orders them out. The anti-gypsy sentiment prevalent throughout the film wasn't restricted solely to the screen; in real life, gypsies numbered among those "undesirable" peoples condemned to death by the Nazis. By 1945 the estimated number of gypsies residing in pre-war Europe (750,000) had been radically diminished.[44] After leaving the inn, Talbot is seized by his lycanthropic transformation, runs off into the woods, kills a Vasarian resident, and is pursued to the ruins of Frankenstein's castle by the angry villagers. Within the icy caverns of the now-deserted dwelling, Talbot finds and releases the Frankenstein Monster from his entombment. Unable to find Frankenstein's records amid the ruins, Talbot arranges to meet Baroness Frankenstein on the pretext of wanting to purchase her father's land. When he reveals the true motive for seeing her, the baroness explains that she doesn't have her father's records; had she, she would have long ago destroyed them.

That evening, at Vasaria's Festival of the New Wine, Talbot meets up with Dr. Mannering (Patric Knowles), the doctor who treated him for his head injury in Cardiff, and who has searched all of Europe for him. Mannering tries to convince Talbot to return to England with him before the next full moon. At this moment, the Monster enters the town, igniting a panic. Taking the Monster with him, Talbot flees aboard a horse-drawn wagon back to the Frankenstein ruins. Once they were back in the safety of the demolished castle, the script originally called for this exchange between Talbot and the Monster:

> TALBOT: Why did you come down to the village? Now they'll hunt us again —.
> THE MONSTER: I was afraid you'd left me — I thought you'd found that diary — and run away —
> TALBOT: You think you're so clever — Frankenstein gave you a cunning brain, did he? But you're dumb! You've spoiled our only chance —
> THE MONSTER (as the Doctor's voice is heard calling Talbot): Don't leave me — don't go! I'm weak.... They'll catch me and bury me alive...!

It was this interchange that resulted in the deletion of Lugosi's dialogue as the Monster from the film, weakening his performance.[45] Maintaining continuity with *The Ghost of Frankenstein, Frankenstein*

Meets the Wolf Man was to feature the nearly sightless Monster with Ygor's brain inside him, still speaking, still harboring visions of global domination:

> Dr. Frankenstein created this body to be immortal! His son gave me a new brain, a clever brain. I shall use it for the benefit of the miserable people who inhabit the world, cheating each other, killing each other, without a thought but their own petty gain. I will rule the world!

The Monster's next dialogue scene was the aforementioned one between him and Talbot as they were hiding from the villagers after they fled from the Festival of the New Wine. The final scene, near the film's conclusion, found the demonic duo awaiting the climactic lab scene: Wearing a white operating gown, sitting motionless "like a Tibetan god," the Monster boasts that his vitality will presently be restored; then, rising, he proclaims: "Then I shall see again—and be fit to rule the world!"

When the time came for the production staff to preview the completed film, Lugosi's talking Monster left the audience in stitches. The reason, explained Siodmak, was that Bela couldn't talk: "They had left the dialogue I wrote for the Monster in the picture when they shot it, but with Lugosi it sounded so Hungarian funny that they had to take it out!" Lugosi, Siodmak added, "was good as Dracula, because it supplied him with a Hungarian part. But a *monster* with a *Hungarian* accent?!"[46] A panic-stricken Waggner decreed the elimination of all of Lugosi's dialogue from the film's final release print, despite the fact that such action would, moreover, eliminate every reference to the Monster's near-blindness, rendering both the character's clumsy way of moving in the film and his opening and closing of his mouth without uttering a sound illogical. Ironically it was Lugosi's portrayal of the Monster—its arms outstretched, its eyes half-shut—that became the model for subsequent Monster imitations.[47]

Eventually, Mannering, the baroness, and Maleva find Talbot and the Monster. The baroness reveals her father's diary's hiding place, and Mannering agrees to drain off the energy of both the Monster and Talbot. However, when the time comes for him to make good on this pledge, Mannering succumbs to the temptation to restore the Monster to its full strength. Revived, the latter tries to abduct the baroness but is thwarted by the Wolf Man. As the baroness and Mannering escape, a titanic battle between the two reigning Universal monsters now ensues, halted when flood waters unleashed by an explosion of the dam above the ruins, set off by one of the villagers, wash through the ruins, drowning the battling fiends (called "phantoms" in the script).[48]

The following year, both Frankenstein's Monster and the Wolf Man were freed from icy prisons for Universal's next "monster rally," *House of Frankenstein,* which added Count Dracula (John Carradine) and Boris Karloff, the latter returning to the series as a mad scientist, Dr. Gustav Niemann. Niemann, who had been imprisoned for trying to insert a human brain into the skull of a dog, escapes with his hunchbacked pal Daniel (J. Carrol Naish), then hides out as the star of a traveling chamber of horrors carnival show, featuring Dracula's skeletal remains. Revived by Niemann, the vampire becomes part of the crazed scientist's plans to wreak vengeance on those responsible for incarcerating him. His plans include transplanting the brain of one of his enemies into the Frankenstein Monster, while the Wolf Man is to become the new receptacle for the Monster's brain; the werewolf's old brain will be "donated" to Niemann's remaining foe. Daniel, who has fallen in love with a gypsy girl, desires that *his* brain be placed in the Wolf Man's body but finds his request denied by Niemann. As the concluding scene plays out, the Monster carries Niemann into quicksand.

Universal's next — and final straight dramatic — spook rally was originally conceived as *The Wolf Man vs. Dracula.* No script bearing such a title has ever materialized, yet a letter from the all-powerful Hollywood censor Joseph Breen to Universal suggests that the scenario in question is far different from what the studio actually delivered to the big screen. Ultimately the production was released as *House of Dracula* and featured a new angle: All the monsters, not just the Wolf Man, now desired to be cured of their supernatural maladies — which the latest film depicts as more scientific in nature. In Larry Talbot's case, his attending physician diagnoses the cause of his affliction as pressure on the brain: "This condition, coupled with your belief that the moon can bring about a change, accomplishes exactly that.... Your reasoning processes give way to self-hypnosis, the glands which govern your metabolism get out of control, like a steam engine without a balance wheel."[49] Looking back on the film, producer Paul Malvern explained what it was like to make it under wartime conditions:

> There was ... a certain amount that we were allowed to spend on sets. I think it was $5,000, so that we could save lumber and nails for the War effort. Universal had the old European village and the Phantom's Opera House and the Notre Dame cathedral, we had our own lake, western villages, just about anything you wanted. But we mostly used the existing sets and kept spending down to a minimum.

Just the name Frankenstein was known to be an instant box office winner. So with *House of Frankenstein* on the big hit list for the previous year it was a natural to follow it up with *House of Dracula*. Only it wasn't called that at first. It was called *Dracula Meets the Wolf Man*.... We found the original story and sent it over to the censors office and they screamed bloody hell. There was so much real violence going on that I guess they were sensitive about what went on the screen ... the picture was shelved but you never really got rid of a good story line.[50]

Released the year World War II ended, *House of Dracula* fittingly provided a cinematic allegory of the time: An operation finally cures Talbot of his werewolf affliction, thus calming the "irrational, violent, European forces" both he and the western Allies had fought so long and hard to vanquish. Now a free man, he and his girlfriend were, in the script's original ending, to walk hand in hand "into the light of the full moon which shines beyond them,"[51] as if they were both entering the brand new world dawning at the war's end. "The Wolf Man's saga was the most consistent and sustained monster myth of the war, beginning with the first year of America's direct involvement, and finishing up just in time for Hiroshima."[52]

Val Lewton's Cat People

RKO Studios provided its take on the "were-animal" theme during the war with *Cat People* (1942), produced by Val Lewton and directed by Jacques Tourneur. In contrast to the blatant visual shocks dominating the standard horror film of the day, Lewton specialized in suggesting, *not showing*, the terror implied in his films, letting the audiences give substance to these shocks with their own imaginations. Of the eleven films he produced for RKO in the period between 1942 and 1946, nine of them fell between the thriller and the horror film, yet each one spurned fantastic elements. "With the exception of the last three ... they were all compact little novellas set in a recognizable modern world," one where the classic monsters of Gothic tradition would have been alien to — and misplaced. The real horror of Lewton's productions stemmed from the genuine dread of that which is unknown, the dark, and of ancient superstition, and what Moncure D. Conway characterized as "the reason of unreason"; instead of featuring tangible ghouls, Lewton's films depicted humanity's fear of them.[53]

"He was not opposed to a good, cheap scare here and there," noted writer-director Guillermo Del Toro. "But ultimately he really understood that the best horror movies are dark mirrors in which you project and reflect the most scary things in you."[54]

Lewton got into the horror business because RKO boss Charles Koerner decided that his studio should have its own horror division, one that would supplement its B mystery films and vie with Universal for the horror fan's dollar.[55] Initially Lewton's first project for Koerner was to be an adaptation of Algernon Blackwood's *Ancient Sorceries*. However, when Koerner attended a party at which someone suggested that, while werewolves and vampires as film subjects had been done to excess, "nothing much has been done about cats," Koerner abandoned the Blackwood story for a title he himself thought up: *Cat People*. Despite his revulsion at both the subject matter, owing to his own atavistic fear of felines, and the sensational title, Lewton plunged ahead with the project. Several stories were considered; ultimately Lewton discarded the notion of adapting a published story in favor of an original concept.[56]

The focus of Lewton's original story was a snowed-in Balkan village, the residents of which are now under the yoke of a Nazi Panzer division. During the day the villagers give their captors no trouble but, at night, they transform into predaceous beasts who annihilate the Nazis. In the wake of the massacre, one of the villagers, a girl, escapes, ultimately reaching New York, and falls in love. Lewton intended to have the girl's dialogue remain incomprehensible to movie-goers, her lines uttered in long shots: "You hear the murmur of her voice, you never hear what she is saying and, if it is necessary to give her words meaning to the audience, I think we can always contrive to have some other character tell what the girl said." Lewton's notion received his RKO superiors' veto.[57]

Lewton ultimately cast aside the Balkan storyline in favor of a plot closer to home: "The characters in the run of the mill weird films were usually people very remote from the audiences' experiences. European nobles of dark antecedents, mad scientists, man-created monsters, and the like cavorted across the screen. It would be much more entertaining if people with whom audiences could identify were shown in contact with the strange, the weird, and the occult." To that end, Lewton created sets that reflected how real people lived. Commenting on the air of authenticity Lewton strove for, film historian Kim Newman observed: "*Cat People* is almost the first horror film to try and be credible. It's set in a real world — at least the people in the film have jobs, they have lives before the scary stuff comes along, before the supernatural intervenes."[58]

The opening shot of *Cat People* features a passage attributed to a work authored by one of the film's characters, Dr. Louis Judd, *The Anatomy of*

Atavism: "Even as fog continues to lie in the valleys, so does ancient sin cling to the low places, the depressions in the world consciousness." We are then introduced to Irena Dubrovna (Simone Simon), a fashion designer of Serbian extraction, who meets Oliver Reed (Kent Smith), a draftsman at a shipbuilding firm, while she is sketching a panther at the zoo. Visiting Irena at her apartment, Oliver asks about a statue of a king on horseback, holding his sword upright, a cat impaled on it. Irena tells him of her Serbian ancestry, how cats in her native country epitomized evil — in this instance "transformed versions of the dreaded enemy, the Mamlukes"—and how King John purged the land of cats. Oliver buys Irena a kitten as a gift but when he presents it to her, the animal reacts violently to her. When they return the kitten to the pet store, the other animals there also become extremely agitated at Irena's presence.

Quickly falling in love, Irena and Oliver marry. At their wedding party at a Serbian restaurant, a mysterious woman (Elizabeth Russell), whom one of the wedding guests describes as looking like a cat, rises and addresses Irena as *Moya sestra,* causing the latter to cross herself. Irena tells Oliver, "She called me sister."

Haunted by the legends of her native land, Irena refuses to consummate her marriage. When she tries to pick up the canary Oliver got as the replacement for the kitten, the bird dies of fright. Taking the bird to the panther's cage at the zoo, she tosses it to the cat. Oliver sends Irena to a psychiatrist, Dr. Louis Judd. Under hypnosis, she tells Judd of the beliefs of her village and of the cat-women who, when they kiss a man or become jealous, turn into great cats — panthers. The key to Irena's condition, Dr. Judd believes, is a childhood experience — the death of her father. As time passes, Irena becomes increasingly jealous of the proximity to Oliver of one of his co-workers, Alice Moore (Jane Randolph): one night, Irena catches the two of them together at a coffee shop adjacent to the firm they work for. As Alice leaves the coffee shop to go home, Irena follows her. As she walks, Alice becomes aware that she's being followed. We then hear the sound of what initially appears to be a panther's growl but, in reality, is the airbrake of a bus screeching as the vehicle stops.

After Alice boards the bus and the latter departs, the zookeeper finds a sheep has been slaughtered. When we next see Irena, she is wiping something from her mouth with a tissue. Presently, the audience is treated to another classic scene. Alice goes swimming in an indoor pool in the basement of her apartment building. As she prepares for the swim, she hears

Actress Simone Simon exudes menace as the title character in Val Lewton's feline take on lycanthropy, *Cat People* (1942) (RKO/Photofest).

a panther's growling coming from the steps. Frightened, she jumps into the pool. The walls of the dark room echo with the animal's growling, while a huge, black shadow is seen. Alice cries for help. The lights come on, and we see Irena, who has been looking for Oliver. When Alice asks for her robe, she finds it has been torn to ribbons.[59]

5. The War Years, Part I

Soon Oliver tells Irena the truth: He loves Alice, and will grant Irena a divorce. Telling Oliver to leave her, Irena rips the back of a couch, clawlike, with her fingers. Later, Irena, now transformed into the panther, confronts Oliver and Alice at their office. Using a T-square as a cross, Oliver drives her off, as though the cross were to Irena as it was to Dracula. Back at Irena's apartment, Dr. Judd, who has amorous designs on his patient, waits for her return. Taking her in his arms and kissing her, he unleashes the beast within Irena. She kills Judd but not before he stabs her with the sword from his cane, breaking it off in her shoulder.

Wounded from Dr. Judd's stabbing, Irena, now reverted back to human form, returns to the panther's cage, releasing the animal, who kills her, then is itself struck dead by a car. The film's concluding scene features the words of John Dunne's *Holy Sonnets V*: "But black sin hath betrayed to endless night; My world, both parts, and both parts must die."

6

The War Years, Part II: Horror Goes to War

Before the war Hollywood had considered making films dealing with the worsening international situation of the late 1930s but had shied away from doing so on account of a number of considerations: "industry policy" concerning films about other nations; Hollywood's dependence on the overseas film market for both revenue from its latest films and those that were no longer viewed in America but reissued to foreign audiences; the profound suspicions of Production Code Administration chief Joseph Breen that Jews in Hollywood, primarily writers, sought to use Nazi persecution of Jews to make propaganda films, which masked Breen's true concern about an attempt to *"capture the screen of the United States for Communistic propaganda purposes."*[1] Taking a lighthearted approach to military life, Hollywood in 1941 released *Buck Privates,* starring the comedy team of Abbott and Costello and featuring the singing trio the Andrews Sisters. "If ... 'Buck Privates' can be considered any criterion," said one review, "a draftee's life is just a jitterbug paradise, where comedians enliven the humdrum of work at camp, and hostesses ... pep up the boys with patriotic songs and boogie-woogie, strictly eight-to-the-bar." Naturally the success of *Buck Privates* spawned the release of other slapstick comedy military films.[2]

Once the United States was finally engulfed in the war, Hollywood, ever mindful of new angles, discarded neutrality, jumping into the war effort with both feet first. Not only was the war applied to comedies, it also found its way into seemingly unlikely genres: gangster, musical, and

Tarzan films.³ This also reflected the bewildered situation studio bosses found themselves in early in the war, what *The New York Times* saw as "...On the one hand studios have feverishly announced pictures about conflict, on the other, studios have already abandoned war stories and decided that pure escapism will be the only acceptable alternative..."⁴ This escapist trend was evident in early films with the Nazi menace. *Enemy Agents Meet Ellery Queen* (1942) had its detective hero thwarting Nazi agents in their quest for a Dutch diamond. Similarly, the Northwest Mounties frustrated the Nazis' in their search for a critical component for a new weapon in *Yukon Patrol* (1942). Not to be outdone by the Canadians, American cowboys frustrated another Nazi scheme, this time to acquire American horses for the service in Hitler's cause in *Phantom Plainsman*.⁵

Given this sort of movie fare, it was only natural that the horror film would be drafted into wartime service. Illustrative of this trend were a pair of 1942 releases, both Poverty Row productions. *Black Dragons* was rushed into production to capitalize on America's entry into the fighting. The film, which began shooting in January 1942, and was released by Monogram Studios, was the result of producer Sam Katzman's ambition to be the first filmmaker to depict Japanese villainy in the wake of Pearl Harbor.⁶ The inspiration for Katzman's film, originally called *The Yellow Menace,* was the real-life Black Dragon Society of Japan. The group, founded in 1901 and whose correct name, the Kokuryukai, or Amur River Association, was popularly incorrectly identified as "Black Dragon Society"— and had a long and violent history. Its members were homicidal zealots whose mission was conquest by war, and who hid their identities from each other by wearing a large overcoat, a broad-brimmed hat covering the wearer's head, and a lengthy, black, curling beard made of dyed silk. The Society's clandestine activities precipitated the 1904 Russo–Japanese War. This was only the beginning of the Dragons' nefarious activities: in the following years they murdered prime ministers who signed naval limitation treaties with the West and other public officials and those who dared oppose or denounce the Society. The assassins, once they had completed their murderous deeds, usually took their own lives as well. In what was the Dragons' boldest action, 3,000 soldiers (splitting up into teams of 60) captured all government offices, police stations and cable, radio and telephone headquarters in Tokyo on February 26, 1936, placing machine guns at every significant street intersection in the city. If a radio account of the Dragons' operations, broadcast in the United States in the immediate

One of Hollywood's first films about World War II following America's entry into the conflict, *Black Dragons*, a 1942 Poverty Row epic starring Bela Lugosi (left, with co-stars Joan Barclay and Clayton Moore), was part of an exploitation trend that characterized Hollywood's depiction of the war during the early months of American participation in the fighting (Monogram Pictures Corporation/Photofest).

pre–Pearl Harbor interval is credible, the Society had decided to extend its violence to the West in the form of a surprise attack against America and Britain, scheduled for August 26, 1941. The broadcast making this assertion aired after this date, and the narrator clarified that, owing to the situation on the German front, the attack had been rescheduled for November 26. Again there was a change in plans for, that day, the narrator was back with word that the Dragons' assault would be launched in early December. The warning received scant notice — until Pearl Harbor day.[7]

The word of the Dragons' planned strike at the western allies, coming as it did just before Pearl Harbor, made the Society a timely subject. The resulting film was characterized by *Variety* "Probably the most incredible of the film productions ... out of Hollywood since [the] outbreak of the war...."[8]

Opening in Washington in the immediate post–Pearl Harbor period, the film depicts a succession of disasters perpetrated by saboteurs — a group of spies sent to the United States with the objective of impeding the war effort. With this as a backdrop, a mysterious gentleman named Colomb (Bela Lugosi) arrives at the home of one of the agents, Dr. Saunders, explaining that he has come a long way to see the latter. Saunders claims not to remember Colomb — only to discover, too late for him, that he has indeed seen his caller before. A scream from Saunders' study brings his compatriots, only to find Saunders calmly telling them everything is fine, prompting the others to leave. Saunders then issues orders to his manservant to prepare the guest room for Colomb. When Kearney, another member of the spy ring who had remained behind to look-in on Saunders and Colomb, boards a cab, he discovers Colomb is sharing it with him! Shortly thereafter, Kearney's body is found on the steps of the now vacant Japanese embassy, a Japanese dagger in his hand.

Saunders' niece Alice returns to see her uncle after a long absence. Asked by her how long he plans to stay at her uncle's residence, Colomb replies, "It depends on circumstances."

Kearney's death is followed by another — that of a man named Wallace, who is also found clutching a Japanese dagger. His body is discovered in his hotel room by two of his fellow spies, Ryder and Van Dyke. The latter, unnerved by Wallace's death, wants to call the police. "You fool," Ryder admonishes. "Do you want them prying around in our business...? Don't you realize we're at war with this country? Brace yourself. We're forewarned, now we're forearmed." When Ryder tries to see Saunders, he tells the latter that Van Dyke is about to crack and is ordered to dispose of him; this he does but both he and Van Dyke fatally shoot each other in a struggle. The dying Ryder is astonished to see Colomb, who laughingly tells him, "You were both very accommodating.... Thank you." Its clear that Colomb arranged to have both men kill themselves, making Colomb's task much simpler.

In an attempt to force the murderer out into the open, the government enlists the aid of one of the remaining spies, a banker named Hanlin, to act as a decoy. Colomb, who had previously left Saunders' residence, returns and murders Hanlin but not before the latter shoots him. Saunders, whom Colomb had drugged and confined to a bedroom, reappears and reveals Colombo's true identity: Dr. Milcher, a Nazi plastic surgeon on loan to the Japanese from Hitler, who was commissioned to transform members of the Black Dragon Society into leading American industrialists as part of a plan to disrupt the American war effort. However, once Milcher's services had been rendered, his Japanese "allies" showed their gratitude by imprisoning him so that the Dragons' true identities would remain secret. Making himself up to resemble a man already occupying the cell with him, Milcher escaped to America, driven, not by loyalty to the Axis' cause, but revenge — murdering each member of the spy ring.

In analyzing Lugosi's role in *Black Dragons,* film historian Rick Worland has concluded that, though Bela was playing a Nazi plastic surgeon, his role was simply an extension of his earlier and most famous characterization: Dracula. To substantiate his argument, Worland observes that *Black Dragons* borrowed a device from *Dracula* to stress Lugosi's sinister presence: closeup shots of his "searing eyes" that originally denoted "the hypnotic threat of the vampire." Worland continues: "Within its limited means, *Black Dragons* thus associates the supernatural threat of Dracula with a popularized caricature of fascist ideology. In one of the most florid lines of the time, Dracula-as-Nazi-fanatic coolly avers, 'Anything I can do to hasten the establishment of our New Order and to destroy the archaic democracies in an honor and a privilege.'"[9]

The Wolf Man's success for Universal clearly inspired *The Mad Monster,* another Poverty Row release, this time from Producers Releasing Corporation (PRC). Filmed in March 1942 and released two months later, the film stands out for two reasons: it boasted America's first *patriotic* mad scientist and was one of the few Poverty Row films dealing with lycanthropy.[10] The film's mad scientist character, Dr. Lorenzo Cameron (George Zucco), extracts blood from a wolf which he then turns into a serum and injects into Petro (Glenn Strange), a naive man-child who works as a hired-hand for Cameron. As the latter watches, Petro transforms into a werewolf— only this time the monster resulted from scientific means, not the supernatural as was the case with Lon Chaney, Jr's Lawrence Talbot. Earlier Cameron had earned the ridicule of his peers in the scientific community over his theory that blood can be transfused from one species to another. His motive for such an experiment is that it will aid the war effort: "You're aware, of course, this country is at war, and our armed forces are locked in combat with a savage horde who fight with fanatical fury." Such fury, Cameron continues, "will avail them nothing when I place my new serum at the disposal of the War Department. Just picture gentlemen: an army of wolf-men — fearless, raging. Every man a snarling animal. My serum will make it possible to unloose millions of such animal-men — men who are governed by one collective thought, the animal lust to kill without regard to personal safety. Such an army will be invincible. Such an army will sweep everything before it."

After administering the antidote to Petro, the latter regains consciousness, saying he had a bad dream: he ran around trying to kill people. "What does a dream like that mean, doctor...? Why should I be trying to kill people...? I ain't got nothin' against nobody." Plot-wise, *The Mad Monster* closely resembles Universal's earlier release, *Man Made Monster:* both films feature an unsuspecting individual who falls into the clutches of diabolical scientists who use them as guinea pigs to fulfill grandiose schemes of conquest. In Petro's case, he is the first recruit in Cameron's proposed "wolf man" army, one who must be taught to overcome his reluctance to kill. The following evening he does just that: sent out into the swamp after another of Cameron's treatments, he kills the daughter of a local resident.

Instead of turning his serum over to the government for the war effort, Cameron unleashes his wolf man creation on those responsible for his ostracism from the scientific community. In this, Cameron resembles Hitler: both are outcasts who seek the destruction of those they felt denied them the realization of their goals. Presently, an unforseen complication arises: beginning to feel killer urges within himself, Petro transforms into the beast without benefit of Cameron's serum. Like a good drill sergeant, Cameron has succeeded only too well in liberating Petro from his natural abhorrence toward killing. Like Dr. Frankenstein's and Dr. Jekyll's creations, Cameron's ultimately turns on him: during a thunderstorm, Cameron's residence goes up in flames when struck by lightening; Petro, in his werewolf form, murders his creator and, in turn, is consumed in the fire.[11]

OWI Enters the Picture

Black Dragons and *The Mad Monster* represented the kind of exploitation fare that dominated Hollywood's war-related films before the creation of the federal government's Bureau of Motion Pictures (BMP). The BMP was part of the Domestic Operations Branch of the Office of War Information (OWI). Created by presidential executive order on June 13, 1942, OWI's mission was to "undertake campaigns to enhance understanding of the war at home and abroad; to coordinate government information activities; and to handle liaison with the press, radio, and motion pictures." The BMP's overriding assignment, as expressed by the slogan "Will This Picture Help Win the War?" was to ascertain if Hollywood productions contributed to or detracted from the government's propaganda program as measured by their impact domestically and abroad, and recommend changes. The OWI lacked the authority to act as a censor, nor were the film studios required to cooperate with it, as evidenced by the fact that Paramount declined to submit just about anything to BMP's scrutiny. The BMP primarily sought to gain Hollywood's cooperation through patriotic entreaties. In 1943, after the OWI's Domestic Operations Branch ceased to exist as a result of losing its funding due to the actions of revitalized congressional Republicans who viewed the department as merely an instrument for advancing the New Deal, the new leader of BMP's Hollywood office, Ulric Bell, allied the bureau with the federal Office of Censorship. The latter, acting on the basis of national security, could decide whether a film was to receive an export license for overseas distribution. When BMP began appraising motion pictures solely in light of what their likely impact would be abroad, Bell increasingly affiliated his bureau with the Office of Censorship — the latter preparing its own more demanding criteria for film exportation. In this new atmosphere, Hollywood had a crucial new incentive to cooperate with OWI: the promise of reopened film markets in those countries the Allies liberated.

The evaluation of a film's merits was conducted, in Worland's words, "on a case-by-case basis. The BMP files indicate that producers were most likely to submit scripts that directly addressed the war in context or genre, though BMP sought to examine a broad selection of stories that could have a bearing on the war information campaign, however indirect or implicit." A process of negotiation characterized the way the BMP and Hollywood conducted their business.

When it came to horror films, the BMP was never instinctively antagonistic toward them, nor was it especially concerned about what unfavorable propaganda influence such films had "per se." Unlike the British government, which imposed a blackout on horror films in mid-1942 — owing to the civilian casualties resulting from the Battle of Britain and British defeats on the battlefield in 1940-1941 — the American government never entertained the thought of cracking down on the horror genre, as the latter's violent and gory aspects fell under the regulation of the

Production Code Administration. After viewing one Universal horror offering, 1943's *Son of Dracula,* a BMP analyst passed it with a clean bill of health: "This is a story of pure fantasy which could not possibly be confused with reality anywhere in the world. In consequence, it has no bearing whatever on the War Information Program, domestic or overseas."*[12]

Where horror films did arouse OWI's misgivings occurred when they utilized the war as a backdrop for "fantasy" productions and racist depictions of non–Caucasian characters — the latter often being the case in wartime zombie films — and false representations of American allies. In such instances, the BMP sought to change the film's content or prevent it from being shown abroad. Such strictures weren't applied exclusively to the horror genre. No matter what category a film fell into, if it violated any of these guidelines, it incurred the BMP's disapproval.

One of the first films to receive BMP's scrutiny was *Invisible Agent.*[13] Release some months after *Black Dragons* and, like the former, a horror-espionage film, *Invisible Agent,* part of Universal's Invisible Man series, was billed as a straight dramatic war film, yet in the words of film historians Tom Weaver and Michael and John Brunas, "is very much a tongue-in-cheek affair" that closely resembles a Saturday afternoon matinee serial. "The studio's decision to upgrade the potboiler storyline into a minor A production with a prominent producer and a strong cast might have been owing to the fact that H. G. Wells was still a literary figure to be reckoned with and that Universal's contract with the author's estate was still in effect." Highly successful at the box office, *Invisible Agent* earned well over $1,000,000 in profits, yet in no way was drawn from Wells' original novel, save for using the name Frank Griffin and the invisibility idea.[14]

Written by Curt Siodmak, the film opens as a group of men, led by Nazi officer Conrad Stauffer (Sir Cedric Hardwicke) and his Japanese confederate Baron Ikito (Peter Lorre), enter the print shop of Frank Griffin (Jon Hall), grandson of the original Invisible Man, who now conceals his identity under an assumed name. Stauffer and Ikito have tracked Griffin down to offer him money for his grandfather's invisibility formula to be used by the Axis powers. When Griffin refuses the offer, his "guests" put his fingers inside his paper-cutter; relenting, Griffin pretends to cooperate, only to knock out the lights in his shop and escape. Asked by his own government for the drug, Griffin again refuses, saying there'll never be a sufficiently critical emergency to justify its use. The sufficiently critical emergency comes in the form of Pearl Harbor. Griffin finally consents to the use of his drug by the Allies — on condition that *he* is the one to use it. Washington accepts his terms: Griffin will be dropped into enemy territory to gather details concerning an Axis plot to disrupt American war production — much the same as in *Black Dragons*.

Flying over Berlin under anti-aircraft fire, Griffin administers himself the invisibility drug, then parachutes out of the plane; floating down to earth as the drug takes affect, he removes all his clothing. Griffin then makes his way to the shop of his Berlin contact, a carpenter, who in turn, furnishes him the name and address of another agent, Maria (Ilona Massey), who will provide him the information on the German war plans he needs. Griffin arrives at her place just in time to witness her dinner with Gestapo operative Karl Heiser (J. Edward Bromberg), who is romantically interested in her. During the course of the dinner, Heiser tells Maria that Hitler himself revealed to him plans and the date for an attack upon the United States. All the while Griffin, unseen by all, uses his invisibility to have fun at Heiser's expense — finally dumping the dinning table and its contents upon him, soiling his uniform. Enraged, Heiser places Maria under house arrest. When Nazi guards manhandle her, Griffin comforts her with an invisible kiss.

"Oh, I wish I could see you," she says.

"Very well, then you shall see me." Applying Maria's cold cream to himself, Griffin makes himself visible, then, under the drug's influence, falls asleep. While he sleeps, his old adversary Stauffer appears, accompanied by Heiser, forcing Maria to remove the cold cream from Griffin's face. Thinking Heiser to be disloyal to the Nazi party, Stauffer has him arrested, then tells Maria he must return to his office to await files concerning the Nazis' plans for the United States — an operation she'll have an important role in.

While Stauffer has been conversing with Maria, Griffin has slipped out and gone to Stauffer's office to find the Axis' plans. Instead he finds himself in a trap set by Stauffer, who knew of Griffin's invisibility and will permit the invisible spy to live in exchange for the invisibility formula. Griffin then starts a fire in Stauffer's office and summons the fire department. In a sequence no doubt intended to make the Nazis look ridiculous, Griffin thwarts their attempts to seize him, then scurries down the fire truck ladder outside, taking with him a list of German and Japanese agents working in America. After giving it to his carpenter contact for immediate transmission to England, he contacts Maria. In the interim,

Stauffer's men search among the litter in his office for the missing list. At this moment Baron Ikito arrives — a sequence revealing the awkward relationship between the two Axis "allies":

> STAUFFER: Allow me to congratulate you upon the speed of your news service, Baron. One minute sooner and you'd have beaten the fire engines.
> IKITO: And perhaps caught Griffin. Tell me, sir, that book listing our agents in the United States — it's still in your possession, of course.... When you asked me to let you have that book, you promised to guard it with your life ... you know, of course, that should the names of so many of our loyal agents fall into the wrong hands, it would cost me my life.... In my country when a man makes a mistake — Uh, would you mind showing me that book? As only one copy exists, its safekeeping would comfort me.
> STAUFFER: Unfortunately, other people's comfort is not my strong suit, Baron.... May I remind you that though we are Axis partners, you are still on German soil. Our code demands that we do only what we consider best for our own welfare.
> IKITO: ... And at the moment, my welfare is not related to yours.
> STAUFFER: You are very discerning, Baron. I cannot allow my judgment to be influenced by consideration of your welfare.
> IKITO: I'm sure that you won't mind, then, my informing the Japanese government about your unique handling of our affairs.
> STAUFFER: Do what you like, Ikito, but you are still in Germany!
> IKITO: I've never been more aware of it.

The next sequence, occurring in Heiser's jail cell, provided Siodmak another opportunity to express the sentiments of war — this time America's view. The Invisible Agent enters Heiser's cell just before he's scheduled to be executed. The disgraced Nazi, reduced to eating "pig slop" after his more exotic diet of lobster, is taunted by Griffin:

> You're only getting what you deserve.... You've sent thousands of innocent people to these rat holes. Now you're in one yourself! In a few hours, you'll be shot. You know how it'll happen, exactly how. You've given the orders yourself too often.... Did you think those murders would help you? You're as good as dead, Heiser.... Most of your victims were driven insane before they died, the way you'll die tonight..... You're going to die, Heiser. You're going to pay for just one of the crimes you've committed in the name of your party — to cover up your own greed and brutality. Your kind doesn't just kill men. You murder their spirit. You strangle the last breath of hope and freedom so that you, the chosen few, can rule your slaves in ease and luxury. You're a sadist just like the others, Heiser, with no resource but violence and no feeling but fear, the kind you're feeling now! You're drowning, Heiser, drowning in the ocean of blood around this barren little island you call "The New Order." One of your own gang pushed you off. Someone else'll push him off. And that's how you'll all go, killing your own, dog eating dog, until only the biggest and hungriest are left. You were a little dog, Heiser, and they're pretending you're mad so they can shoot you tonight.

Peter Lorre (left) and Sir Cedric Hardwicke (center) formed an uneasy Axis partnership in Universal's *Invisible Agent* (1942), starring Jon Hall (right) as the invisible spy (Universal Pictures/Photofest).

In exchange for his freedom, Heiser reveals the plans of the enemy's attack on the United States: an aerial attack on New York, sabotage of American industry, destruction of public utilities. The attack will begin that very night. With this information in hand, Griffin helps Heiser escape.

Returning to the carpenter shop, Griffin walks right into another trap: he's snared in a fish-hook net setup by Baron Ikito who takes both him and Maria prisoner to the Japanese embassy. In exchange for the secret of the invisibility drug, Ikito promises that Maria will be set free. The latter, acting as a member of the German Secret Police, demands that Griffin be turned over to her custody. When Ikito refuses to comply, Maria says, "...You double-crossed your own allies." "Our alliance," Ikito explains, "is desirable only as long as it serves Japan." When Stauffer and his men arrive, Griffin ferrets Maria out while Nazis and Japs flail away at each other.

"May I remind you, sir, that this embassy is Japanese territory?" Ikito admonishes Stauffer.

"Only so long as it suits our purpose, Baron."

As Griffin and Maria escape, Stauffer orders his men after them. "Wait a minute, sir," says Ikito. "Griffin escaped. You won't." Ikito then flips Stauffer, then picks up a dagger. "You have failed, Stauffer. We have both failed.... I'm going to make an honorable man even out of you." After he stabs Stauffer to death, Ikito atones for his own failure by committing hara-kiri. Heiser, who believes he'll succeed Stauffer now that the latter is dead, is ultimately shot as a traitor.

Reaching the airport, Griffin and Maria commandeer a plane and take-off, then bomb the airfield and the bombers set to attack New York, delaying the planned assault by a few hours. Evading German anti-aircraft fire, the duo head for England, only having to parachute out when the British open fire on them. Back in England, Griffin learns that Maria, in fact, is a British agent. Maria, in turn, finally sees Griffin as he truly is now that the effect of the invisibility drug has dissipated.

In addition to being horror-espionage films, *Black Dragons* and *Invisible Agent* share another theme: both films depict the German Nazis and the Japanese as mutually suspicious of one another. In the case of *Black Dragons,* this mutual distrust is tinged with racism. When Lugosi's Dr. Melcher is interred by the Japanese to ensure that the true identities of the Japanese agents he transformed into Americans will remain secret, Melcher declares: "You will pay for this, you apes, you swine. The Fuhrer will wipe you off the face of the Earth." Melcher's use of the word "apes" is quite revealing: during World War II Westerners of all kinds — writers and cartoonists, Allied political and military figures, U.S. Marines — employed simian imagery to characterize the Japanese: "beastly little monkeys," "apes in khaki," "monkeymen," "yellow monkeys," "Japes" (a fusion of the words "Japs" and "apes"). In January 1942, when Japanese forces took Singapore via the Malay Peninsula, rumor had it that the Japanese achieved this victory by swinging from tree to tree. This provided the basis for a cartoon in the British magazine *Punch,* "The Monkey Folk," featuring helmet-clad, rifle toting monkeys swinging through the jungle. Though the simian metaphor was sometimes applied to the Nazis, "this was a passing metaphor, a sign of aberration and atavism, and did not carry the explicit racial connotations of the Japanese ape."[15] Japanese were also depicted as reptiles or insects. "A Lesson in Japanese," an installment of radio's *The*

Treasury Star Parade, utilized both simian and reptilian imagery to characterize America's foe:

> Listen! Have you ever watched a well-trained monkey at the zoo! Have you seen how carefully he imitates his trainer...? The monkey goes through so many human movements so well that he actually seems to *be* human! But under his fur, he's still a savage little beast!
> Now consider the imitative little Japanese ... who for seventy-five years has built himself into something so closely resembling a civilized human being that he actually believes he is just that.
> You know, snakes have the same characteristic — hissing! What a sharp similarity.... The Japanese — some of them painted green — some of them covered with green mosquito netting — wiggling their way across the ground on the plains of Luzon — through the jungles of Java — the hills of Burma — Listen!
> [A soft hissing building under]
> Do you hear them...? Do you hear the little green snakes?[16]

Sir Cedric Hardwicke and Peter Lorre, the Axis villains of *Invisible Agent,* were two of many actors, some of them of German and *Mittel Europa* background, drafted by Hollywood to play Nazis. In Lorre's case, he played Nazi and Japanese rogues.[17] In reviewing the two actors' performances in *Invisible Agent,* Tom Weaver and Michael and John Brunas opined:

> Far and away the best thing about *Invisible Agent* is the casting of Sir Cedric Hardwicke and Peter Lorre as representatives of the Axis. Their scenes are a casebook example of how a bit of stylish acting can transcend routinely written roles. Siodmak couches both characters well within the guidelines of wartime stereotypes: Hardwicke, the steely, ruthless German; Lorre, the insidious, catlike Japanese with a sadistic streak a mile wide....
> A partnership of convenience, Stauffer and Ikito's alliance is an uneasy one at best, roughly parallel to actual German-Japanese relations at the time. At every opportunity, Siodmak depicts them as cutthroats plotting against each other whenever the other's back is turned, their feigned politeness hinting at the mutual contempt lurking beneath the surface. When both rivals fail to deliver the Invisible Man to their governments, Ikito is bound by custom to do the only "honorable thing," disemboweling Stauffer with a hara-kiri knife before turning it on himself. The camera lingers on both their bodies in a bitter political statement that's easily the strongest scene in the film.[18]

Screenwriter Siodmak, having fled Nazi Germany, enjoyed ridiculing the Nazis in his screenplay for the film, which prompted a contemporary reviewer to question whether it was wise to underrate the very genuine menace the Nazis posed. In a scene deleted from the film — an action taken, according to the film's pressbook, owing to an injunction against lodging personal attacks on enemy despots — the Invisible Agent kicked Hitler in the latter's posterior! The monologue Griffin delivers in Heiser's jail cell was clearly indicative of Siodmak's viewpoints.[19]

While Griffin's ability to singlehandedly set Stauffer and Baron Ikito at each other's throat's annoyed the BMP ("[T]he equivalent of Superman vs. the Nazis," complained a reviewer), what truly disturbed the bureau was what Worland called *Invisible Agent's* "comic treatment" of America's Axis adversaries. "German officers and their men become modern Keystone Cops"; "The head of the Secret Police is a burlesque edition of Heinrich Himmler, an awkward nitwit who … in moment of apoplectic rage, jams his cap on backwards." Especially disturbing to the BMP was Baron Ikito's slaying of Stauffer and his own suicide thereafter as these "would serve to prove that the Germans and the Japanese are unwilling partners and really hate each other," when the truth of the matter was that the Nazis and Japanese had no use for each other.[20]

When it came to how Hollywood portrayed non–Western peoples, OWI desired that they not be presented as primitive and superstitious as this suggested white supremacy. In stressing this point, OWI sought to eliminate stereotypes for the purpose of encouraging black Americans to join the war effort as well as rebut Nazi racist doctrines and Japanese propaganda aimed at winning the support of peoples of color. An example of OWI's concerns in this area was the considerable amount of attention it paid to the B level production, *Revenge of the Zombies.* Featuring John Carradine in the villain's role, the film presented the tale of a Nazi scientist, Von Altman, and his attempt to aid the Axis cause by creating an army of zombies. After studying a script draft for the film, BMP, though it lamented the presentation of The Enemy, was more unsettled by the overt racist aspects it contained. Von Altman killed his American wife to expedite his experiments , yet, when she becomes a zombie, proves more resistant than the local blacks, whom Von Altman characterizes as being "of a lower mentality." Von Altman's description is virtually the same as that of the white American hero, who calls the local black people "a lot of ignorant natives."

Branding the screenplay "at variance with our government's war information policy abroad," reviewer Lillian Bergquist wrote: "The Negroes … are presented as a strange, uncivilized and superstitious group of people living in a world quite apart from that of other Americans. They are either comic servants, zombies, or in the case of Manny Beulah, a voodoo-ist. There is not one real Negro American in this story." This demeaning representation of black Americans "serves to confirm Japanese propaganda which tells dark-skinned peoples that under fascism they will receive fairer treatment than under democracy" and "this could also have the effect of alienating our dark-skinned allies from the United Nations' cause." In an internal memo, Bell called the script "the most irresponsible story I have yet seen out of Monogram" and, in Rick Worland's words, "raised the veiled threat of censorship, urging that 'Monogram should be advised that it will in all probability be impossible to obtain an export license for *Revenge of the Zombies,*' a point duly communicated to" Monogram producer Lindsley Parsons.

Evidently Monogram took the hint seriously. After studying the release print in July 1943, a BMP analyst observed that specific objections BMP's study of the film's early draft screenplay had made had been corrected; yet there remained a problem:

> Von Altman no longer makes zombies only of Negroes as was the case in the script. Of his six zombies, three are Negro and three are white, and references to the Negroes' being "ignorant natives" and of "a lower mentality" have been eliminated. Von Altman now refers to "my country" to which he will return for the creation of his zombie army, and nowhere in the film is his nationality named. The obvious inference, however, is that he is a German.
>
> Because the story presents our Nazi enemies unrealistically, the Overseas Branch of OWI cannot recommend its distribution overseas.

True to form, *Revenge of the Zombies* concludes with Von Altman's zombie army revolting against its master. Ironically, this conclusion fell in line with another OWI edict for, as Worland writes, this produces "a weird compliance with OWI entreaties for ethnically mixed combat platoons whose melting-pot democracy would defeat an arrogant 'master' race."*[21]

Another wartime horror film, *The Mummy's Ghost,* released by Universal in 1944, illustrated another point of concern with OWI: the depiction of America's allies. Though the film's storyline in no way pertained to the war, BMP's analyst found the screenplay lacking when it came to how it presented the religion, culture, and peoples of modern Egypt and the Middle East:

> Ahmed Bey, a modern Egyptian, is sworn to carry out the will of the ancient gods. He controls the will of the monster-mummy killer. Besides Amina (the girl of Egyptian descent who shudders at the mention of Egypt), Ahmed Bey, the monster, and the weird priests of Karnak are the only representatives of the Egyptian people in the story.... How would Egyptians (or the many people who look to that country as the leader in the Arab-Moslem world) react to this presentation of the cult of Karnak, which is an actual part of their history...? Could they infer that Amina's reference to Egypt as a place of "dark tombs and passages ... rot, decay and death" is representative of American attitudes toward their country?

... The script should definitely be checked by OWI authorities on the Middle East before any recommendation is made by this office, to avoid any misrepresentation which could prove offensive to our allies in this strategic war theater.

Worland felt this closing recommendation, "quite unusual among BMP reviews," must be considered within the context of the recent Allied victory in North Africa in mid–May 1943 — a triumph in which Egypt had played a strategically significant part — the successful invasion of Sicily, and Mussolini's ouster from power in Italy (July and August), which had focused American attention on the Mediterranean theater of war.

Acting in accord with the recommendation of its Los Angeles reviewer, the Washington office of OWI sought the advice from a gentleman, whose position and credentials made him an unlikely source of counsel for a Hollywood horror programmer — Dr. John S. Badeau. A former American authority on the Near East, Dr. Badeau had, before the war, served as dean of the College of Arts and Sciences at the American University of Cairo, and had recently penned *East and West of Suez: The Story of Modern Egypt*, the latter part of an informational series by the Foreign Policy Association that discussed how the history and culture of that area of the world immediately pertained to the war. Dr. Badeau apparently undertook this newest assignment with gusto! The recommendations he produced were sent to OWI, and were then relayed to the BMP's Los Angeles Office and ultimately to Universal Studios. The latter's front office received a memo from the film's executive producer, Joseph Gershenson: "I have read the OWI comments on our script, *The Mummy's Return* [the film's original title], and whatever specific objections were mentioned, we have tried to correct them." Universal adhered to the majority of Badeau's culturally sensitive recommendations. The name of the ancient Egyptian cult of Karnak became Arkham; the heroine's original name of Amina El-Harun (branded "an Arabic phony" by Badeau) became a more genuine surname provided by Badeau-Mansoury; Ahmed Bey was rechristened Yousef Bey to eschew a specifically Moslem name given a nefarious character adhering to the creeds of the ancients — something Badeau considered heretical to modern Moslems: "[T]o picture a Moslem forsaking his faith to become a priest of the old idol-worship of Egypt would certainly be highly unpalatable to any Moslem audience," a "major difficulty" of the screenplay he stressed that "makes [the movie] practically unusable for Near Eastern countries."

While Yousef Bey would ultimately continue in his characterization

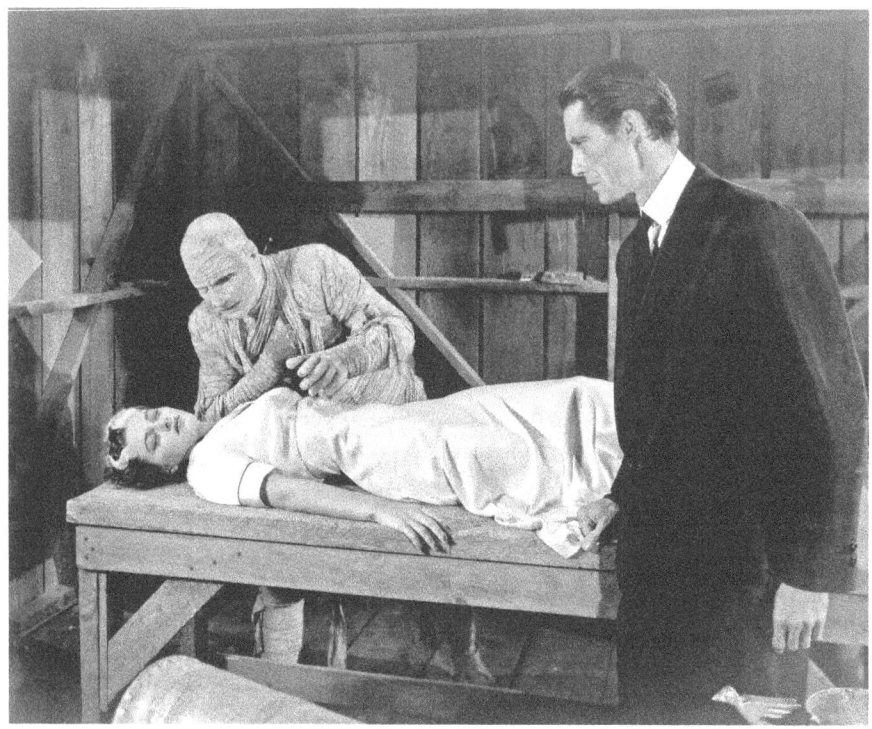

Kharis the Mummy (Lon Chaney, Jr.) views the reincarnation of his long-lost love, Princess Ananka (Ramsay Ames), while Yousef Bey (John Carradine) looks on in *The Mummy's Ghost* (1944) — a film whose depiction of Egypt and its people and religious beliefs drew the concern of the federal government's Office of War Information that it presented a wartime ally in an unfavorable light (Universal Pictures/Photofest).

as a nefarious priest of the mummy cult, Gershenson changed or eliminated numerous objectionable lines of dialogue, among them those describing Egypt with the terms "rot, decay, and death," that had disturbed BMP's initial reviewer. Gershenson concluded that the adherents of the ancient cult signified "a group within a large country [that] is not necessarily recognized by the people in that country, any more than certain gangs and subversive groups in this country are an indication of the general American public." These changes, along with others Universal made in the screenplay, apparently succeeded in placating OWI. "Subsequent internal correspondence praised Universal's cooperation and compliance with government concerns about the project."[22]

The inspiration for another war-themed horror film was a 1943 theatrical revival of *Dracula*, featuring Bela Lugosi, that toured East Coast venues (Boston, Buffalo, Pittsburgh, Philadelphia, Cleveland, and Washington, D.C.), with performances at army camps along the way. That the play was showing its age and the audience was more sophisticated in no way diminished Lugosi's performance; a Cleveland critic noted: "Mr. Lugosi, who is an expert at that sort of thing, was in fine form. His face wore a deep and frightening scowl. His long, slender fingers were always clutching ... clutching. And his eyes were like embers. Even when you knew that this awful blood-sucking vampire or werewolf... was just something someone dreamed up in an unusually wacky moment, Mr. Lugosi made it seem pretty real."[23]

The success of the revived stage production of *Dracula* may have been the impetus for Universal and Columbia to consider producing their own respective vampire films. Universal's entry, the aforementioned *Son of Dracula*, starred Lon Chaney, Jr., in the title role under the name Count Alucard (Dracula spelled backward). Over at Columbia, the writing of their script began in June 1943 on what could have been titled *Dracula and the Wolfman*, as the vampire was joined in his vile activities by a werewolf assistant. Because Universal felt that they owned the rights to the name Dracula, the moniker of Columbia's vampire became Armand Tesla and the film dubbed *Vampires of London*. Before cameras rolled on the production, the title was changed to *The Return of the Vampire*.[24]

Beginning its story shortly before the end of World War I, *The Return of the Vampire* shows how, in October 1918, Lady Jane Ainsley (Freda Inescort) and her mentor, Dr. Walter Saunders, treated a woman for a mysterious ailment. Saunders spends the night studying the writings of a Romanian scientist, Dr. Armand Tesla, who lived two centuries earlier. Unknown to Dr. Saunders and Lady Jane, Tesla still lives as a vampire and was responsible for the attack on their patient; Tesla now attacks Saunders' granddaughter Nicki. Finding Tesla asleep in his coffin sanctuary in an abandoned graveyard, Saunders and Lady Jane destroy the monster and, in so doing, liberate his werewolf slave, Andreas Obry (Matt Willis), from his domination.

Years later, with Britain again at war and London in the midst of the German Blitz, a German bomber drops its payload on the abandoned graveyard, disinterring Tesla's coffin. In the aftermath of the Blitz, two gravediggers find Tesla's body, complete with the metal spike that held him down during all this time; thinking the spike is a bomb splinter, they remove it, thereby reviving the vampire. It doesn't take long for Tesla to find and once more enslave Andreas, whom Lady Jane rehabilitated and now employs as an assistant. Again a werewolf, Andreas helps Tesla pose as Dr. Hugo Bruckner, a refugee scientist Lady Jane helped escape from the Nazis. It is now Tesla's aim to avenge himself against Lady Jane by striking at her through those closest to her. He begins by enslaving Nicki (Nina Foch); under his influence, she attacks her fiancée, John Ainsley, Lady Jane's son. Lady Jane, however, accurately deduces that John's real assailant was Tesla. The latter finally summons Nicki to him, taking her to his hideout among the bombed ruins of London. Just as he is about to complete Nicki's transformation into one of the undead, Andreas, now dying from a police bullet and no longer in Tesla's favor, flashes a cross in front of the vampire, foiling his plans for Nicki. Another German bomb knocks everyone unconscious. Regaining consciousness, Andreas drags Tesla into the sunlight, then drives a stake into his chest. The combination of this and the sun's rays finally end Tesla's vampiric existence and frees Nicki from his spell. Though he too dies, Andreas does so a free man.

The Return of the Vampire can be viewed as an allegorical retelling of British history during the interwar period. Indeed, Armand Tesla's original demise, coming as it did in the closing weeks of World War I, closely parallels the end of that conflict. This was followed by the vampire's long sleep during the interval between the two world wars — one during which both Tesla and the simmering issues left unresolved by the first war awaited their respective opportunities to come to life once more. Finally, the vampire is restored to life in the midst of the German Blitz of London; the monster's resurrection epitomizes the renewal of hostilities in this new conflict. One of the film's main characters, a Scotland Yard inspector, is skeptical of Lady Jane's assertion that Tesla is a vampire. Similarly, British Prime Minister Neville Chamberlain ignored the genuine threat posed by Nazi Germany — at great cost to his country and the world.

The Return of the Vampire offered another wartime metaphor as well: the new role of women, specifically in the form of Lady Jane Ainsley, who assumes the traditionally male role of vampire hunter.

The belief that women lacked the capacity to comprehend machines and that their presence would distract their male colleagues made factory managers initially reluctant to hire women. Of the estimated 750,000 women who applied for jobs in war plants in the six-month period after

Pearl Harbor, only about 80,000 received employment. The manpower shortage the war created made it necessary to revise old-fashioned notions of what a woman's place was: An intensive recruitment drive for female laborers was initiated. Emblematic of this campaign was "Rosie the Riveter"; posters featuring Rosie's image became commonplace, along with feature stories of real-life "Rosies." "If you can drive a car you can run a machine," exhorted a Connecticut ordinance plant in its drive to hire an additional 5,000 female employees.

Not only was women's participation in the labor force a production necessity, it confirmed the total war effort on the home front. "The traditional picture of the all–American girl with the toothy smile was supplanted by the image of a dirt-streaked face beneath hair bound up in a bandanna. Military photographers were often assigned to factories to get that morale-boosting new image to relay to the forces overseas." By the

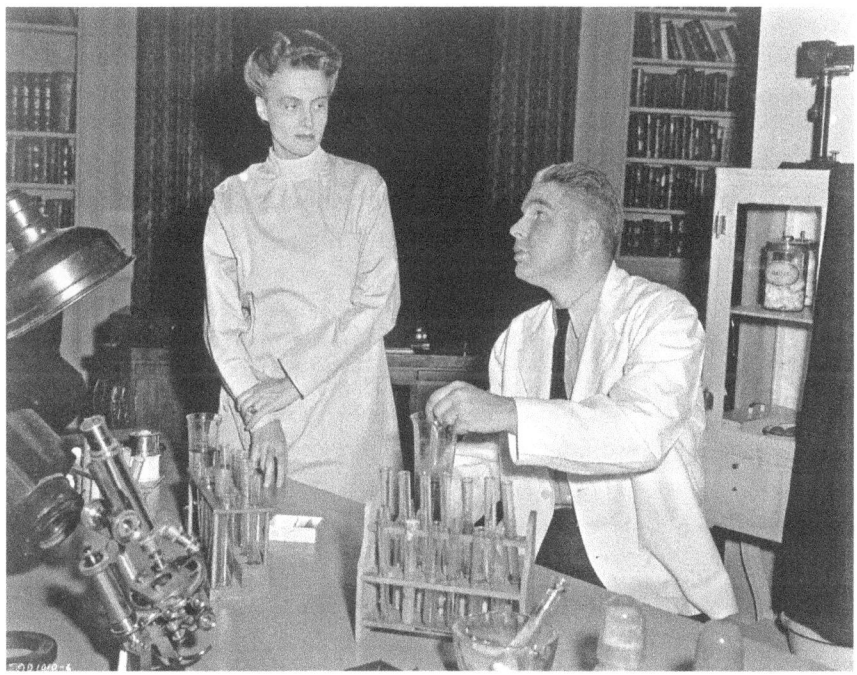

A wartime feminist character. Frieda Inescort (right) played the traditionally male part of vampire hunter in Columbia Pictures' *The Return of the Vampire* (1944). Matt Willis plays her lab assistant, Andreas Obry (Columbia Pictures/Photofest).

war's conclusion, prejudices toward a woman's presence in the workplace had diminished, and the majority of Americans were ready to acknowledge that women doing their part for the war effort had been a vital factor in attaining victory.[25]

Thus, by the time *The Return of the Vampire* was released, the idea of a strong woman vampire hunter wasn't a farfetched notion. The beginning of the film shows how Lady Jane learned the art of vampire hunting from Dr. Saunders, who then disappears completely from the remainder of the film. When Armand Tesla is revived during the London Blitz, it is Lady Jane, with virtually no male assistance, who destroys the monster. Scotland Yard's Sir Frederic Fleet's skepticism toward her claim that the vampire exists renders Sir Frederic a virtually ineffective figure — though his disbelief stems, not from the fact of Lady Jane's gender, but mere rationality; vampires just don't exist. Worland noted that, at the film's conclusion, Lady Jane "pointedly leaves" her injured daughter-in-law to view Tesla's decaying remains in daylight, "showing determination to see the thing though. At this level," Worland believes, the film "has a closer relationship historically and intertextually to movies such as *Mrs. Miniver* and the nurses-in-combat film *So Proudly We Hail!* ... than to *Dracula*."[26]

Contemporary reviews of *The Return of the Vampire* failed to take note of its female vampire slayer — an oversight attributable to a pair of considerations: the low regard horror films were held in and the presence of Bela Lugosi in the film. And the fact that the BMP's film analysis staff, the boss of which was Dorothy B. Jones, and the staff of which was composed mainly of women and "sharply attuned to what women meant to the war and what the war meant to women," did not prevent the film from receiving a blistering condemnation from one staff member, Lillian R. Bergquist, who "failed to note any protofeminist implication in Lady Jane's role":

> *Return of the Vampire* uses the war as a background for a sensational melodrama, mixing the very real horrors of this war with a fantastic story about the supernatural. Much of the action takes place while London is defending itself against the blitz, and there are numerous shots of ruined buildings and homes. Some documentary footage is used in this film. Besides being in extremely bad taste, a picture of this type suggests that Americans fail to take the war seriously and regard it merely as a convenient peg on which to hang a yarn.
> This picture was granted an export license (10/30/43). However this office cannot recommend *Return of the Vampire* for overseas distribution.

While conceding that a film "that showed how to combat a profascist vampire in one's hometown did not treat a significant war problem or issue as defined by OWI," Worland nevertheless contends that "in its portrayal of a competent and resourceful woman in a nontraditional genre and social role, *Return of the Vampire* remains a nonetheless intriguing variation of the horror film in the context of World War II popular culture."[27]

Beating Columbia to the punch, Universal released its *Son of Dracula* in November; consequently, Columbia delayed releasing *The Return of the Vampire* until January 1944.[28] Reviewing the latter film, a New York critic opined: "In a place like England, where according to films the ancient burying grounds are practically sown with the corpses of vampires ... it is a cinch that in the upheavals of the blitz period one of these stale characters should get tangled with the underground."[29]

Horror Stars and the War Effort

In addition to entertaining troops at military bases while touring in *Dracula*, Bela Lugosi was a regular participant in lunch-box bowls staged for the benefit of defense-plant workers along the West Coast. And, according to Buddy Hyde, the special services officer responsible for organizing the tours, when it came to audience response, Bela could outdraw bigger Hollywood names:

> We were going to have Eddie Cantor in the show with Bela at the El Toro Marine Base and then at the Douglas Aircraft Plant in Santa Monica. Bela was the gentlest person you could imagine. He just said to me, "Buddy, put me somewhere nice in the program, because I'm not an entertainer." I just laughed and thought how many great films he had done in his lifetime and said, "Bela, I'll put you between Eddie and the female singer. Just pitch morale, because everybody is here to see you. When you get in front of the microphone they will go wild."
>
> That is exactly what happened too. We played at lunchtime and the men just brown-bagged it. By the time they filed in and out of the auditorium, we had less than thirty minutes for the program, so there really wasn't any time for elaborate sketches. Eddie Cantor needed twenty minutes just to warm up. When Bela came on, the men cheered so long that he barely had time to make his pitch. He just made a quiet appeal; no Dracula takeoff or anything like that, but the audience loved him. I could have put some of Hollywood's glamorous stars out there, but none of them could have upstaged Bela. He got the warmest welcome of anyone connected with the morale program.

Among Lugosi's other wartime services was appearing on *Mail Call,* a weekly radio program whose audience were those armed service personnel fighting in sweltering jungles, and supporting fund-raising benefits in Los Angeles to help war orphans, victims of Nazi barbarism, and resistance groups in Nazi-dominated Europe. On one occasion, he raised $10,000 to assist Hungarian freedom fighters.[30]

There was more to Lugosi's involvement with the war effort than mere patriotism: In some measure, it was also an effort to free himself from the "Dracula curse" that hindered his acting career. His civic activities received faithful coverage in his studio publicity. In press releases, he frequently lauded FDR's democratic ideals; both FDR and Bela shared the same birth year, 1882. "He is constantly extending a helping hand to someone," noted one of his sheet bios released to newspapers in cities where the Hungarian actor appeared. "There is a Hungarian proverb which says you can't receive with a closed fist, and that has been part of his philosophy for life ... Lugosi is a true believer in the democratic principles of our country. Abraham Lincoln is his political ideal. There is a definite Lincolnian air about the strongly civic-minded Lugosi and his activities."[31]

Harboring an interest in political matters, Lugosi ardently perused Hungarian newspapers published in a few major American cities. Very strong political disagreements were an element of the Hungarian-American community: Some supported the semi-fascist government of Admiral Miklos Horthy during the '30s and its subsequent close affiliation with Hitler — an association others denounced. Lugosi, who numbered among the latter camp, had made known his views in 1939 and was outraged when Hungary followed Hitler's lead by declaring war on the United States in 1941. Speaking to a *Boston-Herald* correspondent two years later, Bela declared, "I am an avowed Roosevelt disciple and I think without a doubt the president is the greatest outstanding personality of the day. I am a firm believer in his ideas and ideals, and you can put that down in spades." In a subsequent interview, this time with the *San Francisco Chronicle,* he explained that he was an "extremely liberal democrat." In 1944, Lugosi made appearances before numerous political gatherings and became the president of the anti-fascist Hungarian Council for Democracy, an organization whose aim, in Lugosi's words, was for the "real" people of Hungary to have a say in political matters. Though the Council may have received Communist support, as was the case with numerous liberal groups, during the '30s and early '40s, it is possible that the Council's members and some of its leaders were ignorant of this fact.

For his part, Lugosi despised Horthy and the fascists who ran Hungary and cooperated with Hitler. As the war turned in favor of the Allied cause and the Russians came nearer to Hungary, Hitler feared that Hungary would surrender, prompting the German occupation of Hungary in March 1944, with the result that "leftist journalists, opposition politicians, trade-union officials" began vanishing; by April 5 all Jews had to wear the Star of David and were sent to extermination camps. Cognizant of what Hitler's occupation of Hungary entailed for that nation, Lugosi and likeminded others hoped that in the war's aftermath the nation's assorted forces would combine to create a genuine democratic government. As president of the Hungarian Council for Democracy, Lugosi believed that Hungary's future lay in Count Karolyi, the Socialist who had been removed from power shortly after World War I. This was the topic of a radio appearance Lugosi made in the spring of 1944, at the end of which he said:

> But besides the uniting factor of patriotism, and yearning for *real* democracy, it is my conviction that the plain people of Hungary are united by their faith in a true leader of the people — the long-exiled president of the pre–Horthy Hungarian Republic — Count Michael Karolyi!
> It were the ideals of Karolyi which rallied the people of his country to organize the Resistance in the cities, in the factories, in the mountains, and even inside of the Hungarian army. And now, Democratic Hungarians all over the world, in the United States, in South American countries, in England — all who want to see Hungary liberated so that the people of Hungary may once more be a free nation among free nations — look to Count Karolyi as Hungary's own Abraham Lincoln!

Numerous conservative Hungarians objected to this kind of pro–Karolyi sentiment and what he stood for and made known their opposition. In July 1944, the *New York Daily News* issued a political column citing numerous apparently Communist committees, Lugosi's among them, that were housed in a building that subsequently served as headquarters of the American Communist Party. Concurrently, radio commentator Henry J. Taylor said the Hungarian-American Council for Democracy was a Communist front. Presently Lugosi curbed his utterances regarding his political convictions, yet many of his fellow Hungarian-Americans did not forget his post–World War I political activities or his pro–Karolyi stance near the end of World War II; in the subsequent McCarthy era, when America went crazy over domestic Communism, Lugosi was suspected of being "a fellow-traveler if not, indeed, an actual Communist."[32] When, after the war, the House Un-American Activities Committee (HUAC) began delving into Communist infiltration of the film industry, many people were blacklisted. Lugosi, concerned that he might be in the same trouble, sent a letter to HUAC's chairman:

> My belief in the principles of democracy and personal freedom is firm and unshakable. My entire life in America has been guided by these principles. I am unalterably opposed to the Communist menace against these ideals. Communist totalitarianism has always been abhorrent to me. I have never knowingly or willfully given it aid or comfort in any way. During the war I was one of several artists of Hungarian birth asked to sponsor an organization. Shortly thereafter I learned the so-called Hungarian-American Council for Democracy was in reality a Communist front. I promptly resigned. Its high sounding platform was deliberately phrased to avert suspicion from its true auspices.
>
> My indignation at such deception impelled me to communicate with the FBI. I reported all I knew. My judgment proved correct. Four years later the Attorney-General cited this organization as subversive and disloyal.
>
> Actors are usually too busy to pay much attention to organizations that request their sponsorship. These are times of sharpening conflict between freedom-loving people and Red Fascism. We must act and speak boldly against this brutalitarianism. I urge my fellow-artists to carefully scrutinize groups before giving their endorsement, lest they fall into a Communist booby-trap.

Lugosi's missive may have removed the cloud of suspicion from him, but the chances were now slight that he would have to face HUAC: by now his star had so dimmed that he was scarcely a sufficiently big fish for the members of the Committee to summon. "Their indifference matched that of Hollywood and the legitimate theater."[33]

Lugosi wasn't the only Hollywood bogeyman to lend time and talents in service to the war effort. Along with his wife, Boris Karloff participated in Civilian Defense work. At the time, Karloff was appearing on stage in *Arsenic and Old Lace.* Serving as an air raid warden in the basement of New York's Hotel Beekman every third Thursday from midnight until eight in the morning, Karloff, equipped with a pillow and blanket, used his shift to read, write letters, and enjoy "a lunch ... that would feed an army." Nancy Farrell, a fellow Civilian Defense warden recalled,

> He was always ahead of his time when he reported for his watch, which began at midnight. Our post was in the Beekman Hotel at 63d Street and Park Avenue — a basement room with cement floor and walls and pipes overhead. As Karloff entered, he said, "Good evening. I've brought my *suppah.*" His voice, with its variety of pitch and its resonance, was friendly and reassuring....
>
> In the air raid post, Karloff kept on his conservative coat of good British tweed. He wore rimless glasses. He looked thin and not especially tall. He urged us two wardens to hurry home and assured us he was glad to go on duty early.... I thought only of the calmness and dependability of this courteous man who was responsible for the lives of thousands of his neighbors. I felt that he would rather be an air raid warden in London and that he was imposing on himself the same discipline that he would have observed in the blitz.

Karloff also joined his *Arsenic and Old Lace* castmates in performing the play at West Point, the first time a Broadway production had been performed at the military academy in 139 years. In 1945, under the sponsorship of the USO Camp Shows, Inc., Karloff arrived in Hawaii on the first leg of a tour with *Arsenic* in the Pacific. A requirement for actors entering a war zone was that they learn a simplified version of "basic training"; wearing military fatigues, Karloff earned his stripes as an honorary Marine, receiving instruction in infantry techniques, among them amphibious maneuvers and the correct utilization of weapons. After wrapping up performances at every military base on Oahu, the *Arsenic* troupe proceeded to Midway, the Marshall Islands, Canton, and Christmas Island. En route to the Marshalls, the company stopped at Johnson Island, where they did a two-night run in a theater adjacent to an aircraft loading area. Karloff reminisced that "they used to rev the planes up before they went out on the runways; so always on your best line, there would be a blast of engines ... right next door! It was a wonderful experience.... I wouldn't take anything for it." Another memorable experience for Karloff occurred on Kwajalein Atoll in the Marshalls:

> The Seabees had asked us to play their end of the island and said they'd build us a stage. They were marvels. They built the stage in a couple of hours and erected the set — a Victorian living room. And then the most astounding thing happened — on the dreary, wasted island. A cat emerged from the kitchen door of the set. He looked around the living room — and, bless me, walked calmly out the living room door as if he'd lived there all his life.

After returning to Oahu, Karloff visited hospitalized soldiers.[34]

Lon Chaney, Jr., participated in a flying tour for the purpose of selling war bonds. During a ten-day period, the tour visited thirteen cities, selling $50,911,730 worth of bonds. When, at one stop, the audience failed to enthusiastically respond to an appeal to buy bonds, an enraged Chaney tossed aside his prepared remarks and vented the full force of his fury on the crowd:

> I saw you smiling and grinning when Albert Dekker was talking about the most serious business in the world. Instead of grinning, you ought to be marching over to the bond booth and buying all the bonds you can.
> I'm not going to use this speech given to me by the War Department. I have something else I want to tell you. [Chaney then recounted his meeting with two young U. S. Air Force flyers who had just returned from Guadalcanal.]
> They had been through hell down there and were complete nervous wrecks. While I was talking with them, I asked if they bought bonds. One of them said that in Guadalcanal he put as high as 94 percent of his salary into War Bonds. The other aviator seemed ashamed that he only had been putting about 80 percent of his salary into bonds.
> Then I asked them what other soldiers were putting into bonds. They replied

that the boys in the Southwest Pacific were investing an average of 75 to 80 per cent of their salaries in War Bonds.

Maybe you people can guess how that made me feel. I must have shown how ashamed I was, for one of the boys turned to me and said: "That's all right, Mr. Chaney, you don't need to be ashamed. It seems that the farther away they get from the fighting front, the lower the percentage becomes that is deducted from their salaries for War Bonds."

Don't disappoint our wonderful boys in uniform who are fighting and dying for you. Dig down in your pockets now, and buy bonds for all you are worth. You in that streetcar, get off and buy bonds before it is too late. You up in those buildings, come and buy bonds, bonds, bonds!

The result of Chaney's impassioned plea, according to studio publicity, was that people in the streetcar and the buildings, as well as members of Chaney's own troupe, bought the bonds. While it is a known fact that studio pressbooks have a habit of stretching the truth, most likely the aforementioned incident did occur. In biographer Don G. Smith's words: "Chaney was highly patriotic. Because he undoubtedly experienced guilt and anger regarding his own 4-F status, a crowd such as he faced on that day would have made his blood boil." *Reader's Digest* disclosed another stratagem Chaney employed — one that reflected his evident dislike of reading government-prepared speeches:

During the last Bond Drive at the Beverly Tropics, Lon Chaney, Jr., faced the audience and pulled out a sheaf of papers. "I have here a very long speech which the Treasury Department asked me to read to you. Do you want to hear it?"

The audience screamed, "No!"

"Good," replied Chaney, putting the speech back in his pocket. "By gosh, you people better buy all the bonds you can or I'll come back and read it to you!"[35]

Curt Siodmak, the man who created Chaney's most famous movie character, began his wartime service much as Boris Karloff had by serving as an air raid warden in his California neighborhood, telling his fellow residents to switch off their lights and/or draw their blackout curtains. "I suspect," he later wrote, "I did not do too well as an air raid warden, since my German accent frightened people into believing the Teutons had already landed." From air raid warden, Siodmak rose even higher, compared to Lugosi, Karloff, and Chaney. in service to his country, by being "invited" to join the Office of Strategic Services (OSS), the precursor of the CIA. After undergoing training at El Toro Marine Base near San Diego, Siodmak was sent to Washington, D.C., where he learned that he had been assigned to gather information behind German lines. When this assignment was canceled, he was asked to return to Washington and to give thought to serving in Japan. "I knew a great deal about the Germans. I didn't know anything about the Japanese. I had reason to fight the Nazis, though I was no soldier." After telling his superior that he wouldn't be of value serving in the Far East, Siodmak was directed to return home on the next train.[36]

7

Beyond the Golden Age

The end of World War II marked the beginning of a new world and the end of Hollywood's Golden Age of horror. It was characterized by both ominous shadows and bright promise. On the dark side was the atomic bomb and the new Cold War with the Russians and, closer to home, the threat of domestic Communists at loose subverting America. Against such a backdrop, the old-fashioned horrors of Dracula, Frankenstein's Monster, the Wolf Man, and their ilk were clearly passé. On the other hand, former GIs were going to college, establishing themselves financially, and starting families. They, along with everyone else, were busy enjoying the benefits that peacetime now brought: the end of rationing, new cars, and overall prosperity. Movies were no longer the principal attraction they once were. An added factor in the changing fortunes of post-war Hollywood was the Supreme Court's decision banning the practice of block-booking, whereby the important producers and distributors had compelled theaters to show their entire output. With block-booking now outlawed, the profitability of numerous inexpensive films was no longer assured. The number of productions Universal released were clearly indicative: where it had issued fifty to sixty films yearly in 1941 through 1944, the studio now made forty-six in 1945; forty-two in 1946; thirty-three in 1947; thirty-five in 1948; and twenty-nine in 1949. One of the casualties of this decrease of film production was the usual kind of horror film by all the Hollywood studios.[1]

Americans believed that the can-do spirit of the war years could be applied to the problems of peace — specifically the nation's social ills. Reflecting this mood, postwar Hollywood replaced fantasy with "social problem films" covering such issues as alcoholism, war casualties, rural poverty, civilian readjustment, racism, anti–Semitism, prison reform, and mental illness.²

Finally, there was the impact of a new medium dawning on the postwar horizon: In 1946, there were merely sixty-five hundred television sets nationwide; that number skyrocketed to where, by 1956, there were fifty-two million. Television now offered a more instantaneous form of gratification: During World War II, people had "gone to the movies"—not to see a specific motion picture, but simply to get out of the house to be entertained. Now, with the television revolution, a movie had to generate an extraordinary buzz to draw an audience; otherwise people would stay home to enjoy TV entertainment. Consequently, movie attendance took a radical dive.

Horror films virtually disappeared in the late Forties. In its place came the science fiction boom of the 1950s, characterized by galactic threats (*The Thing from Another World, The War of the Worlds*) and atomic mutations (*Them!*). Still, there was evidence that classic horror had yet to see its final days: In 1951 both *Dracula* and *Frankenstein* were reissued, both doing well, but Hollywood incredibly failed to notice. Not until late in the decade, when England's Hammer Films made *The Curse of Frankenstein, Horror of Dracula*, and a whole wave of remakes (as well as their own horror creations), did a full-fledged horror revival take off.³

By then the monsters of horror's classic age had gained a new lease on life, having been discovered by the emerging television generation. In 1957 Universal sold its enormous library of genre films for viewing on television, where they aired under the title *Shock*. The result was an unanticipated success that far exceeded anyone's expectations: Airing in ninety American cities, *Shock Theater* proved a ratings smash! In New York, it provided strong competition to *The Jack Paar Show* and *The Late Show*. People who, until now, had been totally unfamiliar with Boris Karloff and Bela Lugosi, became instant fans of the classics. The *Shock Theater* phenomenon also made celebrities of horror movie hosts who were employed by the local TV stations to make the less spectacular films more interesting.⁴

Shock Theater gave the classic horror films something they never had before: an element of cultural significance. Now seen as a collective body of work after they had originally been released over many years, they became, particularly to their new, young viewers, important. Along with such monster movie periodicals as *Famous Monsters of Filmland, Shock The-*

ater heralded the beginning of a durable fan base. Universal's monsters, much to the displeasure of the older generation, were becoming their offspring's new heroes.[5] One reason for the younger generation's veneration was the fact that, having grown up during the Cold War, with the ever-present possibility of nuclear devastation a reality, the monster figures, being immortal in nature, offered the prospect of continued existence in the wake of the Bomb.[6]

The younger generation's embrace of monsters had a major effect on Hollywood as well. Horror and science fiction dethroned the traditional Western to become the essential movie genre, with Universal horror trailblazing the way. Indeed, argue Tom Weaver and Michael and John Brunas, the film classic *Psycho* might not have been produced if Alfred Hitchcock hadn't noticed the success of low-budget horror films, "all of which owe a debt to the Universal horror films of the past." *Psycho*'s stupefying success "more than solidified Hitchcock's position as one of the most bankable Hollywood directors. His sharply edged technique and sardonic wit, an almost seamless fusion of art and commercialism, became such an identifiable style that he would surpass such high-profile contemporaries as John Ford, Howard Hawks and William Wyler in terms of directly influencing future generations of filmmakers."[7]

The success of *Shock Theater*, ironically, did not result in the classic horror characters making new screen appearances. For years, Universal's principal efforts concerning its classic monster legacy was limited to such commercial marketing efforts as licensing merchandise and issuing the classics on home video. The studio's faith that its horror franchise could be revived at the box office was negligible. What appearances the monsters made were confined to such television fare as *The Munsters*. It remained for Broadway to convince Hollywood that the old monsters still had life in them when, in 1977, the Hamilton Deane—John L. Balderston version of *Dracula* was revived to great success, due to Frank Langella's performance in the title role. Langella went on to don the count's cape again in Universal's 1979 remake of its pioneering horror classic.

The 1990s witnessed further renewed monster activity on Universal's part when the studio issued *The Mummy* (1999), followed by *The Mummy Returns* (2001). Two other Universal releases, *House of Frankenstein* 1997, the latter a made-for-television movie, and the 2004 release *Van Helsing* recalled the studio's wartime monster rallies.[8] In 2005,

Universal released Peter Jackson's remake of *King Kong,* one more faithful to the spirit and setting of the 1933 original than the 1976 remake.

Despite the ups and downs, the Universal horror classics hold an enduring place in the hearts of film fans and in the history of cinema. As testimony to this, one need only look at such recent developments as the continuing popularity of the classics on home video which have now evolved into the DVD age (DVD sets of Universal's fright films have sold quite well); the astonishing sums that original memorabilia from these films command; and the U.S. Postal Service's commemorative set of postage stamps honoring the classic monsters.[9] The latter, coming from so august a source as the United States government, clearly indicates that horror films have come a long way to achieve such official recognition!

While Universal trailblazed the classic horror film of Hollywood's Golden Age, other studios made their own mark on the genre as well: in addition to Fredric March's *Dr. Jekyll and Mr. Hyde,* Paramount produced *Island of Lost Souls* and *Dr. Cyclops;* MGM *Freaks;* RKO *King Kong* and Val Lewton's films; Columbia *The Return of the Vampire.*

The Golden Age of Horror, along with the actors, producers, writers, directors, and others who made it possible, is long gone, leaving the films themselves. The latter are continually discovered by succeeding generations. Granted, the hi-tech special effects and graphic violence of today's fright films undoubtedly make the classics seem bland to modern audiences. Yet their various incarnations over the years testify to their continuing influence on filmmakers, as witness Jackson's *King Kong.* When it comes to reading hidden messages and subtexts into movies, it is the critics and film historians, not the filmmakers themselves — except for a few instances perhaps — who provide what "social commentary" there is in a film by reading such commentary in themselves. Bearing this in mind, what do the classic horror films tell us about the Great Depression–World War II era when they were made?

To begin with, horror had been a part of American cinema long before *Dracula* and *Frankenstein* arrived on the scene in 1931. What differentiated this spooky pair from earlier screen ghouls was that they introduced and made acceptable the supernatural as an element of American movies. The fact that both films debuted during the early years of talking pictures is equally significant as sound added a new dimension to movie horror; it made it, in Robert Sklar's words, "more real: creaking doors, mysterious howls, wild screams."[10] When it came to the acceptance of supernatural themes, this transformation no doubt owed much to the Great Depression: The new breed of monsters debuted as Americans sought escape at the movies from the harsh reality and burdens hard times had imposed on their lives. Horror films did just that by taking audiences out of their everyday lives into a fantasy realm, one where the characters confronted crises — a vampire's predations, a monster on the loose — that were far worse than that of the economic calamity. The monsters themselves served as metaphors for the age. Not unlike the Depression, Count Dracula weakened and devitalized his victims as well as presented a negative image of the well-to-do who, in pursuit of their own selfish motives, exploited the powerless lower classes. Being an Eastern European, the count further denoted America's fear of immigration and European contamination in the post–World War I era and the Depression. On the other hand, the Frankenstein Monster resembled a downtrodden everyman whose search for acceptance and an understanding of who he was and what his place in the world was mirrored the same question his real-life contemporaries asked: What had happened to our world and what can be done to alleviate our suffering?

This shattering of '20s America's righteous belief in wealth and prosperity discredited the proponents of this creed, rendering faith in experts and technological progress null and void. We had trusted them when they said we were marching toward a better world — only to march right into disaster. Small wonder then that "mad science" films, showing what happened when technology ran amock, were so prevalent during the early '30s when the Depression was at its worst. Frankenstein's creation brought shame and disgrace both to his creator and his descendants. Dr. Jekyll (as Mr. Hyde) and Dr. Mirakle both carried their scientific pursuits to extremes. This skepticism of progress was shared by FDR himself, whose own cynicism toward experts' wisdom grew out of his polio experience, freeing him to tackle the problems of the nation with bold, innovative programs that went against the grain of convention — much as Dr. Jekyll's unorthodoxy placed him at odds with his peers (though in Jekyll's case, the consequences of his unconventionality, unlike Roosevelt's, brought disaster upon him).

Some segments of Depression society, the bonus marchers of 1932 in particular, weren't content to sit back but rose up to demand immediate alleviation of their plight. Such protest, shocking in its day, was viewed by some as the first step toward violent revolution against the status quo.

The freaks of Tod Browning's film and the beast-folk inhabiting Dr. Moreau's island similarly revolted against those social orders they believed treated them unjustly. And while the Depression afflicted mostly the less fortunate class of society, the horror films of the age showed that anyone, regardless of his or her social standing, could suffer, as was demonstrated in *White Zombie* when bride-to-be Madge Bellamy and wealthy plantation owner Robert Frazer both fell into zombie master Bela Lugosi's clutches, becoming mindless automatons like his other victims; the zombie labor force operating Lugosi's sugar mill in the same film was as powerless against him as was the real-life American worker against the heartless titans of big business before the New Deal empowered them to fight for their rights and dignity. The unfairness of life struck Dr. Wilfred Glendon and Lawrence Talbot: Both discovered that their exalted standing failed to shield them from the lycanthropic curse and its accompanying agonies. Dracula's daughter, unlike her father, struggled to overcome her vampiric heritage in favor of a normal life, only to discover in the end that such a release was impossible; her heritage condemned her to a life of misery. *The Invisible Man*'s Jack Griffin, it can be argued, was a victim of fate — though, like Dr. Jekyll, it was one he brought on himself through his own actions. The madness that seized his mind as a result of using the invisibility-inducing drug monocane was his punishment for delving into the forbidden frontiers of science.

The Invisible Man, though an ultimately tragic figure, also held an allure for movie audiences in 1933, that of absolute power — the kind that allowed those possessing it to shatter all obstacles before them, seize the moment, take charge of their destinies, and mold circumstances to their liking. Such a sentiment attracted both those battered by the Depression and those who longed for a strongman — an American Mussolini — to take charge and bring order out of the chaos America faced in 1933. Coming to power that year, Roosevelt proved to be no Mussolini but one who sought to restore the nation through the democratic process. Another movie character of 1933, King Kong, also resonated with Americans' anger and frustration: Kong's rampage through New York City provided audiences a surrogate revery at seeing the very heart of America's financial capital demolished in the midst of the Depression as well as personifying the hostility of those Americans who viewed New York not as a true American city but as a vile, corrupt, and alien environment. After all, only a place like New York would cruelly exploit an outsider like Kong, removed from his native island habitat and brought to Gotham, where he was put on stage, bound in chains, to be gawked at as an entertainment piece.

By the mid–30s, the horror cycle that had commenced in 1931 had petered out — mainly due to the ban imposed on horror films by Great Britain. The genre's 1938–1939 revival occurred just as World War II began. The war produced its own special representative monster — the Wolf Man, whose saga embodied screenwriter Curt Siodmak's experience as a Jewish refugee from Nazi Germany as well as symbolizing the violence the war loosed upon Europe and the efforts to restore peace, signified by Larry Talbot's desperate search for a means to tame the beast within himself.

Once America entered the war, horror, like other film genres, enlisted for the duration. Monsters plugged war bonds, were created by scientists to assist the Allied cause, or were resurrected as part of the wartime setting. More often, these films were dubious efforts, mere exploitation films that capitalized on the war for the sake of doing so. On the other hand, horror stars lent their time and talents to the anti–Axis cause on the homefront.

Whatever hidden sub-texts may have populated the classic horror films — or were read into them by film scholars — what is certain is that their main purpose was to entertain the audiences who packed the theaters to see them. That they did so in their day — and still do long afterward, on television and home video — is a testament to their enduring magic and popularity.

Chapter Notes

Preface

1. Robert S. McElvaine, *The Great Depression: America, 1929–1941* (New York: Times Books, 1984), 208.
2. Quoted in William E. Leuchtenberg and the Editors of *Life*, *The Life History of the United States. Volume 11: 1933–1945. New Deal and Global War* (New York: Time Inc., 1964), 61.
3. Thomas Doherty, *Pre-Code Hollywood: Sex, Immorality, and Insurrection in American Cinema, 1930–1934* (New York: Columbia University Press, 1999), 297.
4. Michael Brunas, John Brunas, and Tom Weaver, *Universal Horrors: The Studio's Films, 1931–1946* (Jefferson, North Carolina: McFarland, 1990), 27.
5. Doherty, *Pre-Code Hollywood*, 297.
6. *Ibid.*, 298.
7. Quoted in David J. Skal, *Screams of Reason: Mad Science and Modern Culture* (New York: W. W. Norton, 1998), 174.
8. Brunas, Brunas, and Weaver, *Universal Horrors*, 581.

Chapter 1

1. Gene Smith, *The Shattered Dream: Herbert Hoover and the Great Depression* (New York: William Morrow, 1970), 65–66.
2. The Editors of *American Heritage*, *The American Heritage History of the 20's & 30's* (New York: American Heritage Publishing, 1970), 177.
3. Smith, 68.
4. Doherty, 299.
5. David J. Skal, *The Monster Show: A Cultural History of Horror* (New York: W.W. Norton, 1993), 81–82, 83.
6. *Ibid.*, 81.
7. Joseph Maddrey, *Nightmares in Red, White and Blue: The Evolution of the American Horror Film* (Jefferson, North Carolina: McFarland, 2004), 11, 18.
8. Skal, *The Monster Show*, 82.
9. "The Seduction of Renfield." http://everything2.com/index.pl?node_id=1928413&displaytype=printable&lastnode_id=0, July 13, 2008.
10. Skal, *The Monster Show*, 82.
11. "The Seduction of Renfield." splaytype=printable&lastnode_id=0, July 13, 2008
12. Skal, *The Monster Show*, 82.
13. Arthur Lennig, *The Count: The Life and Films of Bela "Dracula" Lugosi* (New York: G. P. Putnam's Sons, 1974), 63.
14. Skal, *The Monster Show*, 83.
15. Skal, *Screams of Reason*, 60.
16. *Nightmare: The Birth of Victorian Horror. Dracula with Christopher Frayling* (A Wall to Wall Production in Association with the BBC for A&E Network, 1996).
17. "Feature Commentary with Film Historian David J. Skal," *Dracula*, Universal Studios Classic Monster Collection, 1999. Skal's assertion that Dracula is an anti-Semitic character had already been sounded by cultural historian Bram Dijkstra: "Dracula may not officially have been one of those horrid inbred Jews everyone was worrying about at the time Stoker

wrote his novel, but he came close, for he was very emphatically Eastern European ... like [George] du Maurier's 'filthy back Hebrew,' Svengali." Quoted in David J. Skal, *Hollywood Gothic: The Tangled Web of Dracula from Novel to Stage to Screen* (New York: W.W. Norton, 1990), 27.

18. Quoted in Skal, *Hollywood Gothic*, 25.
19. Raymond T. McNally and Radu Florescu, *In Search of Dracula: A True History of Dracula and Vampire Legends* (Greenwich: The New York Graphic Society, 1972), 181.
20. Skal, *Screams of Reason*, 94–97.
21. *Ibid.*, 99–100.
22. "The Road to Dracula."
23. "The Road to Dracula."
24. Mark A. Vieira, *Hollywood Horror: From Gothic to Cosmic* (New York: Harry N. Abrams, 2003), 16–17.
25. Lennig, *The Count*, 64–65.
26. Vieira, *Hollywood Horror*, 18.
27. McNally and Florescu, 166.
28. Skal, *Hollywood Gothic*, 68–78.
29. Lennig, *The Count*, 66.
30. Skal, *The Monster Show*, 84, 86–89.
31. Gary Don Rhodes, *Lugosi: His Life in Films, on Stage, and in the Hearts of Horror Lovers* (Jefferson, North Carolina: McFarland, 1997), 7–8, 10, 19–20.
32. Skal, *The Monster Show*, 89.
33. Robert Cremer, *Lugosi: The Man Behind the Cape* (Chicago: Henry Regnery, 1976), 103.
34. Lennig, *The Count*, 66–67, 69.
35. *Ibid.*, 78–80.
36. Howard M. Sachar, *A History of the Jews in America* (New York: Alfred A. Knopf, 1992), 358–59.
37. "Production Background by Gregory Wm. Mank," Philip J. Riley, editor, *MagicImage Filmbooks Presents* Frankenstein. *Universal Filmscripts Series. Classic Horror Films–Volume 1* (Absecon, New Jersey: MagicImage Filmbooks, 1989), 11–12.
38. "Production Background," *MagicImage Filmbooks:* Frankenstein, 12–13.
39. Thomas Schatz, *The Genius of the System: Hollywood Filmmaking in the Studio Era* (New York: Pantheon Books, 1988), 82–85.
40. Schatz, 86–89.
41. Vieira, *Hollywood Horror*, 29–30.
42. *Ibid.*, 30–31.
43. *Ibid.*, 32.
44. Cremer, *Lugosi*, 116.
45. Skal, *Hollywood Gothic*, 124, 125.
46. *Ibid.*, 126.
47. *Ibid.*, 140, 142.
48. David J. Skal and Elias Savada, *Dark Carnival: The Secret World of Tod Browning, Hollywood's Master of the Macabre* (New York: Anchor Books, 1995), 157.
49. Michael W. Phillips, Jr., "The Fall of the House of Dracula." http://goatdog.com/articlePage.php?articleID=24, July 13, 2008.
50. Doherty, *Pre-Code Hollywood*, 300.
51. T. H. Watkins, *The Great Depression: America in the 1930s* (Boston: Little Brown, 1993), 79–80.
52. "Feature Commentary with Film Historian David J. Skal."
53. Skal, Hollywood Gothic, 142.
54. "Our Horror, Ourselves." sevenF.html July 13, 2008.
55. Watkins, 26–28, 33.
56. The congressman's opinions aired in the same installment of *Between the Wars* that featured Prof. Winks' observation. Like Dracula, other screen monsters — the Wolf Man, the Mummy and Frankenstein's Monster — originated beyond America's shores. Those Americans who held immigrants responsible for the nation's problems during the Depression found confirmation of their fears in the movie monsters of the time. The immigrants themselves were of divided mind about what the films signified for them. For those who had grown up with the superstitions that formed the basis of them, these films reminded them of the native lands they wished to return to. Others found horror films justification for why they had left their homelands for a place like America that was "more realistic and reasonable." Finally, horror films gave substance to the anxieties of those people who feared that one day they would discover that their parents' fears and anxieties weren't all that implausible. "How the Horror Movies of the Great Depression Reflected the History of the Time." www.associatedcontent.com/pop_print.shtml?content_type=article&content_type_id ... July 12, 2008.

57. *Between the Wars: The Great Depression and Foreign Affairs,* 1978, Alan Landsberg Productions.
58. John D. Hicks, *Republican Ascendancy, 1921–1933* (New York: Harper Torchbooks, 1963) 278; Alan Brinkley, *The Unfinished Nation: A Concise History of the American People* (New York: Alfred A. Knopf, 1993), 675.
59. Oscar Theodore Barck, Jr. and Nelson Manfred Blake, *Since 1900: A History of the United States in Our Times* (New York: Macmillan, 1965) Fourth Edition, 453–54.
60. David M. Kennedy, *Freedom from Fear: The American People in Depression and War, 1929–1945* (New York: Oxford University Press, 1999), 133. In his book about Roosevelt's Hundred Days, Jonathan Alter contends that Hoover never uttered such a remark; further that the "custom" of a retiring president returning his successor's courtesy call was nonexistent. Jonathan Alter, *The Defining Moment: FDR's Hundred Days and the Triumph of Hope* (New York: Simon & Schuster, 2006) 199–200.
61. "Our Horror, Ourselves." sevenF.html July 13, 2008.
62. Vieira, *Hollywood Horror,* 35.
63. Philip J. Riley and George Turner, "Production Background," *MagicImage Filmbooks Presents* Dracula *(The Original 1931 Shooting Script)* (Absecon, New Jersey: MagicImage Filmbooks, 1990), First Edition, 19–20.
64. Skal, *Hollywood Gothic,* 147, 151.
65. Vieira, *Hollywood Horror,* 35.
66. Mank, "Production Background," *MagicImage Filmbooks:* Frankenstein, 14.
67. Mank, "Production Background," *MagicImage Filmbooks:* Frankenstein, 22.
68. Skal, *Screams of Reason,* 118, 119.
69. *Ibid.,* 119–20.
70. Lennig, *The Count,* 115.
71. Mank, "Production Background," *MagicImage Books:* Frankenstein, 24.
72. Skal, *Screams of Reason,* 123; *Heroes of Horror: Bela Lugosi: Hollywood's Dark Prince,* ID0687FSDVD, Image Entertainment, 2003.
73. Mank, "Production Background," *MagicImage Filmbooks:* Frankenstein, 23.
74. Schatz, 92.

75. Mank, "Production Background," *MagicImage Filmbooks:* Frankenstein, 27.
76. Vieira, *Hollywood Horror,* 37.
77. Skal, *Screams of Reason,* 125.
78. Peter Underwood, *Karloff: The Life of Boris Karloff* (New York: Drake Publishers, 1972), 15; Denis Gifford, *Karloff: The Man, the Monster, the Movies* (New York: Curtis Books, 1973), 19.
79. Mank, "Production Background," *MagicImage Filmbooks:* Frankenstein, 29–30.
80. Vieira, *Hollywood Horror,* 37–38.
81. Skal, *Screams of Reason,* 126.
82. Mank, "Production Background," *MagicImage Filmbooks:* Frankenstein, 30; Vieira, *Hollywood Horror,* 38.
83. Mank, "Production Background," *MagicImage Filmbooks:* Frankenstein, 32, 34.
84. *Ibid.,* 34, 40.
85. James Curtis, *James Whale: A New World of Gods and Monsters* (Boston: Faber and Faber, 1998), 151.
86. Skal, *Screams of Reason,* 129–30.
87. Doherty, 303.
88. Quoted in Skal, *Screams of Reason,* 131.
89. "Our Horror, Ourselves." sevenF.html July 13, 2008.
90. Mark A. Vieira, *Sin in Soft Focus: Pre-Code Hollywood* (New York: Harry N. Abrams, 1999), 43.
91. Curtis, 153–54.
92. Mank, "Production Background," *MagicImage Filmbooks:* Frankenstein, 40.
93. Mank, "Production Background," *MagicImage Filmbooks:* Frankenstein, 40.
94. Scott Allen Nollen, *Boris Karloff: A Gentleman's Life* (Baltimore: Midnight Marquee Press, 1999), 46; Paul M. Jensen, *Boris Karloff and His Films* (Cranbury, New Jersey: A. S. Barnes, 1974), 44.
95. Gregory William Mank, James T. Coughlin, and Dwight D. Frye, *Dwight Frye's Last Laugh: An Unauthorized Biography* (Baltimore: Midnight Marquee Press, 1997), 110.
96. Quoted in Skal, *The Monster Show,* 139.
97. Jensen, *Boris Karloff and His Films,* 44.
98. Skal, *Screams of Reason,* 130.

Chapter 2

1. Vieira, *Hollywood Horror,* 41.
2. Skal, *The Monster Show,* 162–63.
3. Nelson B. Bell, "Thoughts on Horror Era, Renaissance and Miss Ulric," *The Washington Post,* February 21, 1932, 1.
4. Doherty, 307–08; Skal, *Screams of Reason,* 139–40.
5. Margaret Mackay, *The Violent Friend: The Story of Mrs. Robert Louis Stevenson* (Garden City, New York: Doubleday, 1968), 207.
6. Skal, *The Monster Show,* 139.
7. "Commentary by Gregory William Mank," *Classic Double Feature: Dr. Jekyll and Mr. Hyde,* Warner Home Video, 2004.
8. Skal, *The Monster Show,* 240.
9. Denis Gifford, *Movie Monsters* (New York: E. P. Dutton, 1969), 120.
10. Skal, *The Monster Show,* 140.
11. Gifford, *Movie Monsters,* 120.
12. Skal, *The Monster Show,* 141.
13. "Commentary by Gregory William Mank," *Classic Double Feature: Dr. Jekyll and Mr. Hyde.*
14. Vieira, *Hollywood Horror,* 41.
15. Skal, *The Monster Show,* 142.
16. Vieira, *Hollywood Horror,* 41.
17. Alter, 66, 328.
18. Quoted in Annalee Newitz, "A Lower-Class, Sexy Monster," *Bright Lights Film Journal,* #15, 1995, 14.
19. William Manchester, *The Glory and the Dream: A Narrative History of America, 1932–1972* (New York: Bantam Books, 1975), 46–47.
20. Newitz, 14.
21. *Ibid.,*15.
22. *Ibid.,*16.
23. *Ibid.,* 17, 50.
24. Skal, *The Monster Show,* 159.
25. Gregory William Mank, *Women in Horror Films, 1930s* (Jefferson, North Carolina: McFarland, 1999), 91.
26. Frank J. Dello Stritto, "Are We Not Men? The Evolution of Darwin in Hollywood," *Cult Movies* #41, 74.
27. Skal, *Screams of Reason,* 136.
28. Dello Stritto, 74.
29. Lennig, *The Count,* 116–17.
30. Skal, *Screams of Reason,* 133–34.
31. Mank, *Women in Horror Films, 1930s,* 107, 109–10.
32. Lennig, *The Count,* 118; Mank, *Women in Horror Films, 1930s,* 110.
33. Lennig, *The Count,* 122–25.
34. Skal, *Screams of Reason,* 140.
35. Alter, 50, 92–93.
36. Hugh Gregory Gallagher, *FDR's Splendid Deception* (New York: Dodd, Mead, 1985), 215.
37. Carlos Clarens, *An Illustrated History of the Horror Film* (New York: Capricorn Books, 1968), 70; "Freaks: The Sideshow Cinema," *Freaks,* Turner Entertainment Co. and Warner Bros. Entertainment, 2004.
38. Bob Thomas, *Thalberg: Life and Legend* (Garden City, New York: Doubleday, 1959), 187–88.
39. Chris Steinbrunner and Burt Goldblatt, *Cinema of the Fantastic* (New York: Galahad Books, 1972), 37–38.
40. Skal, *The Monster Show,* 146.
41. Mank, *Women in Horror Films, 1930s,* 124; Skal and Savada, 167–68.
42. Mank, *Women in Horror Films, 1930s,* 124; Skal and Savada, 168.
43. Samuel Marx, *Mayer and Thalberg: The Make-Believe Saints* (New York: Random House, 1975), 180.
44. Mank, *Women in Horror Films, 1930s,* 126.
45. Skal and Savada, 174.
46. Skal, *The Monster Show,* 155.
47. Skal and Savada, 174–75.
48. Skal and Savada, 175.
49. Mank, *Women in Horror Films, 1930s,* 126–27.
50. Skal and Savada, 175.
51. "Freaks: The Sideshow Cinema."
52. Skal and Savada, 177–78.
53. Skal and Savada, 180; Mank, *Women in Horror Films, 1930s,* 127.
54. "Commentary by David Skal," *Freaks.*
55. Skal and Savada, 181.
56. Leuchtenburg and the Editors of *Life, The Life History of the United States. Volume II,* 8.
57. Doherty, 312.
58. *Ibid.,* 308.
59. McElvaine, 92–93.
60. Ernest R. May and the Editors of

Life, The Life History of the United States. Volume 10: 1917–1932. War, Boom and Bust (New York: Time, 1964), 137.

61. *The Presidents: Wilson to Franklin D. Roosevelt (1913–1945)* (AAE-71742 A&E Television Network, 2005).
62. May and the Editors of *Life, The Life History of the United States. Volume 10*, 137.
63. Skal, *The Monster Show* 156, 158.
64. Steinbrunner and Goldblatt, 48.
65. Carlos Clarens, *An Illustrated History of the Horror Film* (New York: Capricorn, 1968), 87–88.
66. Lennig, *The Count*, 127.
67. Daniel Cohen, *A Natural History of Unnatural Things* (New York: McCall Publishing, 1971), 129.
68. Skal, *The Monster Show*, 169.
69. Gary D. Rhodes, *White Zombie: Anatomy of a Horror Film* (Jefferson, North Carolina: McFarland, 2001), 70–86.
70. Lennig, *The Count*, 126; Rhodes, *White Zombie*, 92–93.
71. Lugosi's line was echoed by San Francisco reviewer Katherine Hill in referring to the Depression. She further observed that "real" zombies were positioned all over the theatre lobby–a publicity gimmick on the part of the theatre management. "To my genuine horror," Hill said, "I discovered a lady zombie in the retiring room. Did you ever try to telephone with a zombie right behind you? It's too terrible, really." Skal, *The Monster Show*, 169.
72. Rhodes, *White Zombie*, 141–42, 143, 145, 146–47.
73. *Ibid.*, 46–48.
74. Dello Stritto, 78–79.
75. Doherty, 309.
76. Lennig, *The Count*, 147–48.
77. Charles Higham, *Charles Laughton: An Intimate Biography* (Garden City, New York: Doubleday, 1976), 39.
78. Mank, *Women in Horror Films, 1930s*, 204.
79. Doherty, 310–11.
80. Skal, *The Monster Show*, 171.
81. Doherty, 311–12.
82. Mank, *Women in Horror Films, 1930s*, 204; Skal, *The Monster Show*, 171.

Chapter 3

1. Kenneth S. Davis, *FDR: The New York Years, 1928–1933* (New York: Random House, 1985), 446; Davis W. Houck, *FDR and Fear Itself: The First Inaugural Address* (College Station, Texas: Texas A & M University Press, 2002), 127; Mark Sherwin and Charles Lam Markham, *One Week in March* (New York: G. P. Putnam's Sons, 1961), 60.
2. Davis, 446.
3. Brinkley, 675; James D. Horan, *The Desperate Years: A Pictorial History of the Thirties* (New York: Bonanza Books, 1962), 95; Sherwin and Markman, 57.
4. Ray Morton, *King Kong: The History of a Movie Icon: From Fay Wray to Peter Jackson* (New York: Applause Theatre & Cinema Books, 2005), 78; "Commentary by Ray Harryhausen and Ken Ralston with Merian C. Cooper and Fay Wray," *King Kong*, Warner Bros. Home Video.
5. Doherty, 293; Paul M. Jensen, *The Men Who Made the Monsters* (New York: Twayne Publishers, 1996), 82.
6. "*I'm King Kong! The Exploits of Merian C. Cooper.*"
7. *RKO Production 601: The Making of the Eighth Wonder of the World*, Warner Home Video in association with Wingnut Films, Pellerin Multimedia and Sparkhill Productions.
8. Morton, 85.
9. David Zinman, *50 Classic Motion Pictures* (New York: Crown Publishers, 1970), 171.
10. Clarens, 91–92.
11. Vieira, *Hollywood Horror*, 66.
12. Morton, 29.
13. Doherty, 289.
14. Noel Carroll, "*King Kong*: Ape and Essence," Barry Keith Grant, editor, *Planks of Reason: Essays on the Horror Film* (Metuchen: The Scarecrow Press, 1984), 232–33.
15. Morton, 66.
16. Carroll in Grant, 239–40.
17. Doherty, 292.
18. When Fay Wray permitted her own children to watch *King Kong*, they were more concerned about Kong than her mother. Wray's seven-year-old daughter said Kong

"had no intention of hurting me but just liked me and never should have been shot at by those airplanes." Wray continued:

> That confirmed a belief I developed during the filming and which has been reinforced as the years pass by, that *Kong* should be classed as an adventure fantasy, not as a horror film. If Kong were purely a horrifying and horrible fellow, the sympathy he evokes when, finally, he is struck down wouldn't exist. There is no doubt about such sympathy. Even I, seeing the film a year or so ago, felt a great lump in my throat in behalf of Kong.... When I'm in New York, I look at the Empire State Building and feel as though it belongs to me ... or is it vice versa?

When Wray died in 2004, the Empire State Building dimmed its lights for fifteen minutes in her honor. Fay Wray, "How Fay Met Kong, Or the Scream That Shook the World," *New York Times,* September 21, 1969, D17; Morton, 83.

19. Orville Goldner and George E. Turner, *The Making of* King Kong*: The Story Behind a Film Classic* (Cranbury: A. S. Barnes, 1975), 192.
20. Vieira, *Hollywood Horror,* 66.
21. Morton, 78; Doherty, 293.
22. Goldner and Turner, 9.
23. Doherty, 290–91.
24. Goldner and Turner, 9.
25. Andrew Bergman, *We're in the Money: Depression America and Its Films* (Chicago: Ivan R. Dee, 1992), 19–21.
26. *Ibid.,* 69.
27. Carroll in Grant, 241–42.
28. Goldner and Turner, 9; Morton, 84, 85–86.
29. "Commentary by Ray Harryhausen and Ken Ralston with Merian C. Cooper and Fay Wray."
30. Houck, 142, 143.
31. Leuchtenburg, 10.
32. Frank Freidel, *Franklin D. Roosevelt: Launching the New Deal* (Boston: Little, Brown, 1973), 205, 207–08.
33. James MacGregor Burns, *Roosevelt: The Lion and the Fox* (New York: Harcourt Brace Jovanovich, 1956), 184.
34. Alter, 3–4.
35. Manchester, 57.
36. Skal and Savada, 146; Alter, 186*n.*
37. Manchester, 58.
38. Alter, 4, 6.
39. *Ibid.,* 227.
40. Sherwin and Markman, 59; Richard D. White, Jr., *Kingfish: The Reign of Huey P. Long* (New York: Random House, 2006), 167–68.
41. "Now You See Him: The Invisible Man Revealed." *The Invisible Man: The Legacy Collection,* Universal Studios, 2004.
42. Don G. Smith, *H. G. Wells on Film: The Utopian Nightmare* (Jefferson, North Carolina: McFarland, 2002), 59.
43. Frank McConnell, *The Science Fiction of H. G. Wells* (New York: Oxford University Press, 1981), 99–100.
44. Curtis, 205*n.*
45. Jensen, *The Men Who Made the Monsters,* 37–38.
46. Michael Sevastakis, *Songs of Love and Death: The Classical American Horror Film of the 1930s* (Westport, Connecticut: Greenwood Press, 1993), 113.
47. Smith, *H. G. Wells on Film,* 68–69.
48. Brunas, Brunas, and Weaver, 73; Jensen, *The Men Who Made the Monsters,* 40.

Chapter 4

1. Schatz, 228–232.
2. Brunas, Brunas, and Weaver, 125; Philip Riley, editor, The Wolf Ma*n (The Original 1941 Shooting Script*) (Absecon, New Jersey: MagicImage Filmbooks, 1993), 24.
3. Vieira, *Hollywood Horror,* 79.
4. Brunas, Brunas, and Weaver, 125; Vieira, *Hollywood Horror,* 79.
5. Brunas, Brunas, and Weaver, 125–26.
6. Brunas, Brunas, and Weaver, 130.
7. Schatz, 232–34.
8. Cremer, 175.
9. Tom Johnson, *Censored Screams: The British Ban on Hollywood Horror in the Thirties* (Jefferson, North Carolina: McFarland, 1997), 112–13, 123, 124–25.
10. Skal, *The Monster Show,* 194–95.
11. *Ibid.,*191.
12. Cremer, 175.
13. Lyndon W. Joslin, *Count Dracula Goes to the Movies: Stoker's Novel Adapted, 1922–1995* (Jefferson, North Carolina: McFarland, 1999), 126.

14. Brunas, Brunas, and Weaver, 163.
15. Editors of Time-Life Books, *This Fabulous Century. Volume IV: 1930–1940* (New York: Time-Life Books, 1969), 156–57.
16. Vieira, *Hollywood Horror*, 91.
17. Schatz, 234–35.
18. Vieira, *Hollywood Horror*, 91; Schatz, 235; Gregory William Mank, *Karloff and Lugosi: The Story of a Haunting Collaboration* (Jefferson, North Carolina: McFarland, 1990), 160.
19. Brunas, Brunas, and Weaver, 3; Scott Allen Nollen, *Boris Karloff: A Critical Account of His Screen, Stage, Radio, Television, and Recording Work* (Jefferson, North Carolina: McFarland, 1991), 163.
20. Johnson, 7.
21. Cremer, 175–76.
22. Gary Don Rhodes, "A Hunger for Horror: The 1938 Revival of a Genre," email to Melvin E. Matthews, Jr., January 27, 2007. This article was originally published in *Scarlet Street* magazine in 1997 and 1998.
23. Mank, *Karloff and Lugosi*, 164.
24. Cremer, 187.
25. Rhodes, "A Hunger for Horror," email to Matthews.
26. Skal, *The Monster Show*, 204.
27. Rhodes, "A Hunger for Horror," email to Matthews.
28. Mank, *Women in Horror Films, 1930s*, 379.
29. Skal, *Screams of Reason*, 162.
30. Skal, *Screams of Reason*, 162; Mank, *Karloff and Lugosi*, 179, 181.
31. Mank, *Karloff and Lugosi*, 197–98.
32. Gifford, *Karloff*, 56.
33. Brunas, Brunas, and Weaver, 184–85; Vieira, *Hollywood Horror*, 97–98.
34. Drake Douglas, *Horror!* (New York: Macmillan, 1966), 135.
35. Rhodes, "A Hunger for Horror," email to Matthews.
36. "The Son of Frankenstein Starts a New Horror Cycle," *Look*, February 28, 1939, 39.
37. The Editors of *American Heritage, The American Heritage History of the 20's & 30's*, 380. An additional factor in explaining the scare was the American people's trust in radio — a confidence neatly summarized in the words of one listener: "We have so much *faith in broadcasting*. In a crisis it has to reach all people. That's what radio is here for." Gerd Horten, *Radio Goes to War: The Cultural Politics of Propaganda during World War II* (Berkeley: University of California Press, 2003), 27.
38. Robert Edwin Herzstein, *Roosevelt & Hitler: Prelude to War* (New York: Paragon House, 1989), 116.
39. Rhodes, "A Hunger for Horror," email to Matthews.
40. Skal, *Screams of Reason*, 161.
41. *Ibid.*,164.
42. Alonzo L. Hamby, *For the Survival of Democracy: Franklin Roosevelt and the World Crisis of the 1930s* (New York: Free Press, 2004), 427–28.
43. Richard M. Ketchum, *The Borrowed Years: 1938–1941. America on the Way to War* (New York: Random House, 1989), 203.
44. Hamby, 428–29; Skal, *Screams of Reason*, 165.
45. Hamby, 429.
46. Richard Bojarski, *The Films of Bela Lugosi* (Secaucus, New Jersey: The Citadel Press, 1980), 174.
47. Skal, *Screams of Reason*, 168.
48. Brunas, Brunas, and Weaver, 243, 244, 245, 527; Mank, *Karloff and Lugosi*, 235; David Zinman, *Saturday Afternoon at the Bijou* (New Rochelle, New York: Arlington House, 1973), 46–47.
49. Skal, *Screams of Reason*, 176.
50. Mank, *Women in Horror Films, 1940s*, 18.
51. Brunas, Brunas, and Weaver, 249.

Chapter 5

1. Ketchum, 768; Geoffrey Perrett, *Days of Sadness, Years of Triumph: The American People 1939–1945* (Baltimore: Penguin Books, 1974), 203.
2. Leuchtenburg, 114.
3. William K. Klingaman, *1941: Our Lives in a World on the Edge* (New York: Harper & Row, 1988), 427–29.
4. James MacGregor Burns, *Roosevelt: The Soldier of Freedom* (San Diego: Harcourt Brace Jovanovich, 1970), 172.
5. Ketchum, 792.
6. Ross Gregory, *America 1941: A Na-*

tion at the Crossroads (New York: The Free Press, 1989), 284.

7. Burns, *Roosevelt: The Soldier of Freedom*, 175.

8. Mank, *Women in Horror Films, 1940s*, 57.

9. Riley, *The Wolf Man*, 92.

10. Ibid., 92.

11. Ibid., 92.

12. Riley, *The Wolf Man*, 93; Mank, *Women in Horror Films, 1940s*, 57.

13. "Monster By Moonlight: The Immortal Saga of the Wolf Man," *The Wolf Man,* Universal Studios *Classic Monster Collection,* 1999.

14. Brunas, Brunas, and Weaver, 267.

15. Irena Gallier, "In Memory: Curt Siodmak, Creator of *The Wolf Man,* August 10, 1902–September 2, 2000," July 26, 2002.

16. Curt Siodmak, *Wolf Man's Maker: Memoir of a Hollywood Writer* (Lanham, Maryland: The Scarecrow Press, 2001), revised edition, 275–276.

17. Curt Siodmak, "Introduction to My Screenplay, *The Wolf Man,*" Riley, *The Wolf Man,* 13.

18. Ibid.,14.

19. Skal, *The Monster Show,* 213, 215.

20. Siodmak 262.

21. Siodmak in Riley, *The Wolf Man,* 14.

22. Skal, *The Monster Show,* 216, 218.

23. Patrick Sierchio, "Interview With a Wolf Man," By/1299/siodmak.html July 26, 2002. In a tribute to Siodmak, written at the time of his death, Irene Gallier wrote: "The Wolf Man, Siodmak was fond of explaining, was a man doomed to be outcast, a man who did not choose his fate or nature but had it thrust upon him as an inescapable curse and was persecuted for it. Siodmak's Wolf Man, at the mercy of the rising moon, was symbolic of himself at the mercy of the rising Hitler Regime [sic], and 'the mark of the werewolf,' a pentagram which appeared on the werewolf, was an unsubtle substitute for the Star of David with which Jews were branded by the Nazis." Film historian Jan-Christopher Horak also noted that *Under Wolf People,* the German title of Siodmak's autobiography, refers to those Germans who became Nazis and "turned from very likeable people into monsters." Gallier, "In Memory: Curt Siodmak, Creator of *The Wolf Man,* August 10, 1902–September 2, 2000," July 26, 2002; "Monster By Moonlight."

24. Robert G. L. Waite, *The Psychopathic God: Adolf Hitler* (New York: Basic Books, 1977), 28.

25. Nollen, *Boris Karloff: A Critical Account...*, 241–43.

26. Skal, *Screams of Reason,* 172.

27. "Production Background" by Gregory Wm. Mank, Philip J. Riley, editor, The Ghost of Frankenstein (*The Original Shooting Script*) (Absecon, New Jersey: MagicImage Filmbooks, 1990), 27, 28, 30.

28. "Production Notes," *The Ghost of Frankenstein.*

29. Noting that the film was released on April 3, 1942, just as the initial disclosures of Nazi barbarity in Eastern Europe were being made, Susan Tyler Hitchcock believes *The Ghost of Frankenstein* foreshadowed the Holocaust, particularly in the film's closing moments when Bohmer activates the switch, unleashing the lethal gas that overcomes the townspeople. Hitchcock also draws another connection between *Frankenstein* and the war by noting that wartime editorial cartoons employed the Frankenstein metaphor to depict Hitler's fortunes as they rose and fell in relation to the war he instigated. One of the earliest of these cartoons, drawn by Pultizer Prize winner Clifford K. Berryman, and appearing in the June 6, 1940, edition of a Washington paper — at a time when the Nazi war machine strode triumphantly over the European continent — portrayed the Fuhrer as a heavily armed military colossus dwarfing his fellow dictators Mussolini and Stalin. The latter pair are shown asking "Are WE Frankensteins?"— clearly implying that they sired Hitler. In characterizing Hitler in his cartoon, Berryman drew upon elements from the novel and Boris Karloff's screen appearances as well as his own interpretations. Berryman's Fuhrer is shown attired in a tank equipped with turret guns, and carried a smoking gun in one hand, "a skull-adorned swastika in the other." By 1943 and 1944, when the war was running against Hitler, editorial cartoonists were using the Frankenstein metaphor to depict the German blitzkrieg as turning against Hitler,

just as Frankenstein's Monster revolted against its creator. These cartoons, Hitchcock writes, characterized "key elements in the rise and fall of Adolf Hitler and the dynamics of World War II. Victor Frankenstein may have been a recluse in the novel, working in isolation, but to many living in the 1940s, his story resonated with world events as despots rose, commanded, and then fell victim to their own designs." Susan Tyler Hitchcock, *Frankenstein: A Cultural History* (New York: W. W. Norton, 2007), 193–97, 200–01.

30. "Production Notes," *The Ghost of Frankenstein*.

31. Tom Weaver, Michael Brunas, and John Brunas, *Universal Horrors: The Studio's Classic Films, 1931–1946* (Jefferson, North Carolina: McFarland, 2007), 275.

32. Pressbook, Riley, *The Ghost of Frankenstein*, unpaged.

33. Skal, *The Monster Show*, 215–16. Almost a year before the United States entered the war, the Joint Army and Navy Public Relations Committee contemplated investing $50 million for the establishment of "complete censorship of publications, radio and motion pictures within the U.S.A." Though FDR characterized this "a wild scheme," he did little to relax the military's hold on information once the United States became a belligerent. During the first twenty-one months of American participation in the conflict, no photograph of dead American military personnel was published lest such images precipitate a public demand for a premature peace. Finally, in September 1943, the censors, aided by *Life* magazine, reversed their policy of withholding such images, a decision motivated by several factors: first, a series of home front events—labor agitation, race riots, and political infighting between the powerful of Washington—made it seem that "business as usual" still prevailed in America; second, there were concerns that Italy's capitulation would cause Americans to believe the war was almost over; third, Hollywood war films, the scripts of which received careful scrutiny from the Office of War Information (OWI), showed few American casualties. "Washington," writes historian Thomas Fleming, "became concerned that Americans might conclude that only Germans and Japanese were willing to die for their country." That September an issue of *Life* featured on its cover a picture of three dead American soldiers on the beach in Buna, New Guinea, a demolished landing craft behind them. *Life* published an editorial accompanying the images proclaiming that it was time for Americans to face "war's terror." The nation's dead were in danger of dying meaninglessly "if live men refused to look at them." By the time this issue of *Life* hit the newsstands, tens of thousands of Americans had already been notified that a loved one had given his life in action. In praising the *Life* picture, the *Washington Post* maintained that the time had come for the government to treat the American people as adults, terming government manipulation of the people's emotions "intolerable." Having said this, the *Post* then opined that "an overdose of such photographs would be unhealthy." Shortly afterward, an OWI poll, conducted in the New York area, revealed that 75 percent of those canvassed endorsed the publication of pictures showing American dead. "In fact, the OWI concluded that the public had been barraged with so much preachy propaganda, they were somewhat immune to it." Only "hate pictures" sufficiently motivated the public to purchase war bonds. "Topping this bizarre conclusion was a telegram to the OWI from New Orleans: *Please rush airmail gruesome photos of dead American soldiers for plant promotion Third War Loan.*" Thomas Fleming, *The New Dealers' War: Franklin D. Roosevelt and the War Within World War II* (New York: Basic Books, 2001), 128, 380–81.

34. Skal, *The Monster Show*, 217.

35. Brunas, Brunas, and Weaver, 336; Skal, *Screams of Reason*, 172–73.

36. Brunas, Brunas, and Weaver, 336; Siodmak, 269.

37. Curt Siodmak, "Foreword" in Philip J. Riley, editor, Frankenstein Meets the Wolf Man (*The Original Shooting Script*) (Absecon, New Jersey: MagicImage Filmbooks, 1990), 8.

38. Lennig, *The Count*, 254.

39. Riley, *Frankenstein Meets the Wolf Man*, 11, 14, 15; Lennig, *The Count*, 255.

40. Riley, *Frankenstein Meets the Wolf Man,* 16–17.
41. *Ibid.,* 19, 22, 23.
42. *Ibid.,* 25.
43. Skal, *The Monster Show,* 217.
44. Douglas, 59.
45. Riley, *Frankenstein Meets the Wolf Man,* 24.
46. Weaver, Brunas, and Brunas, *Universal Horrors,* 326–27; Riley, *Frankenstein Meets the Wolf Man,* 23.
47. Weaver, Brunas, and Brunas, *Universal Horrors,* 327.
48. Riley, *Frankenstein Meets the Wolf Man,* 120, 126.
49. Weaver, Brunas, and Brunas, *Universal Horrors,* 502; Gregory Wm. Mank, "House of Dracula Production Background," Philip Riley, editor, House of Dracula (*The Original Shooting Script*) (Absecon, New Jersey: MagicImage Filmbooks, 1993), 26; Skal, *Screams of Reason,* 175.
50. "Foreword by Paul Malvern," Riley, *House of Dracula,* 13.
51. Riley, *House of Dracula* script, 104.
52. Skal, *The Monster Show,* 218.
53. Clarens, 111–12.
54. *Shadows in the Dark: The Val Lewton Legacy,* 2005, Warner Bros. Entertainment.
55. Joel E. Siegel, *Val Lewton: The Reality of Terror* (New York: The Viking Press, 1973), 21.
56. George E. Turner, editor, *The Cinema of Adventure, Romance & Terror* (Hollywood: The ASC Press, 1989), 233–34.
57. Edmund G. Bansak, *Fearing the Dark: The Val Lewton Career* (Jefferson, North Carolina: McFarland, 1990), 123; Turner, 234. The idea of a supernatural force confronting Hitler's legions wasn't solely Lewton's. In 1943, in the wake of *Cat People*'s release, Manly Wade Wellman penned the short story "The Devil Is Not Mocked," in which a Nazi general, von Grunn, and his men bivouac in a Balkan castle — the latter to be utilized as a command post for a German offensive. The castle's occupant, a man dressed in black, with "a pale, sharp face and brilliant eyes," welcomes the general and his men, acting as von Grunn's steward. At midnight, von Grunn's men are slaughtered by wolves. Too late, von Grunn discovers the identity of his host — Count Dracula! Twenty eight years later, Wellman's story was adapted for an installment of *Rod Serling's Night Gallery,* starring Helmut Dantine, who portrayed Nazis in Hollywood films during World War II, as the ill-fated general, and Francis Lederer as Dracula. The story is told in flashback, as Dracula, now a grandfather, tells his grandson how he served his country during the war. Despite his evil reputation, Dracula was a patriot as he explains: "[W]hile many are the terrible charges made against our ancestors, let no man deny our patriotism." John Pelan, editor, *The Devil Is Not Mocked and Other Warnings: Selected Stories of Manly Wade Wellman, Volume 2* (San Francisco: Night Shade Books, 2001), 5–10.
58. Bansak, 125; *Shadows in the Dark.*
59. In a deleted sequence that was to open the swimming pool episode, Alice checks in with a desk clerk at the apartment. The clerk was to have said that she was too busy with Civilian Defense work to go on a date, further "them Japs and Nazis is whittling down her love life." The latter phrase raised objections from the Breen Office, which requested that the line be changed to "social life." The entire line was discarded. "Commentary by Greg Mank with Simone Simon."

Chapter 6

1. Clayton R. Koppes and Gregory D. Black, *Hollywood Goes To War: How Politics, Profits, and Propaganda Shaped World War II Movies* (New York: The Free Press, 1987), 15, 21, 22.
2. Gregory, 232.
3. Koppes and Black, 60, 61.
4. Richard R. Lingeman, *Don't You Know There's a War On? The American Home Front 1941–1945* (New York: G. P. Putnam's Sons, 1970), 176.
5. Koppes and Black, 281.
6. Arthur Lennig, *The Immortal Count: The Life and Films of Bela Lugosi* (Lexington, Kentucky: The University Press of Kentucky, 2003), 304; Bojarski, 180–81.
7. Tom Weaver, *Poverty Row Horrors! Monogram, PRC and Republic Horror Films of the Forties* (Jefferson, North Carolina: McFarland, 1993), 57.

8. Rhodes, *Lugosi*, 123; Bojarski, 180.
9. Rick Worland, "OWI Meets the Monsters: Hollywood Horror Films and War Propaganda, 1942 to 1945," *Cinema Journal*, Vol. 37. No. 1 (Autumn 1997) July 20, 2008, 49.
10. Weaver, *Poverty Row Horrors!*, 74–75.
11. In pursuit of his goal, Cameron toils in secrecy in a swampland plantation, justifying his reclusive existence to his daughter's journalist boyfriend by saying, "I buried myself in this out-of-the-way place so I could work undisturbed — away from snooping reporters who only ridicule what they have not the intelligence to understand." The secrecy that Cameron and his ilk surrounded themselves with wasn't solely a characteristic of wartime cinematic fare, the real-life effort to perfect the atomic bomb being an obvious example. Additionally, those individuals who happened upon the mad scientist's secret project suffered Draconian consequences for their meddling. "Part of the message conveyed by Hollywood horror pictures was that it was better not to poke around laboratories, ask too many questions, or interfere with technoscientific prerogatives generally." Skal, *Screams of Reason*, 176.
12. Apparently the analyst failed to take note of the racist line of dialogue in one of the film's scenes involving plantation mistress Katherine Caldwell (Louise Allbritton), who has arranged for the count to come to America with the intention of becoming a vampire herself, then turning her fiancé into a member of the undead ranks so the two of them can live together forever. When one of the black servants handling the count's luggage tells her the latter is "amazingly heavy," Caldwell replies, "Then get some of the other *boys* [italics added] to help you."
13. Worland, "OWI Meets the Monsters," July 20, 2008, 50–52.
14. Weaver, Brunas, and Brunas, *Universal Horrors*, 295; Smith, *H.G. Wells on Film*, 79.
15. John W. Dower, *War Without Mercy: Race and Power in the Pacific War* (New York: Pantheon Books, 1986), 84–87.
16. Dower, 81; Horten, 55.
17. Lingeman, 189–90.
18. Weaver, Brunas, and Brunas, *Universal Horrors*, 297.
19. Brunas, Brunas, and Weaver, 306.
20. Worland, "OWI Meets the Monsters," July 20 2008, 52; Leuchtenburg, 115*n*.
21. Another zombie film that met with BMP chief Ulric Bell's disapproval was Val Lewton's *I Walked with a Zombie*: In its portrayal of West Indian voodoo, it appeared to depict an acute distinction between the races. Bell apparently failed to see any harm in one of the film's character's acceptance of voodoo as a potent instrument but the film nevertheless unsettled him. On February 4, 1943, the studio invited OWI to preview *I Walked with a Zombie*—one day after it had received clearance for foreign exhibition. Koppes and Black, 127–28.
22. *Ibid.*, 53–55.
23. Bojarski, 37.
24. Lennig, *The Immortal Count*, 322.
25. Ronald H. Bailey and the Editors of Time-Life Books, *World War II. The Home Front: U.S.A.* (Alexandria, Virginia: Time-Life Books, 1977), 85–86, 90.
26. Worland, "OWI Meets the Monsters," July 20, 2008, 57, 59, 58.
27. *Ibid.*, 60–61.
28. Lennig, *The Immortal Count*, 327.
29. Skal, *The Monster Show*, 223.
30. Cremer, 199–200.
31. Frank J. Dello Stritto, "Lugosi in Politics," in Rhodes, *Lugosi*, 61.
32. Lennig, *The Immortal Count*, 336–38.
33. *Ibid.*, 376–77.
34. Nollen, *Boris Karloff: A Gentleman's Life* 139, 141–43, 157–59, 161.
35. Don G. Smith, *Lon Chaney, Jr.: Horror Film Star, 1906–1973* (Jefferson, North Carolina: McFarland, 1996), 70–71.
36. Siodmak, 268, 300–01, 305, 317, 329.

Chapter 7

1. Lennig, *The Immortal Count*, 349.
2. Bansak, 305–06.
3. Lennig, *The Immortal Count*, 350.
4. Weaver, Brunas, and Brunas, *Universal Horrors*, 561–62.

5. *Ibid.,* 2.
6. Skal, *The Monster Show,* 278.
7. Weaver, Brunas, and Brunas, *Universal Horrors,* 2–3.
8. *Ibid.,* 562–63.
9. *Ibid.,* 1.
10. Robert Sklar, *Movie-Made America: A Cultural History of American Movies* (New York: Vintage Books, 1975, 1994), revised and updated, 179.

Bibliography

Books

Alter, Jonathan. *The Defining Moment: FDR's Hundred Days and the Triumph of Hope.* New York: Simon & Schuster, 2006.

Baily, Ronald H., and the Editors of Time-Life Books. *World War II. The Home Front: U.S.A.* Alexandria: Time-Life Books, 1977.

Bansak, Edmund G. *Fearing the Dark: The Val Lewton Career.* Jefferson, North Carolina: McFarland, 1990.

Barck, Oscar Theodore, Jr., and Nelson Manfred Blake. *Since 1900: A History of the United States in Our Times.* Fourth Edition. New York: Macmillan, 1965.

Bergman, Andrew. *We're in the Money: Depression America and Its Films.* Chicago: Ivan R. Dee, 1992.

Bojarski, Richard. *The Films of Bela Lugosi.* Secaucus, New Jersey: Citadel Press, 1980.

Brinkley, Alan. *The Unfinished Nation: A Concise History of the American People.* New York: Alfred A. Knopf, 1993.

Brunas, Michael, John Brunas, and Tom Weaver. *Universal Horrors: The Studio's Classic Films, 1931–1946.* Jefferson, North Carolina: McFarland, 1990.

Burns, James MacGregor. *Roosevelt: The Lion and the Fox.* New York: Harcourt Brace Jovanovich, 1956.

_____. *Roosevelt: The Soldier of Freedom.* San Diego: Harcourt Brace Jovanovich, Publishers, 1970.

Clarens, Carlos. *An Illustrated History of the Horror Film.* New York: Capricorn Books, 1968.

Cohn, Daniel. *A Natural History of Unnatural Things.* New York: McCall Publishing, 1971.

Cremer, Robert. *Lugosi: The Man Behind the Cape.* Chicago: Henry Regnery, 1976.

Curtis, James. *James Whale: A New World of Gods and Monsters.* Boston: Faber and Faber, 1998.

Davies, Kenneth S. *FDR: The New York Years, 1928–1933.* New York: Random House, 1985.

Doherty, Thomas. *Pre-Code Hollywood: Sex, Immortality, and Insurrection in American Cinema, 1930–1934.* New York: Columbia University Press, 1999.

Douglas, Drake. *Horror!* New York: Macmillan, 1966.

Dower, John W. *War Without Mercy: Race and Power in the Pacific War.* New York: Pantheon Books, 1986.

Editors of *American Heritage*. *The American Heritage History of the 20's & 30's*. New York: American Heritage, 1970.
Editors of Time-Life Books. *This Fabulous Century. Volume IV: 1930–1940*. New York: Time-Life Books, 1969.
Fleming, Thomas. *The New Dealers' War: Franklin D. Roosevelt and the War Within World War II*. New York: Basic Books, 2001.
Freidel, Frank. *Franklin D. Roosevelt: Launching the New Deal*. Boston: Little, Brown, 1973.
Gallagher, Hugh Gregory. *FDR's Splendid Deception*. New York: Dodd, Mead, 1985.
Gifford, Denis. *Karloff: The Man, the Monster, the Movies*. New York: Curtis Books, 1973.
_____. *Movie Monsters*. New York: E. P. Dutton, 1969.
Goldner, Orville, and George E. Turner. *The Making of* King Kong: *The Story Behind a Film Classic*. Cranbury: A. S. Barnes, 1975.
Grant, Barry Keith, editor. *Planks of Reason: Essays on the Horror Film*. Metuchen, New Jersey: Scarecrow Press, 1984.
Gregory, Ross. *America 1941: A Nation at the Crossroads*. New York: Free Press, 1989.
Hamby, Alonzo L. *For the Survival of Democracy: Franklin Roosevelt and the World Crisis of the 1930s*. New York: Free Press, 2004.
Herzstein, Robert Edwin. *Roosevelt and Hitler: Prelude to War*. New York: Paragon House, 1989.
Hicks, John D. *Republican Ascendancy, 1921–1933*. New York: Harper Torchbooks, 1963.
Higham, Charles. *Charles Laughton: An Intimate Biography*. Garden City, New York: Doubleday, 1976.
Hitchcock, Susan Tyler. *Frankenstein: A Cultural History*. New York: W. W. Norton, 2007.
Horan, James D. *The Desperate Years: A Pictorial History of the Thirties*. New York: Bonanza Books, 1962.
Horten, Gerd. *Radio Goes to War: The Cultural Politics of Propaganda During World War II*. Berkeley: University of California Press, 2003.
Houck, Davis W. *FDR and Fear Itself: The First Inaugural Address*. College Station: Texas A&M University Press, 2002.
Jensen, Paul M. *Boris Karloff and His Films*. Cranbury: A. S. Barnes, 1974.
_____. *The Men Who Made the Monsters*. New York: Twayne Publishers, 1996.
Johnson, Tom. *Censored Screams: The British Ban on Hollywood Horror in the Thirties*. Jefferson, North Carolina: McFarland, 1997.
Joslin, Lyndon W. *Count Dracula Goes to the Movies: Stoker's Novel Adapted, 1922–1995*. Jefferson, North Carolina: McFarland, 1999.
Kennedy, David M. *Freedom from Fear: The American People in Depression and War, 1929–1945*. New York: Oxford University Press, 1999.
Ketchum, Richard M. *The Borrowed Years: 1938–1941. America on the Way to War*. New York: Random House, 1989.
Klingaman, William K. *1941: Our Lives in a World on the Edge*. New York: Harper & Row, 1988.
Koppes, Clayton R., and Gregory D. Black. *Hollywood Goes to War: How Politics, Profits, and Propaganda Shaped World War II Movies*. New York: Free Press, 1987.
Lennig, Arthur. *The Count: The Life and Films of Bela "Dracula" Lugosi*. New York: G.P. Putnam's Sons, 1974.
_____. *The Immortal Count: The Life and Films of Bela Lugosi*. Lexington: University Press of Kentucky, 2003.

Leuchtenberg, William E., and the Editors of *Life*. *The* Life *History of the United States. Volume 11: 1933–1945. New Deal and Global War.* New York: Time, Inc., 1964.
Lingeman, Richard R. *Don't You Know There's a War On? The American Home Front 1941–1945.* New York: G.P. Putnam's Sons, 1970.
Mackay, Margaret. *The Violent Friend: The Story of Mrs. Robert Louis Stevenson.* Garden City, New York: Doubleday, 1968.
Maddrey, Joseph. *Nightmares in Red, White and Blue: The Evolution of the American Horror Film.* Jefferson, North Carolina: McFarland, 2004.
Manchester, William. *The Glory and the Dream: A Narrative History of America, 1932–1972.* New York: Bantam Books, 1975.
Mank, Gregory William. *Karloff and Lugosi: The Story of a Haunting Collaboration.* Jefferson, North Carolina: McFarland, 1990.
_____. *Women in Horror Films, 1930s.* Jefferson, North Carolina: McFarland, 1999.
_____. *Women in Horror Films, 1940s.* Jefferson, North Carolina: McFarland, 1999.
_____, James T. Coughlin and Dwight D. Frye. *Dwight Frye's Last Laugh: An Unauthorized Biography.* Baltimore: Midnight Marquee Press, 1997.
Marx, Samuel. *Mayer and Thalberg: The Make-Believe Saints.* New York: Random House, 1975.
May, Ernest R., and the Editors of *Life*. *The* Life *History of the United States. Volume 10: 1917–1932. War, Boom and Bust.* New York: Time, Inc., 1964.
McElvaine, Robert S. *The Great Depression: America, 1929–1941.* New York: Times Books, 1984.
McNally, Raymond T., and Radu Florescu. *In Search of Dracula: A True History of Dracula and Vampire Legends.* Greenwich, Connecticut: New York Graphic Society, 1972.
Milne, Tom. *Rouben Mamoulian.* Bloomington: Indiana University Press, 1969.
Morton, Ray. *King Kong: The History of a Movie Icon: From Fay Wray to Peter Jackson.* New York: Applause Theatre & Cinema Books, 2005.
Nollen, Scott Allen. *Boris Karloff: A Critical Account of His Screen, Stage, Radio, Television, and Recording Work.* Jefferson, North Carolina: McFarland, 1991.
_____. *Boris Karloff: A Gentleman's Life.* Baltimore: Midnight Marquee Press, 1999.
Pelan, John, editor. *"The Devil Is Not Mocked" and Other Warnings: Selected Stories of Manly Wade Wellman, Volume 2.* San Francisco: Night Shade Books, 2001.
Perrett, Geoffrey. *Days of Sadness, Years of Triumph: The American People 1939–1945.* Baltimore: Penguin Books, 1974.
Rhodes, Gary Don. *Lugosi: His Life in Films, on Stage, and in the Hearts of Horror Lovers.* Jefferson, North Carolina: McFarland, 1997.
_____. *White Zombie: Anatomy of a Horror Film.* Jefferson, North Carolina: McFarland, 2001.
Riley, Philip J., editor. Frankenstein Meets the Wolf Man (*The Original Shooting Script*). Absecon, New Jersey: MagicImage Filmbooks, 1990.
_____, editor. The Ghost of Frankenstein (*The Original Shooting Script*). Absecon, New Jersey: MagicImage Filmbooks, 1990.
_____, editor. House of Dracula (*The Original Shooting Script*). Absecon, New Jersey: MagicImage Filmbooks, 1993.
_____, editor. *MagicImage Filmbooks Presents* Dracula (*The Original 1931 Shooting Script*). Absecon, New Jersey: MagicImage Filmbooks, 1990.
_____, editor. *MagicImage Filmbooks Presents* Frankenstein. *Universal Filmscripts Series. Classic Films–Volume 1.* Absecon, New Jersey: MagicImage Filmbooks, 1989.
_____, editor. The Wolf Man (*The Original 1941 Shooting Script*). Absecon, New Jersey: MagicImage Filmbooks, 1993.

Sachar, Howard M. *A History of the Jews in America.* New York: Alfred A. Knopf, 1992.
Schatz, Thomas. *The Genius of the System: Hollywood Filmmaking in the Studio Era.* New York: Pantheon Books, 1988.
Sevastakis, Michael. *Songs of Love and Death: The Classical American Horror Film of the 1930s.* Westport, Connecticut: Greenwood Press, 1993.
Sherwin, Mark, and Charles Lam Markman. *One Week in March.* New York: G.P. Putnam's Sons, 1961.
Siegel, Joel E. *Val Lewton: The Reality of Terror.* New York: Viking Press, 1973.
Siodmak, Curt. *Wolf Man's Maker: Memoir of a Hollywood Writer.* Revised edition. Lanham, Maryland: Scarecrow Press, 2001.
Skal, David J. *Hollywood Gothic: The Tangled Web of Dracula from Novel to Stage to Screen.* New York: W.W. Norton, 1990.
_____. *The Monster Show: A Cultural History of Horror.* New York: W.W. Norton, 1993.
_____. *Screams of Reason: Mad Science and Modern Culture.* New York: W.W. Norton, 1998.
_____, and Elias Savada. *Dark Carnival: The Secret World of Tod Browning, Hollywood's Master of the Macabre.* New York: Anchor Books, 1995.
Sklar, Robert. *Movie-Made America: A Cultural History of American Movies.* New York: Vintage Books, 1975, 1994.
Smith, Don G. *H.G. Wells on Film: The Utopian Nightmare.* Jefferson, North Carolina: McFarland, 2002.
_____. *Lon Chaney, Jr.: Horror Film Star, 1906–1973.* Jefferson, North Carolina: McFarland, 1996.
Smith, Gene. *The Shattered Dream: Herbert Hoover and the Great Depression.* New York: William Morrow, 1970.
Steinbrunner, Chris, and Burt Goldblatt. *Cinema of the Fantastic.* New York: Galahad Books, 1972.
Thomas, Bob. *Thalberg: Life and Legend.* Garden City, New York: Doubleday, 1959.
Turner, George E., editor. *The Cinema of Adventure, Romance and Terror.* Hollywood: ASC Press, 1989.
Underwood, Peter. *Karloff: The Life of Boris Karloff.* New York: Drake Publishers, 1972.
Vieira, Mark A. *Hollywood Horror: From Gothic to Cosmic.* New York: Harry N. Abrams, 2003.
_____. *Sin in Soft Focus: Pre-Code Hollywood.* New York: Harry N. Abrams, 1999.
Waite, Robert G.L. *The Psychopathic God: Adolf Hitler.* New York: Basic Books, 1977.
Watkins, T. H. *The Great Depression: America in the 1930s.* Boston: Little, Brown, 1993.
Weaver, Tom. *Poverty Row Horrors! Monogram, PRC and Republic Horror Films of the Forties.* Jefferson, North Carolina: McFarland, 1993.
_____, Michael Brunas and John Brunas. *Universal Horrors: The Studio's Classic Films, 1931–1946.* Jefferson, North Carolina: McFarland, 1990. (A second edition was published in 2007.)
White, Richard D., Jr. *Kingfish: The Reign of Huey P. Long.* New York: Random House, 2006.
Zinman, David. *50 Classic Motion Pictures.* New York: Crown Publishers, 1970.
_____. *Saturday Afternoon at the Bijou.* New Rochelle, New York: Arlington House, 1973.

Articles

Bell, Nelson B. "Thoughts on Horror Era, Renaissance and Miss Ulric," *The Washington Post*, February 21, 1932.
Dello Stritto, Frank J. "Are We Not Men? The Evolution of Darwin in Hollywood," *Cult Movies* #41.
Gallier, Irena. "In Memory: Curt Siodmak, Creator of *The Wolf Man*, August 10, 1902–September 2, 2000," July 26, 2002.
"How the Horror Movies of the Great Depression Reflected the History of the Time," www.associatedcontent.com/pop_culture.shtml?content_type=article&content_type _id... July 12, 2008.
Newitz, Annalee. "A Lower-Class, Sexy Monster, *Bright Lights Film Journal* #15, 1995.
"Our Horror, Ourselves," sevenF.html July 13, 2008.
Phillips. Michael W., Jr. "The Fall of the House of Dracula," July 13, 2008.
Rhodes, Gary Don. "A Hunger for Horror! The 1938 Revival of a Genre," email to Melvin E. Matthews, Jr., January 27, 2007, originally published in *Scarlet Street* magazine in 1997 and 1998.
"The Seduction of Renfield," http://everything2.com/index.pl?node_id=1928413&displaytype=printable&lastnode_id=0. July 13, 2008.
Sierchio, Patrick. "Interview With a Wolf Man," Written By/siodmak.html. July 26, 2002.
"The Son of Frankenstein Starts a New Horror Cycle," *Look*, February 28, 1939.
"Vampires, Monsters, Horrors!" *The New York Times*, March 1, 1936.
Worland, Rick. "OWI Meets the Monsters: Hollywood Horror Films and War Propaganda, 1942 to 1945," *Cinema Journal*, Vol. 37. No. 1 (Autumn 1997). July 20, 2008.
Wray, Fay. "How Fay Met Kong, Or the Scream That Shook the World," *The New York Times*, September 21, 1969: D17.

Index

Adamic, Louis 5
All Quiet on the Western Front (1930) 13, 14, 15, 16
Allbritton, Louise 195*n*.
Alter, Jonathan 87
Amalgamated Clothing Workers' *Advance* 59
American Film Institute (AFI) 77
American Hungarian Defense Federation 141
American Legion 86, 87
Ames, Leon (Waycoff) 47
Ames, Ramsay 166
Ancient Sorceries (Blackwood) 146
Ankers, Evelyn 127, 129, 130
The Ape Man (1943) 133
Arlen, Richard 69
Arsenic and Old Lace 174–175
Asher, E.M. 46
Ates, Roscoe 52
Atkinson, G.A. 33
atomic bomb 4, 122–123, 124, 195*n*.
Atwill, Lionel 113, 122, 124, 125, 135

Baclanova, Olga 52
Badeau, Dr. John 165
Bain, Reed 38, 39
Balderston, John L. 11, 16, 17, 95, 180
Banking crisis of 1933 76–77, 87
Barclay, Joan 152
Barrymore, John 40
Behlmer, Rudy 77
Bell, Nelson B. 38
Bell, Ulric 156, 164, 195*n*.
Bellamy, Madge 62, 183
Bellamy, Ralph 127, 129, 131
Bergman, Andrew 83
Bergquist, Lillian 163, 170

Berry, Wallace 45
Berryman, Clifford K. 192*n*.
Bioray 31
Birmingham Daily Mail 101
The Black Cat (1934) 95
Black Dragons (1942): inspiration for 151–152; Lugosi's role in compared to *Dracula* 154, 161; plot of 153–154
Black Friday (1940) 114
Black Moon (1934) 3
Blackwood, Algernon 146
Blumberg, Nate J. 110, 114
BMP *see* Bureau of Motion Pictures
"bonus marchers" ("Bonus Expeditionary Force") 59, 65, 182
Borland, Carroll 17
Boston Herald 172
Breen, Joseph 73, 103, 112, 144, 150, 194*n*.
Bride of Frankenstein (1935) 95, 101–102, 103
British Board of Film Censors 102, 103, 109, 112
British horror ban 3, 101–103, 109
Bromberg, J. Edward 158
Bromfield, Louis 16, 17
Broun, Heywood 116
Browning, Tod 15, 16, 17, 52, 57, 59–60, 103
Bruce, Nigel 134
Brunas, John 157, 162, 180
Brunas, Michael 157, 162, 180
Buck Privates (1941) 150
Bureau of Motion Pictures (BMP), evaluation of films and attitude toward wartime horror films 156–157, 163–166
Burke, Kathleen 73
Butler, Nicholas Murray 86

203

Butler, Gen. Smedley 86
Byington, Spring 98
Byron, Lord 6, 7

Cabot, Bruce 79, 84
Cantor, Eddie 171
Cantril, Hadley 116
Capra, Frank 108
Carradine, John 27, 144, 163, 166
Carroll, Noel 84
Cat People (1942): original conception for 146; plot of 146–149; realistic characters of 146; war reference in deleted from 194*n*.
The Cat and the Canary (1927) 15
Censorship of photographs of American casualties of World War II 193*n*.
Chamberlain, Neville 168
Chandler, Helen 22
Chaney, Lon 2, 15, 16, 17, 26, 52, 86, 110, 122
Chaney, Lon, Jr. 122, 124, 125, 127, 128, 129, 130, 133, 134, 135, 136, 139, 154, 166, 167; member of war bond tour 175–176
Churchill, Marguerite 106
Cinema Progress 110
Clapper, Raymond 5
The Climax 138
Cochrane, Robert H. 108, 110
Coley, Thomas 120
Colin, Clive 96
Colton, John 97, 100
Conway, Moncure D. 145
Cooper, Merian C. 77, 78, 80, 84
cosmic rays as commercial products 31
Cowdin, J. Cheever 101, 108
Creation 78
Creelman, James 78
Cremer, Robert 109
Cromwell, Louise 114
Crowther, Bosley 135
Cry of the Werewolf (1944) 133

Dade, Francis 20
Dantine, Helmut 194*n*.
Darwin, Charles 8, 46
Darwin, Maj. Leonard 46
Deane, Hamilton 10–11, 17, 180
Dearborn, Michigan (protest march of 1932) 58–59
De Carlo, Yvonne 138
Dekker, Albert 119, 120, 175
Del Toro, Guillermo 145

"The Devil Is Not Mocked" (Wellman) 194*n*.
Dijkstra, Bram 185–186*n*.
Dione, Rose 52
Dr. Cyclops (1940) 119, 121, 181
Dr. Jekyll and Mr. Hyde (1920 silent version with John Barrymore) 40
Dr. Jekyll and Mr. Hyde (1932 sound version with Fredric March) 41–43, 181
Doherty, Thomas 58, 70, 79, 82, 83
Douglas, Drake 115
Dracula (Stoker novel) 7–8; anti-immigrant attitudes signified by 7–8
Dracula (1931 film) 2, 12–13, 15–18, 103, 109, 111, 112, 179, 181; anti-immigration sentiment and 20–23; compared to *King Kong* 79; Depression metaphors of 18–20; Hoover-Roosevelt clash represented by 23–24; plot of 18–20, 24
Dracula (1943 theatrical revival of) 167
Dracula's Daughter (1936) 103–107, 108, 109
Dracula's Death 9
Dunne, John 149
Durbin, Deanna 108, 114

Earles, Daisy 52
Earles, Harry 52
Early, Steve 126
East and West of Suez: The Story of Modern Egypt (Badeau) 165
East Side of Heaven 114
Eck, Johnny 52
Edison, Thomas 8
Emery, Gilbert 104
Endore, Guy 96
Enemy Agents Meet Ellery Queen (1942) 151
Esper, Dwain 58
eugenics (*Murders in the Rue Morgue*) 46; *Freaks* 57
experts, popular distrust of during the Depression 38

Famous Monsters of Filmland 179
Fantasmogoriana 6
Faragoh, Francis Edwards 47
Farrell, Nancy 174
Farson, Daniel 8
fascism advocated as remedy for the Depression 86
Fermi, Enrico 122–123
Fields, W.C. 114
Film Daily Yearbook (1939) 110

Fish, Hamilton, Jr. 86
Fithian, T.B. 35
Fleming, Thomas 193*n*.
Florey, Robert 25–26, 46, 47; dropped as director of *Frankenstein* 27
Foch, Nina 168
"food riots" during 1931 19
Ford, Ford Maddox 83
Ford, John 108
Ford, Wallace 52
Forry, Steven Earl 7
Fort, Garrett 17, 26
Foster, Susanna 138
The Four Feathers (1929) 77
Fox, Sidney 47
Fox Criterion (Los Angeles) 54
Francis, Arlene 49
Frankenstein (Edison film) 8
Frankenstein (1931 film) 2, 13, 25, 103, 109, 111, 112, 179, 181; approved for viewing in Canada 34–35; metaphor for Hoover-Roosevelt clash and the Depression 32, 33–34, 35–36
Frankenstein Meets the Wolf Man (1943): anti-gypsy sentiment in compared to Nazi persecution of 142; genesis of 138–139; Lugosi's dialogue deleted from 142–143; plot of 141–144; war parallels to 141
Frankenstein Monster metaphor for combat injuries 137–138
Frankenstein; or the Modern Prometheus (Shelley novel) 7
Frayling, Christopher 7
Frazier, Robert 63, 66, 183
Freaks (1932) 51, 52–54; backlash against 56–58; Depression metaphors of 58–59, 181; plot of 54–56
Freeman, Harold 16
Freund, Karl 100
Frye, Dwight 22, 111
Frye, Dwight, Jr. 111
Fussell, Paul 137

Gallier, Irene 192*n*.
Gerrard, Charles 22
Gershenson, Joseph 165, 166
The Ghost of Frankenstein (1942) 139; war-themed contest urged by pressbook for 137; war metaphors of 135
The Ghoul 112
Gifford, Denis 40
Il Giornale d'Italia 85
Goebbels, Joseph 82

Goldbeck, Willis 51–52
Goldner, Orville 84
Grable, Betty 138
Grauman, Sid 82
Grauman's Chinese Theater 82
Great Expectations 97
Green, Betty 53
Grey, Nan 106
Griffies, Ethel 100

Hall, Jon 157, 160
Halperin brothers *(White Zombie)* 62
Hamby, Alonzo L. 118
Hammer Films 179
Hardwicke, Sir Cedric 135, 137, 157, 160, 162
Harlow, Jean 52
Harmatia 131
Harrigan, William 89
Harron, John 62
Harryhausen, Ray 77
Hays, Will 37
Hays Office 2
Hays Production Code 2, 3
Heath, Percy 41
Helm, Fay 130
Higham, Charles 71
Hill, Katherine 189*n*.
Hilton, Daisy 53
Hilton, Violet 53
Hinds, Samuel S. 122
Hitchcock, Alfred 180
Hitchcock, Susan Tyler 192–193*n*.
Hitler, Adolf 85, 172; equated with title character in *Dr. Cyclops* 121, 122; rise and fall of equated with *Frankenstein* 192–193*n*.; wolf obsession of 133–134
Hobson, Valerie 97
Hoffenstein, Samuel 41
Holden, Gloria 104, 105
The Hollywood Reporter 127, 141
Holton, Charles 119, 120
Hoover, Herbert 5, 23, 59; post-election clash with Roosevelt 23–24
Hopkins, Anthony 45
Hopkins, Miriam 45
Horak, Jan-Christopher 192*n*.
Horror decline after World War II 178–179
Horror revival of the late 1930s 111–112
Horthy, Admiral Miklos 172
House of Dracula (1945) 133, 144–145

House of Frankenstein (1944) 144
House of Frankenstein 1997 180
House Un-American Activities Committee (HUAC) 173, 174
Hull, Cordell 117
Hull, Henry 97, 99
The Hunchback of Notre Dame 15
hunger marches 59
Hungarian-American Council for Democracy 173
Hungarian Council for Democracy 172, 173
Huntley, Raymond 10–11
Hutton, Barbara 106
Hyams, Leila 52, 71
Hyde, Buddy 171

I Walked with a Zombie 195n.
Imitation of Life 96
Inescort, Freda 167, 169
Insull, Samuel 58, 66
Invisible Agent (1942): BMP's evaluation of 163; plot of 157–161; portrayal of German and Japanese allies 159, 160–161, 162
The Invisible Man (1933 film): personification of Superman concept 91–92; plot of 89–91, 92–93
The Invisible Man (Wells) 87–88; interpretations of 88
The Invisible Man Returns (1940) 114
The Invisible Woman (1940) 114
Irving, Henry 8
The Island of Dr. Moreau (Wells) 68–69
Island of Lost Souls (1933) 68, 69–73, 181; British ban of 74

Jackson, Peter 1, 181
Japanese (racist attitudes toward during World War II) 161–162
Jensen, Paul M. 36, 91
Joint Army and Navy Public Relations Committee 193n.
Jones, Dorothy B. 170
Josephine/Joseph 53
Joy, Colonel Jason 37–38, 73

Kansas City Star 2
Karloff, Boris 179; appears in *Arsenic and Old Lace* at West Point and in the Pacific 174–175; early life and career and chosen to play the Frankenstein Monster 27–28, 29, 30, 36, 95, 110, 112, 113, 114, 115, 134, 138, 139, 144, 192n.; wartime service as air raid warden 174
Karolyi, Count Michael 173
Katzman, Sam 151
Kilian, Victor 120
Kinematograph Weekly 101
King Kong (1933) 111, 112, 130; anti–New York sentiments and 83, 84, 183–184; death equated to the Depression 82; epitomizes dangers of upward mobility 84; inspiration for 77–78; opens during banking crisis 77; plot of 78–82; rampage through New York symbolic of moviegoers' powerlessness during the Depression 81; symbolic meanings attributed to 82–83
King Kong (2005) 181
Knowles, Patric 127, 131, 142
Koerner, Charles 146
Koo Koo 53
Krueger, Otto 104
Ku Klux Klan (revival during the 1920s) 21, 23

Laemmle, Carl 13, 101, 108
Laemmle, Carl, Jr. 13–14, 15, 16, 25, 26–27, 34, 95–96, 107, 108
Lanchester, Elsa 74, 96, 101
Langella, Frank 180
La Rose, Rose 82
The Last Warning (1929) 15
Laughton, Charles 69, 70–71, 72
Le Borg, Reginald 134
Lederer, Francis 194n.
Lee, Gypsy Rose 82
Lee, Rowland V. 114, 115
Legion of Decency 108
Leni, Paul 15
Lennig, Arthur 7, 62, 70
Lerner, Max 50
Lewis, David 27; on *Frankenstein*'s Santa Barbara preview 34
Lewton, Val 3, 145, 181, 195n.
Library of Congress 77
Lichtman, Al 14
Life 193n.
Life Without Soul (1915) 8–9
Lippmann, Walter 86
Liveright, Horace 11, 16, 17
Logan, Janice 120
London After Midnight 103
The London Times 102–103
Long, Huey 87
Look 115

Lorre, Peter 157, 160, 162
Loy, Myrna 52
Lugosi, Bela 11–12, 16, 179, 183; activities on behalf of the war effort 171–172; chosen to play Dracula 17, 25; political activities during the war 172–173, 174; refuses to play the Frankenstein Monster in 1931 26–27, 36, 46, 47, 49, 66, 70, 95, 103, 110, 111–112, 113, 115, 118, 127, 129, 130, 136, 139, 140, 141, 142, 143, 152, 153, 167

MacArthur, Douglas 59, 87, 114
MacDonald, Marie 138
The Mad Monster (1942) 154–155
The Magic Island (1929) 61
Magnificent Obsession 96, 101, 107
Mail Call 171
Malvern, Paul 144–145
Mamoulian, Rouben 40, 41
Man Made Monster (1941) 115, 121–125, 155; title character symbolizes America's loss of innocence in World War II 123–124
The Man Who Laughs (1928) 15
Mank, Gregory William 114
Mansfield, Richard 40
March, Fredric 41, 45, 181
Mark of the Vampire (1935) 103
Markey, Morris 5, 6
The Mask of Fu Manchu (1932) 3
Massey, Ilona 154–155
Matthews, Lester 97
May, Joe 114
Mayer, Louis B. 57
Mayfair Theatre (New York) 35, 47
McConnell, Frank 88–89
McElvaine, Robert 2
Melford, George 46
Mercury Theater on the Air 110, 115–116
Meredith, Burgess 122
Miracles for Sale (1939) 60
Mitchell, Charles 58, 66
Montagne, Eddie: on *Frankenstein*'s Santa Barbara preview 34
Moore, Clayton 152
Morris, Leland 127
Morris, Martha 54
Morris Theatre (Illinois) 84
Morton, Ray 84
Moscow Art Theater 52
Motion Picture Daily 57
Motion Picture Herald 35, 53, 62, 77, 127

Motion Picture Producers and Distributors Association (MPPDA) 37, 38
Mrs. Miniver 110
The Mummy (1999) 180
The Mummy Returns (2001) 180
The Mummy's Ghost (1944) 164–166
The Mummy's Hand (1940) 114
Munich crisis of 1938 115–116
The Munsters 180
Murder by the Clock (1931) 37
Murders in the Rue Morgue (1932) 25, 46–40
Murnau, Friedrich Wilhelm 9–10
Muse, Clarence 12, 67–68
Music Box Theater (Seattle) 65
Mussolini, Benito 85, 87, 165, 192*n*.

Nagel, Anne 125
Naish, J. Carroll 144
Naldi, Nita 40
The Nation 83
National Film Registry 77
National Recovery Administration (NRA) 90
New Orleans *Times-Picayune* 67
New Roxy Theatre 78, 82
"New Universal" 108
New York (sentiments against) 83–84
New York Board of Censors 57
New York Daily News 173
The New York Herald Tribune 3, 73
The New York Mirror 12
The New York Post 12
The New York Times 12, 85, 110, 127, 135, 151
New York World's Fair of 1939–1940 116–118
Newitz, Annalee (analysis of 1932 *Dr. Jekyll and Mr. Hyde*) 43–45
Newman, Kim 146
Nosferatu—A Symphony of Horror (1922) 9–10, 16

O'Brien, Willis 78, 80
O'Conner, Francis 52
O'Connor, Una 89
Of Mice and Men 122
Office of Censorship 156
Office of Strategic Services (OSS) 176
Office of War Information (OWI) 155–156, 163–166, 193*n*.
Ogle, Charles 8
Oland, Warner 97

Ouspenskaya, Maria 127, 129, 131
OWI *see* Office of War Information

Palmer, A. Mitchell 21
Parsons, Lindsley 164
Parsons, Louella O. 56, 82
Pasternak, Joe 108
Pearl Harbor, attack on 126
The Phantom Creeps (1939) 118–119
The Phantom of the Opera 15
Phantom Plainsman 151
Photoplay 112
Pichel, Irving 40, 104
The Picture of Dorian Gray 40
Pierce, Jack 28, 30, 127
Poe, Edgar Allan 46, 47
Polidori, John 6, 7
Producers Releasing Corporation 154
Production Code 16, 37
Production Code Administration (PCA) 73, 108, 157
Psycho 180
Punch 161
Pye, Merrill 53

Questal, Mae 20

Racial issues in horror films: *Black Dragons* 161; *Frankenstein* 33–34; *King Kong* 83; *White Zombie* 67–68
Radio City Music Hall 76, 78, 82
Rains, Claude 15, 89, 92, 110, 127, 129, 130
Randian, Prince 53
Randolph, Jane 147
Rapf, Harry 53
Rathbone, Basil 112, 113, 134
The Raven (1935) 102, 109, 112
Reader's Digest 176
Reed, David A. 86
Regina Theatre (Los Angeles) 111
Reno, Milo 59
Return of the Ape Man (1944) 133
The Return of the Vampire (1944) 181; allegory of British history between the wars 168; Lady Jane Ainsley as model of the new woman 168, 170–171; plot of 167–168
Revenge of the Zombies 163–164
Rhodes, Gary D. 61, 62, 67, 68
Rialto Theater (New York) 64, 73, 125
Ribbentrop, Joachim von 127
Rivoli Theater (New York) 64–65, 114
RKO Studios 78, 145

Robbins, Tod 52
Rod Serling's Night Gallery 194n.
Roderick, Olga 53
Rogers, Charles R. 108, 110
Rogers, Will 108
Rooney, Mickey 108
Roosevelt, Eleanor 85
Roosevelt, Franklin D. 43–44, 59, 66, 92, 94, 98, 107, 117, 182, 183; Bela Lugosi's support of 172; distrust of experts resulting from polio experience 50–51; inauguration of 85, 86; leaves New York for inauguration 75–77; post-election clash with Hoover 23–24; rejects fascism 87; work with polio patients similar to Dr. Jekyll's work with charity ward patients 42
Rose, Ruth 78
"Rosie the Riveter" 169
Rossitto, Angelo 53, 54
Rothaphel, S.L. "Roxy" 17, 82
Roxy Theatre (New York) 25, 78, 82; *Dracula*'s debut at 17–18
Russell, Elizabeth 147

St. Louis Post 67
San Francisco Chronicle 172
The Saturday Evening Post 136, 137
Schatz, Thomas 108
Schayer, Richard 26
Schlesinger, Arthur M., Jr. 2
Schlitze 52
Schoedsack, Ernest B. 77, 78
Schulberg, B.P. 73
"Scientists as Citizen" see *Social Forces*
scientists, public distrust of during the Depression 50
Seabrook, William B. 61–62
Selznick, David O. 78
Sevastakis, Michael 93, 94
Shelley, Percy 6
Shelley, Mary 6
Sherriff, R.C. 91, 94
Shock Theater 179–180
Show Boat 96, 100, 101, 107
The Silence of the Lambs 45
Simone, Simon 147, 148
Siodmak, Curt 4, 127, 128, 131, 133, 138–139, 143, 157, 159, 162, 184; likens himself to the Wolf Man 133, 192n.; original conception of *The Wolf Man* 129; wartime service in the OSS 176–177
Skal, David J. 8, 19, 36, 50, 56, 57,

59–60, 88, 117, 121, 129, 132, 134, 137, 141
Sklar, Robert 181
Smith, Al 43–44, 86
Smith, Don G. 88, 94, 176
Smith, Jack C. 118
Smith, Kent 147
So Proudly We Hail! 170
Social Forces 38–39
Son of Dracula (1943) 157, 167, 171, 195*n*.
Son of Frankenstein (1939) 115; plot of 112–114
Son of Kong 111
"Spurs" (Robbins) 52
Stahl, John 96
Stalin, Joseph 192*n*.
Standard Capital Corporation 101, 108
Steinbeck, John 122
Stephani, Frederick "Fritz" 16
Stevenson, Robert Lewis 39
Stoker, Bram 7–8
Stoker, Florence 10, 11, 16, 17
Strange, Glenn 115, 154
The Strange Case of Dr. Jekyll and Mr. Hyde (Stevenson) 40
Strickfaden, Kenneth 31
Stuart, Gloria 89, 92
Studio Relations Committee 37, 73
Sullivan, Thomas Russell 40
Sutter's Gold 101, 107
Svengali (1931) 37

Taylor, Henry J. 173
Temple, Shirley 108
Thalberg, Irving 14, 51–53, 53
The Thirteenth Chair 16, 17
Three Smart Girls (1937) 108
Three Smart Girls Grow Up 114
Tilbury, Zeffie 100
Tourneur, Jacques 145
Travers, Henry 89
The Treasury Star Parade 161–162
Turner, George E. 84

Ullman, Emil 111
The Undying Monster (1942) 133
The Unholy Three (1925) 52
Universal Pictures 13–15, 114; financial problems of during the 1930s 25, 95–96, 100–101; Laemmles lose control of 108; relegates horror production to B films during World War II 134
The Unknown (1927) 52

The Vampyre (1819) 7
Vanity Fair 86
Van Sloan, Edward 22, 35, 103
Variety 2, 12, 50, 68, 107, 108, 112, 125, 127, 141, 152
Veidt, Conrad 15
Victor, Henry 52
Vieira, Mark A. 41
Villa Diodati 6
Viner, Roland 84

Waggner, George 125, 127, 129, 138–139, 143
Waite, Robert G.L. 133
Wallace, Edgar 78
War of the Worlds radio broadcast 115–116
The Washington Post 38, 193*n*.
Waterloo Bridge 27
Watkins, T.H. 21
Watts, Richard, Jr. 73
Weaver, Tom 157, 162, 180
Webb, Kenneth 62
Weber, Harry 16
Weird Tales 110
Welles, Orson 110, 115–116
Wellman, Manly Wade 194*n*.
Wells, H.G. 68, 71, 74, 87, 94, 157
werewolf movies as symbolic of Nazi brutality 132–133
WereWolf of London (1935) 96, 112, 127, 128; plot of 97–100
The Werewolf of Paris (Endore) 96
Weston, Garnett 62
Whale, James 27, 89, 95, 100, 101, 107
White Zombie (1932) 60, 183; labor-management metaphors and portrayal of blacks in 65–68; plot of 62–64; reviews of 65
Wilde, Oscar 40
Wilder, Billy 128
Wilkinson, J. Brooke 112
William, Warren 127, 129
Williams, Clark 97
Willis, Matt 167, 169
Winchell, Walter 65
Winks, Robin W. 23
The Witch's Tale 110
The Wolf Man (1941): critical reaction to 127; plot of 130–132; relevance of to Siodmak's own life 133; version of England in compared to wartime reality of 129–130

women's contribution to the war effort 168–170
Work, Cliff 110, 114
Worland, Rick 154, 156, 164, 165, 170
World War I and the end of the Progressive era 20–21
World War II: beginning of 117; escapist quality of films after American entry into 151; horror films as escapist entertainment during 128, 136–137
Wray, Fay 79, 84, 189–190*n*.

Yaconelli, Frank 120
You Can't Cheat an Honest Man 114
Yukon Patrol (1942) 151

Zinman, David 77
Zombie (Webb play) 62
Zombies, creation of and popular culture history of before *White Zombie* 60–62
Zucco, George 154

www.ingramcontent.com/pod-product-compliance
Ingram Content Group UK Ltd.
Pitfield, Milton Keynes, MK11 3LW, UK
UKHW042000140426
5217IPUK00015B/909